THE SECRET LIFE OF VULNERABLE CHILDREN

Edited by
Ved P. Varma

London and New York

This book is dedicated, by the editor,
with affection and esteem, to
all secretive, vulnerable children,
(the late) Dr D.W. Winnicott,
David Stonestreet,
Waveney Bushell,
and Christopher Reev

First published in 1992
by Routledge
11 New Fetter Lane, London EC4P 4EE

Simultaneously published in the USA and Canada
by Routledge
29 West 35th Street, New York, NY 10001

Reprinted 1993

Typeset by Selectmove Ltd, London
Printed and bound in Great Britain by
Mackays of Chatham PLC, Chatham, Kent

British Library Cataloguing in Publication Data
The secret life of vulnerable children.
1. Maladjusted children. Psychiatry
I. Varma, Ved P. (Ved Prakash) 1931–
618.9289

Library of Congress Cataloging in Publication Data
The Secret Life of Vulnerable Children/edited by Ved P. Varma. p. cm.
Includes index.
1. Mentally ill children. I. Varma, Ved P.
RJ499.S4817 1992
618.92'89–dc20

90–23426
CIP

ISBN 0-415-04744-7
0-415-05982-8 (pbk)

THE SECRET LIFE OF VULNERABLE CHILDREN

Most children have secret worlds, but for some these worlds contain secrets that are both permanent and damaging. Within their secret lives, these vulnerable children are often emotionally confused, anxious and angry, and yet many of them put out clear signs of wanting to be understood.

This moving account of the secret lives of vulnerable and disturbed children will enable professionals working with these children to find out what is going on in their minds – what they are thinking, what they are feeling, why they behave as they do. The contributors draw on a wide range of disciplines – psychiatry, paediatrics, clinical psychology, bereavement counselling and psychotherapy – to show how vulnerable children can be assessed and helped. They describe children who are depressed, neurotic, autistic, bereaved and hyperactive, and children who have been physically, emotionally and sexually abused. Practical in their approach, they also deal with the art of communicating with such children and discuss the difficulties of relating to vulnerable adolescents.

The Secret Life of Vulnerable Children provides the key to understanding how such children think and feel, enabling them to be helped more effectively. It will be invaluable to all who work with vulnerable children, whether as educational or clinical psychologists, as psychiatrists, therapists or counsellors.

Ved P. Varma has worked as an educational psychologist with the Tavistock Clinic, London, and for the London Boroughs of Brent and Richmond. He has edited many books, including *Anxiety in Children* and *The Management of Children with Emotional and Behavioural Difficulties*.

CONTENTS

Notes on contributors   vii
Preface   ix
Ved P. Varma

1   THE SECRET LIFE OF THE DEPRESSED CHILD
   Robin Higgins   1

2   THE SECRET LIFE OF THE NEUROTIC CHILD
   Robin Higgins   20

3   THE SECRET LIFE OF AN EXCESSIVELY PASSIVE
   AUTISTIC BOY
   Anne Alvarez   37

4   THE SECRET WORLD OF BEREAVED CHILDREN
   Susan Wallbank   62

5   THE SECRET LIFE OF CHILDREN WHO HAVE
   EXPERIENCED EMOTIONAL ABUSE
   Sheila Melzak   75

6   THE SECRET LIFE OF CHILDREN WHO HAVE
   EXPERIENCED PHYSICAL AGGRESSION AND VIOLENCE
   Sheila Melzak   101

7   THE UNBEARABLE TRAUMATOGENIC PAST: CHILD
   SEXUAL ABUSE
   Gerrilyn Smith   130

8   THE SECRET LIFE OF HYPERACTIVE CHILDREN
   Alan Franklin   157

9   ON RELATING TO VULNERABLE ADOLESCENTS
   Anton Obholzer   170

CONTENTS

10 THE ART OF COMMUNICATING WITH VULNERABLE
   CHILDREN
   Francis Dale   185

   Name index   210
   Subject index   213

CONTRIBUTORS

Anne Alvarez was educated at the University of Toronto, Canada and Indiana University, USA, in Clinical Psychology. She was also a collaborator in research with Dr Graham Foulds at Runwell Hospital, Essex, UK, on problems of paranoid and depressive psychosis when she read the work of Melanie Klein. She trained in psychotherapy at the Tavistock Clinic, London, in the early 1960s and has been teaching there ever since. Her title is Principal Child Psychotherapist, Child and Family Department, Tavistock Clinic, London.

Francis Dale is a Principal Child Psychotherapist and trained at the Tavistock Clinic, London. He has worked in various child guidance settings as well as at the Marlborough Family Service and as a consultant to staff in residential settings. He has been involved in organising and running training courses for adult psychotherapists at the London Centre for Psychotherapy and is currently the Director of a one-year training course in psychodynamic psychotherapy run by Torbay Health Authority in South Devon.

Alan Franklin was born in 1933 in London. As a wartime evacuee he had a rather disturbed childhood. He won a scholarship to a public school in London, then to University College and the West London Hospital, qualifying in 1960. After resident junior hospitals posts in London and Lancashire he settled first in North London and then, on obtaining a consultant post, in Essex. He has been in Chelmsford since 1972. Although appointed as a general paediatrician he has always been interested in chronic childhood problems, especially allergic diseases, which led him to take a particular interest in the hyperactive child and to be asked to be medical adviser to the hyperactive children's support group and to devote a small weekly clinic to trying to help both children and their families to come to terms with their not inconsiderable problems.

Robin Higgins (MB, B.Ch., DPM, B.Mus.) was educated at Highgate School, King's College Cambridge (Choral Scholar) and University College Hospital. He was Consultant Child Psychiatrist at community-based Child and Family Consultation Centres from 1963 to 1987 and Psychiatrist to Goldsmiths' College from 1965 to 1982.

Sheila Melzak became a Child Psychotherapist at the Anna Freud Centre in 1983, after academic training in child psychology to MSc level, and after twelve years working with disadvantaged families living under considerable stress in the East End of London. Her principal work interests are first, working therapeutically with children and parents who have experienced abuse, with children who are separated from their biological families and with the Social Services staff who have care and statutory responsibilities for these children. Second, she is involved in working with the children of refugees, particularly those from repressive regimes. She works on a regular basis with children and parents at the Medical Foundation for the Care and Treatment of Victims of Torture.

Anton Obholzer, after training in medicine spent some years in general practice. He then trained as a general Psychiatrist and, after that, as a Child and Adolescent Psychiatrist at the Tavistock Clinic. He is a Child and Adult Psychoanalyst and was Chairman of the Adolescent Department of the Tavistock Clinic from November 1979 until March 1985. His particular interests are in writing and lecturing about the relevance of psychoanalytic ideas to everyday life.

Gerrilyn Smith is a Clinical Psychologist and Lecturer at the Institute of Child Health, Academic Department of Child Psychiatry, where she organises the Department of Health sponsored Postgraduate Training in Child Sexual Abuse. She trained at the Maudsley Hospital, Institute of Psychiatry, and at the Tavistock Clinic as a family therapist. She began her work in the field of sexual violence as a counsellor at the London Rape Crisis Centre in 1979. Her current clinical work is with the Child Sexual Abuse Team at Great Ormond Street Hospital. She formerly worked in Child Guidance, Medway, Kent and in Social Services in the London Borough of Haringey. Together with colleagues she ran the Child Sexual Abuse Consultation Service before taking up her current post. She is also a tutor at the Institute of Family Therapy.

Susan Wallbank is a bereavement counsellor. For the last twelve years she has worked as part of the counselling team at the national headquarters of the charitable organisation, Cruse – Bereavement Care. Her work there has included both group and individual counselling. Originally she studied graphic design at Twickenham Art School, before undertaking a counselling training at the Universities of London, Student Health Centre. She has devised and presented special lecture courses on the problems of telephone-counselling. She has lectured, in the UK and abroad, on the subjects of widowhood, sexuality and bereavement and has written extensively on the effects of a death on children and young adults.

PREFACE

I commend this book to you. It is a forthright and in-depth study of vulnerable children. You will find as you read it that vulnerable children share some, or all, of the following characteristics: they are easily wounded, they lack self-confidence in the extreme, they have little or no emotional robustness or resilience. Often, there is almost a peculiar quality of fragility, rather a brittleness about them, that makes one more than usually careful about how one relates to them. I think and feel and find that they are more than usually secretive, from themselves and others, either consciously, or unconsciously. They do not 'open up', unlock or reveal themselves easily. As Robin Higgins says in the book, the word 'secret' comes from the Latin participle of the verb 'secernere' meaning to put apart, sunder, to sever, to separate. If you don't believe that they do so, you are a rarity. But if you do, this original book is for you.

But the book is not about prying into the 'secret' world of the vulnerable child. Any child, whether vulnerable or not, like any adult, frequently enjoys a secret life, and has every right to expect that this secret life will be respected. This book is about the fact that, within the secret life itself, as a part of it, or outside it, vulnerable children are emotionally confused, anxious and angry. Many of them put out clear signs of wanting to be understood. Their secret dreams, their language, their imaginary abodes and friends, indeed their enchanted worlds, often arise as attempts to make sense of the world around them.

However, if such children are attempting to communicate words, images, snatches from their secret worlds, from the other side most adults seek to make sense of the puzzle which the vulnerable child presents. They want to know what is going on in such children's minds – what they are thinking, what they are feeling, why they behave as they do. This book deals with secrets in children that are more permanent, more debilitating, more serious than is usually the case. It alerts us to how to recognise and handle secretive vulnerable children.

ix

The content is warm, innovative, interesting and practical. The distinguished contributors include two child psychiatrists, a paediatrician, a clinical psychologist, a bereavement counsellor and three psychotherapists. They outline how depressed, how neurotic and autistic, how bereaved and hyperactive, how physically, emotionally and sexually abused children should be assessed and helped widely, deeply, closely. This book deals in depth with the art of communicating with such children and further deals with how to relate to vulnerable adolescents.

I wholeheartedly commend this book to you. It is the story of secretly weeping children. The grim reality and authors' conclusions are touching, puzzling and disturbing. This book has a message for each of us; somewhere in it we will all recognise a part of ourselves.

Should you find yourself in it, be kind to others, and be kind to yourself. The world belongs to those who work for the suffering. Thus I say good-bye to you, to Elizabeth Schmitz, to Rajni, Margaret, Neil, Victoria, Abdul, to Gyan, Harish, Dharaya Vati, to Mary, Edward, Ian and John, to David, Mr Secret, Master Frank, Dr Vulnerable, to Professor Vernon, Sir William and to Lord Kingsbury. So on and on. And thank you to you as well. Thank you for reading it.

Ved P. Varma
London

FURTHER READING

Varma, Ved. P. (ed.) (1974) *Psychotherapy Today*, London: Constable.

1

THE SECRET LIFE OF
THE DEPRESSED CHILD

Robin Higgins

Wir haben, wo wir lieben, ja nur dies:
einander lassen; denn dass wir uns halten,
das fällt uns leicht und ist nicht erst zu lernen.
(Rainer Maria Rilke)[1]

'SHE'S SUCH A HAPPY LITTLE THING UNDER IT ALL'

Barry[2] aged 6 was walking with his mother through a graveyard. Reading the repeated inscriptions on the stones that so-and-so had 'passed peacefully to sleep', he said: 'This seems an awfully sleepy place. Perhaps we better get out of here before we fall asleep too.' He searched his mother's face for some enlightenment.

Sheila, aged 3, told that her mother had 'gone away', continued to believe for years that she'd come back any day. When eventually told that her mother had died, she wouldn't accept the statement. If they'd lied to her once, they could lie again. Somewhere, she was convinced her mother was still around, being kept hidden by a stepmother, whom Sheila never took to. In fact, she vowed secretly to give her stepmother Hell till her own mother was retrieved.

As a general rule, we try to give our children a happy time. We don't like the idea of their being sad or depressed. Childhood is a time of hope. In our children, we hope to relive our own childhood in a better way, avoiding the mistakes our parents perpetrated on us. We don't want our hopes blighted. We want to protect our children from the pain of sadness. But in doing so, we also deny them their capability of coping with sadness and depression. (The variation in this attitude according to race, culture, class, or historical period would make a study in itself, but take us far beyond the confines of this chapter where the limit is to late twentieth-century metropolitan England, the only setting I am familiar

1

with in any depth.)

Staying with this position for a moment, we soon find the parental feelings more secret and complex than appears at first sight. It's not just our children we want to protect from depressing experiences but ourselves. We resist facing the painful and the depressing. We are apt to shun the gift of tears.[3] We thus deny[4] a whole range of experience. In protecting our children from depression, we are protecting ourselves not just from their effect on us, not just from our guilt that we haven't been good enough parents, but from the guilt and shame that coloured our own childhood and that contain vital clues as to why we are what we are.

What is the effect on the child of this parental embargo on the harbouring or the display of sad and depressing feelings? First, children who are quick to pick up from the adult world an image of what they are expected to be may obligingly hide their sadness and retreat to it only in secret. They may be adept at tuning into a sad or depressing atmosphere (a mother depressed after childbirth, or a pending divorce) but they keep their tunings to themselves. They bottle up their feelings. But, second, they may find these same feelings not so easily disposed of. The child runs into the problem of dissimulation, of putting on a false front, assuming a false self. In the more extreme instances, this may lead them to simulate the inverse of sadness, a hyperexcitable jocularity verging at times on the manic (a point to which we will return).

Third, as was apparent with Barry and Sheila, adult euphemisms designed to protect the child may just fall on deaf ears. A credibility gap opens up between the generations. Curiosity is stirred. (*Why* is everybody falling asleep? *What* have they done with my mum?) The secret search is on, with secret pacts and all the segregation of secrecy including the impossibility of sharing one's pride and joy with those most close to you.

Fourth, being children they are likely to engage in the game of tit for tat. The parents confused us; why shouldn't we confuse them?

Richard's parents had done their best to persuade him all through the four years of his life that he was a loving child and they were loving parents who hated to see him sad and bad. Troubles started over toilet training when he was a year old.

'He'd been trained for the past six months', his mother said 'He knew perfectly well what the score was. Suddenly out of the blue he deposits this enormous turd in the middle of the living room carpet. He knew it was wrong. Just did it to test me out I suppose. Anyhow I pretended it was a joke and got him to help me clear it up and reminded him of the proper place which at this time was his potty. But he said he didn't want to use that any more and kept asking me to take him to the loo. I thought it was a step forward till his next move hit me. He found he could lock himself in and the cunning little devil mixed my best bath oil and powder with the the scourer and sprayed the lot all over the floor. I was at my wit's end. This time you've gone too far, my lad. That's not a funny game. But he just laughed like a delinquent. At the week-end his dad suggested a game of hide-and-seek. I knew in my bones this was risky but I didn't want to spoil their fun. They see so little of each other. Well, while John had his eyes closed counting up to a hundred, do you know what the little monster did? Set fire to his dad's armchair. There could have been a horrible accident.'

This situation can quickly slip into a vicious circle, the two parties becoming increasingly infuriated with each other as hidden meanings are set up against hidden meanings, confusions added to confusions. In such circumstances, parents may be driven to rifle their child's private drawers in search of clues to incomprehensible behaviour. 'I think you should read these diaries,' a mother will say to the therapist and high-hand over her daughter's personal account of her love-life, grossly intruding (with the best intentions) on the girl's privacy and jeopardising relations all round: one route into chaos.

THREE BASIC DISTINCTIONS

To tease out some of the threads in this embattled situation, I would like first to look at three interrelated issues.

The first concerns the difference between sadness and depression. In studies on emotion for some time now it has been customary to separate sadness from depression and link the latter with clinical states.[5] Sadness, *Weltschmerz*, is a universal, empathic, quiet, conflict-free emotion in which we are aware of often inescapable pain. It goes with a capacity to weep and to be alone,[6] to separate oneself off from someone else, to be aware of having, holding and sometimes losing. For the most part, the feelings we have when we are sad are congruent with events which prompt them. We can quickly feel in tune with a child who chooses to keep secret his feelings about the death of someone close to him or about an incident where he lost face or self-esteem. Once we can appreciate what lies behind his sadness, we can understand his feelings and his wish to keep them secret. Both sadness and secrecy make sense, seem reasonable.

This is not always so with depression where the very word starts out with the core idea of 'pressing down' as an action (I am pressing down on something) or as a state (I am being pressed down on, lowered or sunk by something). When applied to the emotions this

3

word 'depression' came to signify being in low spirits, gloomy or melancholy. It also implied that two (or more) people are involved. Someone is depressing or being depressed by someone else. There arises the possibility of conflict which is absent from sadness, and along with the conflict goes aggression and more complicated moves such as the turning of aggression against oneself (see further pp. 12–17). As a result, in depression there is often not the same rapport, the same congruency between the feelings and the events which cause them as there is in the case of sadness. The reasons for children's depression are often as obscure to them as to those looking on from outside, trying to understand them. In this respect depression, because of its hidden meanings, can antagonise all parties, depressed and un-depressed alike.

The distinction between sadness and depression applies across the board of personality measures including gender identity and the way the opposite sex is treated. (It thus provides an index for later marital relations.)

> Sophia was an only child, arriving after several miscarriages. Her mother never enjoyed good health and Sophia came to trust her father to fulfil both parental functions as he to trust her to be both son and daughter. Her favourite dress was the clan costume he made for her to wear on special days. She loved it partly because when she put it on she saw how proud he was of her, partly because the dress struck a chord deep inside her, resonating the roots she shared with him. He was to her someone in whose arms she could feel utterly safe and loved and protected. This same feeling never deserted her in the doldrums which hit the family (her father's lost job and the family's move south from Aberdeen) nor in the friendships she made with boys and girls alike. When Sophia loved someone it was with an unswerving and wholly-committed loyalty. Any half-heartedness or deceit on their part was not taken as a betrayal or let-down. It was just not understood. When a teacher once accused her of lying, Sophia was confused and took weeks to sort out the affair. For it had never occurred to her to act that way.
>
> The good father/(mother) she had inside her ensured that though at times she might become deeply and painfully sad, Sophia never sought to deny or distort the feelings. She held on to her sadness and after a while was usually able to put a finger on what was bringing it about. To succeed in this detection might mean spending long hours on her own.

Sophia knew sadness but rarely depression and never clinical depression. Joan presented a different picture.

All through her childhood Joan, now 13, saw a gap where she felt her father should have been. The last of her parents' five children, she reckoned she must have been the straw that broke her father's back. For he chose the week of her birth to leave home and go to live with the woman he'd been courting all through her mother's pregnancy. He kept in touch with the first two children in the family (both boys) but all Joan could remember of her contact with him were cancelled meetings and forgotten birthdays, disappointments and disillusions. The father she built up in her mind was one she had, as she put it, to suck out of her thumb: an ideal, rather brittle figure who owed a lot to the TV programmes she was always watching and one whom the boys she met never came anywhere near emulating. Joan was edgy with boys. She longed to be loved, hated being left on her own, but would always end up teasing the boy who took her fancy, discountenancing him and laughing at his predicament.

Joan was rarely sad. She spent a lot of time feeling angry, betrayed and depressed and twice made a half-hearted attempt at suicide.

The immediate significance of this distinction between sadness and depression emerges when we consider the second basic distinction: namely that between secrets which we know about and can control and secrets which turn out to be hidden from ourselves (or, as we say, unconscious secrets).

Justin was 7 when his mother died. His immediate response was to withdraw, say nothing to anyone and leave the family table as soon as possible having eaten very little. When he came to see me, he sat by the window looking out and we both noticed a blackbird on one of the bare branches of a tree on the other side of the road. I said: 'It's his favourite spot.' It was the only remark that passed between us on this occasion. When he came again he started to draw: a black house. And for 7 weeks he repeated this picture without comment. Occasionally he'd let out a long sigh but for the most part we sat together in silence because we both knew on one level what his sadness was all about. As it began to lift, his house started to change colour. First it became grey and then streaked with dark blue. In an upstairs window appeared at first a yellow curtain and then a face: his face, looking out. Then he began to talk.

Only Dad, he said, was at home now; Dad and this new woman called Aunty Ethel whom Justin couldn't stand. She was always talking about God and Jesus (the family was Catholic) and how they love people. Justin didn't believe in God or Jesus any more.

They're liars and hypocrites like the Ethel woman. As a matter of fact, he didn't believe in anything any more; wasn't interested in anything either, he said, as his right hand slowly and faintly drew a picture of the truck his mother gave him for his birthday two weeks before she died.

Essentially Justin wanted to share his secret sorrow, pain and anger, and over time he did so. With Mark the situation and outcome were different.

Mark was 10 when his mother died. She and his father had (according to Mark) never loved each other. He'd heard his father say as much. 'Once the boy came, you only had eyes for him', he'd heard his father shout, 'With him here I've served my purpose.' His mother had confided in Mark a year before she died that she was going to leave his father. All that year, Mark found himself torn and guilty that he knew more about his mother than her husband did.

When she died, he felt 'numb and dumb'. He couldn't get at his feelings. If he sat down to draw he only did bits of things, a head here or a boat there without any sails. He spoke disparagingly about his school and the boys and he saw no point in coming to see me. Why should he be treated like a nutter when there was nothing wrong with him?

His visits were very irregular but on one of them he let out that he felt betrayed by his mother ('led on and betrayed') and on another that he wished he could stop feeling, well, not exactly responsible for her death but certainly connected with it somehow, 'very much part of the tragedy, if you see what I mean'.

This distinction between knowing secrets and finding them hidden is by no means watertight. Often the known and the hidden are mixed. In Richard's ambiguously motivated games, the behaviour his mother found 'incomprehensible' almost certainly combined conscious and unconscious drives. For some of the time he knew what he was doing. For some of it, he was also swept up by forces over which he had little control and which surprised and confused him as much as their outcome did his parents. So it is with many children's secret actions.

The third basic distinction lies in the nature of secrecy itself. One has only to consider for a moment the experience of loneliness to see at once that secrecy is Janus-faced and may be evaluated in two very different ways. Positively, it points to privacy, to a personal imaginative space we can call our own, and to all the advantages that go with a capacity to be alone. Negatively, secrecy points to isolation and neglect: to the discovery of an old person's death by mounting piles of milk bottles on the doorstep, or to a Maria Calwell.

Both these faces of secrecy are apparent in our social response to one of the commoner causes of depression in children: a death or a separation in the family. Neighbours may respect the family's privacy; they resist intruding on family grief. They may also be at a loss over what to say to family members who thus slip into feeling like pariahs.

CHILDHOOD OBSERVED: OCCASIONS OF SADNESS, DEPRESSION AND SECRECY

Through the sheer process of growing up, children have to cope with many painful experiences which they may choose to keep secret or which, willy-nilly, they bury without knowing they do so. The change from being a sessile millimetre transplant on the mother's uterine wall to being an independent unit entails some of the most momentous moves in our existence. Of most of their details we remain sublimely unaware – how the transplant takes, the degrees of mutual accommodation trust and rejection, the rhythmic entrainment and synchronicity – these and other issues, central to our development, only filter vaguely and indirectly to our later consciousness.

> Some three months before Eliza's birth, her mother suffered a minor stroke. The event left no obvious mark on the mother or the baby. But the pair never settled again into the comfortable rhythm they'd enjoyed together before. Years later, when she had just learnt to swim, Eliza nearly drowned. No one knew quite why. The girl said it was because she suddenly lost confidence. Eliza could never believe in her assured survival. Her favourite nursery rhyme was Rock-a-bye Baby.

An extensive literature now exists which aims to uncover the secret world of the infant from birth onwards. Of the many terms used,[7] all are designed to describe the slow and often painful process of separation and individuation, the balance between Knowing and Being, and all bear closely on the overt or hidden expression of sadness and depression.

The most obvious separation occurs when a parent dies.

> John's mother died when he was 9 and for years he carried a secret burden of remorse: 'If only I'd been better . . . if only I could have amused her more . . . told her more of the stories she loved to hear before she became too ill to listen . . . if only I hadn't tormented her by fighting all the time with my sister.' When it became

7

unbearable for him to hold this remorse in himself any longer, he blurted out to his father: 'I didn't kill her, did I? It wasn't my fault she died.' His father understood at once what his son had gone through. He took him in his arms and said: 'No it wasn't your fault.'

But the loss doesn't have to involve a death. As Bowlby and others[8] have pointed out, for a small child a separation may evoke feelings and phantasies indistinguishable from those evoked by a death. The idea that objects can return once they've disappeared is one that is only learnt slowly.

It was, as his mother said, most unfortunate that the time Jim's nanny accidentally dropped him from the top of the stairs coincided with the time he was taking his first steps. He broke his leg and had to go into hospital for six weeks and when he came out seemed confused and barely recognised anyone. As soon as he got his bearings his behaviour became uncontrollable. He took a delight in smashing things. His mother wondered if he'd damaged his brain. The nanny who dropped him had only been looking after him for two weeks. The other nanny who'd been with him from his birth left suddenly on the day after his first birthday.

Looking at the situation through Jim's eyes, we can see that what he had to cope with were two successive separations placed quite close to each other in time. The first was from a nanny who had been with him from his birth; the second separation was from all familiar figures and surroundings when he went into hospital. The two 'unnatural' separations occurred at the time he was consolidating an important 'natural' break towards independence (his first steps in the upright position) and were accompanied by the pain and discomfort of breaking his leg and having to have it immobilised (insults to the key component in this step towards independence). Small wonder that this set of events caused a corresponding set of hidden emotions and phantasies which influenced his subsequent development for years.

With the break-up of one marriage in three, with the frequency in turn over which goes with *au pairs* and nannies, with the availability of fostering, adoption and boarding-schools, many children from early on may find the love and trust they placed in a parent or substitute severely tested, ending in a sort of death and inducing the same sort of depression described in the folksong:

> I leaned my back up against some oak
> Thinking that he was a trusty tree.
> But first he bended and then he broke
> And so did my false love to me.

Samantha was proud of her golden curls and her name. When she was 4, she could remember her father taking her on his knee and admiring those curls and telling her how she bewitched him. 'That's why we gave you the name,' he said. 'It was after a series on the Telly about a white witch.'

Samantha thought of herself secretly like the white witch and tended as a result to overestimate her capacity to get herself and others out of impossible stews.

When she was 7 and her parents separated, they couldn't decide where she should live. At first, she chopped and changed between her old house with her mother and the new one her father set up with his girl-friend. Samantha used all her witch powers trying to get her parents back together again, but to no avail. Before long the father's new girl-friend said she didn't want Samantha staying with them any more. So the child stayed all the time with her mother and only saw her father once a month on a Sunday when they spent most of the time on the top of a bus.

But by now her mother was on drugs which she used to leave around the house. One day, Samantha tried out a few and had to be taken to hospital.

After this she was fostered, first short-term then with a long-term family who lived 10 miles out on a triangle near the airport. Samantha stole a cycle and rode it along the motorway back to her mother. There was another hearing and they said she must go back to the foster-home and never do it again.

The good white witch began to plot some other devilish tricks and in the end the foster-home threw her out. Everyone said she was violent and they put her in what they called a Secure unit.

The loss which triggers the depression may not be of a person at all but of a thing: a favourite long-established toy, a room, a house, a school, a way of thinking or life.

(Sharon's mother describes the loss of her child's Pooter.)
When we got home from Africa, we found we'd left her Pooter on the plane. We didn't give it a further thought. It had been a ghastly flight with delays and turn-backs and we were all so relieved to be back. Besides, she had cupboards full of dolls. But that night she was inconsolable. She wouldn't listen to reason.

'I'll get you another tomorrow, Sharon,' Bob said, 'Just like the one you lost. We'll go to the shop together.'

'But don't you understand? It's not the same. I've had him for years.'

'But he was falling to bits for God's sake.'

'He was mine, wasn't he?'

Whatever we said seemed only to make things worse. It was as though she'd left half of herself behind with this Pooter. In the end we shut her in her room and she cried herself to sleep and mourned the wretched thing for a whole week.

Binh was a 4-year-old Vietnamese boy who, with his 18-month-old brother, was among the few survivors of a village raid. When the pair were picked up by the UN forces, Binh was trudging along the mud track with his brother asleep on his back. He was pushing in front of him a toy lorry to which he kept saying: 'Come on now, go. The Lorry will save us. It won't let us down.' The soldier who picked him up said it was as though his belief in his power to animate that lorry was the one thing that kept him going.

For a long time that term his parents thought Derek was worried about moving up into the senior school with the bigger children. It was only when his father kept insisting he'd soon be all right, soon find his feet, that Derek finally exploded.

'Don't you see, I don't want to leave. I don't want to say goodbye.'

'But your friends are coming with you,' his father said hoping to comfort him.

'It's not the same. It'll never be the same. Everything's broken.'

The loss may be of self-esteem or status.

Charles had lived all his eight years alone with his mother. She was an ardent feminist with no intentions of marrying any of the men she was always attracting. She and Charles were very close. One tea-time when he was fooling with his friends and his mother asked him to stop, he told her to shut up. She smacked him hard across his face and sent his friends home. From then on, his school work that she was so proud of fell away. It's as though he just can't be bothered, she told one of her girl-friends.

Charles and his mother were unable to avoid being drawn into a web which entangled many aspects of themselves, not least their gender identities. There were times when they mutually recognised him as her 'husband', a position which, on the basis of its prematurity alone, proved distinctly precarious. His falsely blown-up self-esteem was correspondingly vulnerable and when on this occasion his mother/wife humiliated him in front of his friends, she inadvertently exposed and to some extent exploded the shaky base on which their relations, including his interests and his motivations, had rested.

The depression of a sexually abused child often arises in a similar fashion. There may be the same confusion of roles, the same playing out of phantasies, the same vulnerable identities, the same shattering of (false) self-esteem and the same potential move out of an impasse.

On a less dramatic note, in any family there are likely to be constant shifts of status: the eldest losing the privilege of being the only one; the youngest, that of the baby. Children sometimes deal with these losses by the construction of phantasy families with a new set of siblings or (especially in adolescence) a new set of parents.[9]

Or the loss may involve some physical disability which one tries unsuccessfully to keep secret: facial disfigurement, acne, glasses, a crippling defect or, in more extreme instances, the prospective loss of life.

In passing, we should note that the root meanings of the word 'secret' reflect some parallels with these root experiences in sadness and depression. For 'secret' comes from the past participle of the Latin verb *secernere* meaning to put apart, sunder, sever or separate. (I will deal with one aspect of this root, namely 'splitting' in chapter 2). Here we are concerned with such aspects as: separateness, remoteness; solitariness, loneliness; what is apart from things that belong to it, wanting, being deprived of, living without.[10] All these root meanings of the word 'secret' clearly parallel the experiences of sadness and depression we have been considering so far.

A sense of loss is not the only experience lying behind a child's depression. Another set of feelings, overlapping but not co-terminous with loss involves a sense of hopelessness: a despairing assessment of one's self, one's past experience and future prospects. These are pressing feelings but not the sort one would be in a hurry to parade. Why jeopardise an already vulnerable position? The feelings and their expression constitute a real paradox for the child.[11]

By its very nature, childhood is a vulnerable time for all species, but particularly for the human. Born prematurely, we require much longer than do other species to reach a point where we can fend for ourselves. In addition to this developmental lag, we are endowed from our earliest years with a capacity to reflect on and assess our condition, to compare how things might be with how they are.

At the age of 3, Kim had a sharp eye for life's inequalities. He resented the big difference in size he saw existed between himself and his father. He resented all the things which his father could do and he couldn't and which went along with this size discrepancy. His favourite game was to be Big Foot and 'IN

11

CHARGE', setting me down, a captive audience, to listen to his ritually repeated performances of 'THE ROYAL RESISTANCE'. For these performances, he would hump his props to and from our sessions in his father's haversack which he insisted he strap on to his back though it was as big as him.

Such constraints are imposed by our human biology. They are the Givens from which there is no escape. But in addition, the lot of childhood is further clouded by issues laid down by society (particularly our Western society in the twentieth century). To name but a few such issues of particular relevance to children: our disrespect for ecology (including natural biological rhythms); the pressures on parents to distribute their time between work and raising a family ('finding time – space for the child'); the blurring of roles particularly the role of childhood (including what a child sees, is told, learns about and the discrepancy between knowledge picked up on the media from that provided more formally by parents and teachers).

We can begin to see why the lot of being a child today, despite its greater recognition and exposure, can be even more vulnerable than in the past. The need for secrecy may be correspondingly enhanced. After years of work with deprived children and their families, one is sometimes tempted to paraphrase the title of a recent book on childhood depression:[12] Why isn't Johnny crying . . . or paranoid?

THE UNEXPECTED FACES OF DEPRESSION IN CHILDREN

The expression of sadness and depression, in children as in adults, can take many forms. We have already met some of these: denial, fury, the ambiguous suppression of fury. I will now fill out the account.

A useful outline guide follows the universal phases that have been described for mourning:[13] numbing with outbursts of rage; yearning and searching for the lost figure; disorganisation and despair; reorganisation. Rage arises from a sense of the injustice of life, from finding a loved person taken away from one without any good reason. In childhood, where such experiences are not uncommon and where feelings so quickly spill over into behaviour, depression is often shown by an uncontrollable outburst, a fact which presents problems for those with a yen for neat classification of pathological syndromes.[14]

The fury, for many reasons, may be redirected. In particular, it may be turned on to oneself. Indeed the state of depression in large part arises from these feelings of anger being redirected on to oneself in one form or another. Along with this in-turning of aggression goes another move which has received much attention in the psychoanalytic literature. This move entails the taking-in, the 'internalising', of images, ideas, feelings and the building up of these inside us into a world of 'internal objects'. These 'objects' we use to interpret the world about us and in due course project our interpretation out again on to this same world though we may well not be fully aware of the steps involved. The circular process is described further in chapter 2. Here we need consider only a child whose feelings of depression arise from some point in the circle. He may have tuned into a depressed mother and retained the feelings he picked up from her long after they have lifted in her. His feelings may have taken on a persecutory (and delusional) quality and he may interpret some of her gestures as rejection when, for her part, no such rejection was intended.

The classical case is that of Dido. When she first realised that Aeneas was deserting her, she was furious with him. But in a short time, she began to build up a world of hostile internal images which took the form of nightmares, where the fury she felt towards him was now turned about. In her sleep he was the furious one, pursuing her, and driving her wild as she travelled in search of friends through a deserted land.[15] Later still, the murderous urges towards him were turned into murderous (suicidal) urges towards herself and ended in her self-immolation on the immense pyre built to her own design.

So it is with children who, instead of venting their fury openly and directly, may turn it first into a secret or overt depression and then into a variety of behavioural responses known to accompany depression and which, like depression, paralyse their own resources and enjoyment.

Any one or more of these 'masking' responses may dominate the picture: a difficulty in finding thoughts or in finding them quickly enough, or in getting to places on time; a generalised loss of interest, zest or fun in doing things; feeling dead inside; a string of self-reproaches often assuming delusional proportions in their intensity. Or the complaints may be about not being able to drop off to sleep or of sleep being interrupted by the sort of nightmares that plagued Dido; or of not being able to eat or release their stools. Attempts to compensate a sense of emptiness may lead to over-eating and vomiting; and paradoxically stools, if retained long enough, result in an enforced and messy release, an overflow incontinence.[16]

In more extreme forms, this withdrawal from a painful world, this sabotage of one's own life, may lead to long hours curled up in bed, asleep or dozing ('I just don't feel like waking up') or to the sudden suicidal attempt which often takes everyone by surprise and forces a look at the child's till then secret depression. Here's a note that Philip, aged 7, left, fortunately in a place where it could easily be found and action taken before it was too late.

I don't want to live any more. I'm no use to anyone. Dad syas we're all a brudon on him. I want to make it eysier for him. He can have the money in my pig-bank. John can have all my toys.

Philip was depressed but, as so often in a suicidal attempt by a child, other secret motives contributed: the assumption of the role of sacrificial victim, and of feeling himself *'de trop'*; a plea that his presence in the family be re-established (brother John, two years younger, had stolen the limelight from the moment of his birth); a child's shifting assessment of the reality of death, including the phantasy of reunion in a re-created heaven on earth.[17]

Sometimes a secret symbiotic relation with a parent's depression results in an actual or (as here) a thwarted suicidal pact.

Cassius, aged 10, hated himself for looking like a girl. He blamed his mother for keeping him so close to her, but he could never openly rebel. She had a power over him. He was aware of being more scared of her than he need be, but he couldn't do anything about it. She was always talking about death and dying and being miserable and there being no point in going on. Of course this made him sad at times but beyond the sadness, outweighing it somehow was this grey fear. He couldn't say of what. They lived together on their own in a detached cottage at the end of the street. People called them the odd couple but nobody took much notice of them.

The day she put her plan into action was the day he'd come down with measles and was feeling groggy and giddy. He watched her pour out some medicine for him, stand over him while he took it and tuck him up in bed. Then she told him what she'd done and how she was going to take the same dose. 'We're both going to die', she said 'It'll be easier that way. You wouldn't be able to manage without me.' She poured out her dose and drank it and didn't listen to him crying that he didn't want to die.

When she left the room for a moment Cassius, shaking with fear and his illness, managed to vomit the dose she'd given him down the toilet and get back to bed before she returned. She was groggy now and wanted to hold him. He let her till he saw she was asleep. Then he crept away and phoned her sister and told her to come quick. Her sister wouldn't believe him but came all the same which was as well because she only just arrived in time.

Cassius went into Care and would only come to see me on condition I wouldn't try to take away his secret fears. 'After all, my fears saved my life, didn't they?'

There are two further major ways in which depression may be expressed in an obscured or masked form. The first is through the substitution of one activity normally associated with depression by one not so obviously connected.

Instead of bursting into tears, Theodore would stage an asthmatic attack, wheezing replacing crying, and the battle to get rid of his breath winning the concern which any crying child demands. He'd stumbled on this ploy by accident once when he had a severe cold which 'went on to his chest' as his family doctor put it. Once found, Theodore held on to the ploy if only because his parents found his wheezing much more acceptable than the 'blubbering' which by 6, they (and the teachers at his boarding school) considered he should have grown out of.

Susan, aged 9, had on the side of her neck where she'd been burned a patch of skin which heralded a bout of depression by breaking down and beginning to 'weep' (like the old Grenadier's wound in the Heine/Schumann song when he heard of his Emperor's capture).

Many activities and body-parts may be drawn into these substitutions and are widely reported in the literature of psychosomatic complaints.[18]

The final form occurs when the features which make up the mask are the opposite of those we usually see in depression. Hilarity replaces the sad sombre mood, hyperactivity the retardation. An irrepressible flood of ideas replaces the sense of drying-up and emptiness, self-aggrandisement replaces self-reproach and an ebullient audacity the loss of confidence.

Helene at 6 was 'the life and soul of the party' in a family which was haunted by the spectre of Loss (deaths through suicide on the father's side, incarceration and insanity on the mother's). Her older sister Lucille set the younger child an undented example of painstaking conscientiousness. Helene was for having none of it. Uninvited, she took on the role of the *farceuse* and turned her sister's good example on its head at every possible opportunity both at home and at school. One vignette must suffice to illustrate her role as the Lady of Misrule. It occurred in the art class when an enthusiastic young man unleashed Helene and her fellows on the tubes of acrylic. To begin with, all went smoothly and everyone got on with their individual painting. Then in one corner (Helene's) murmurs of unwelcome jollity began to arise. The individual efforts had fused into a group production. The young man went over to investigate. He was dutifully wearing the sort of apron he insisted they all wore and which Helene strongly resented. His front was thus protected but not his back and, stooping over the group production, the unprotected expanse afforded Helene an opportunity she couldn't resist. A diabolic third eye was lightly stamped on the seat of his pants in bright and unremovable red. It was only when he entered the staff room that the trick was discovered but Helene was immediately identified as the culprit.

When she wasn't testing everyone's patience to the limit, Helene desperately sought to make amends, and be everything to everybody.

Helene was brought to see me because of her excessive liveliness, hyper-excitability and distractibility. Her pranks, what her mother called her 'crazy happy carry-on' ('she's such a happy little thing underneath it all') were the price the family demanded (unwittingly of course) for its continuing to function.

Put more generally and less clinically, the part assigned to Helene may be read as equivalent to the satire in the trilogy of Greek tragedies or to the scherzo as the leaven in the symphony. Her part was important since it established a balance in the system, albeit a precarious one. The system is the family's overall response through sadness and depression to a run of tragic events. The response is closely linked with catharsis. Sometimes the response is quite open. Family members make no attempt to hide their sorrow. More often, as in Helene's family, secret and hidden responses mix with more open expressions of grief.

Suffering, the coping with tragic events, is as unavoidable for adults and children alike as the experience of joy. How we cope, the secret or open expression of sorrow, will vary with each person and each family. *Ubi dolor, ibi digitus*; where there's pain, there's the pointing finger. The finger points not just at the pain, but at how it is managed in the system. In Helene's family (and there are many like it) there were strong pressures for some relief from gloom. Helene at 6 was swept into running the Relieving Operation. For a time she was the appointed directress of the digit, whether she wanted to be or not.

The question of coping with sadness and depression in ourselves and our children is caught up with the circular process of taking-in and projecting, which was touched on earlier and which will be more fully explored in chapter 2. Crucial figures for the children in this circular process are their parents or someone standing in for the parents. The circular process goes with a sense of being held, released and held again. When real people prove insufficient, children are thrown back on their own imaginative figures, which may complement or substitute for the real ones. These complements and substitutes become the basis for all creative activity. Sometimes the most we parents can do for our children is to provide a space where they can feel well enough held to tune into themselves, to move forwards or backwards at their own pace in their own world. To do this is not as easy for either generation as it sounds.

NOTES

1   We need in love to practice only this:
letting each other go. For holding on
comes easily. We do not need to learn it.

Rainer Maria Rilke 'Requiem for a friend', from *Selected Poems*, edited and translated by Stephen Mitchell 1982, p. 84.

The quotation has wide-ranging reference. Its relevance to sadness and depression through the ideas of attachment and loss explain its place at the start of this chapter. But beyond these, it covers more fundamental issues in our experience: holding and falling; moments of confluence combined with moments of catastrophe; transcendence; detachment and its more extreme form of ecstasy (ek-stasis). All these issues bear on the rhythm of our secret and overt development but can only be hinted at in the space of this chapter.

2 To preserve confidentiality, details in the case studies in this and the next chapter have been changed and in this sense fictionalised. The points they exemplify however are all based on fact.

3 See Jones (1985) chapter 4.

4 The exercise of denial is among the most fundamental moves in our psychic make-up. What we deny by intention or by default (unconsciously) often turns out to be the most revealing gesture in everyday behaviour, in a work of art or in a system of thought. Certainly this principle of denial is central to secrecy. In this chapter, it is not possible to consider the full scope of denial in relation to secrecy. But here are some examples of its activity which may impinge on the depressed child: in basic human relations the denial of the 'whole' person with the introduction of part-objects; in a marriage, the denial of mutual rights, mutual viewpoints, with resulting mutual vilification; in political systems, the denial of human rights, of oppositions; more generally, the denial of double binds or limits (such as the impossibility of establishing the exact facts about certain events such as child abuse), the denial of paradox, of anxiety, of doubt.

5 For definitions of sadness and depression in general, see Rycroft (1968).

6 See Winnicott (1965) 'The capacity to be alone', from *The Maturational Processes and the Facilitating Environment*, p. 29.

7 Some of the concepts now in common use among psychoanalysts and psychotherapists working with children are narcissism, part – and whole-object, introjection and projection, projective identification, internal object, true and false self, the good-enough mother, transitional object. The list is by no means offered as all-embracing. For definitions of these and other terms see Rycroft (1968).

For a recent summary of these theoretical concepts, see a series of articles in the *British Journal of Psychotherapy* vols 4 and 5 (1988/9) especially Waddell (1989).

8 See Bowlby (1969, 1973 and 1980) and Robertson J&J Film series *Young Children in Brief Separation* (1967–73).

9 See Rycroft (1985) chapter 22, p. 214, 'On the ablation of the parental images or the illusion of having created oneself'.

10 Instances of this last use of *secernere* are to be found particularly in Lucretius e.g. in *De Rerum Natura* 1.194: 'Nec porro secreta cibo Natura animantum propogare genus possit' (Lacking food, animals cannot reproduce their kind or sustain life).

11 See Jung and Kerenyi (1963).

12 See McKnew, Cytryn and Yahraes (1983). See also the various reports on the world-wide abuse of children: their incarceration, commercialisation and exploitation. For a glaring instance, see the articles in *The Independent* of 13 May 1989 entitled 'Four Found Guilty of Killing Boy in Homosexual Orgy' and 'Children who Sell Sex to Survive'. These articles referred to events occurring in London.

13 See Bowlby (1980) p. 85.

14 Whether such a child should be labelled as suffering from 'depression' or from a 'non-delinquent conduct disorder' (see Rutter and Herzov 1976) and if from 'depression', whether it is 'exogenous' or 'endogenous', 'unipolar' or 'bipolar' depends on a number of issues which are (fortunately) only tangentially related to this chapter. Such issues include: the need for such classifications in the first place; the associated need to operate a medical model with an 'accurate diagnosis' of an 'illness' and its 'appropriate treatment' by drugs; the bias experienced by the operator towards reading any piece of behaviour as 'sad' or 'bad'; the depth of search into feelings and their context. See further in Cantwell and Carlson (1983) and Knight *et al.* (1988).

15 Virgil further describes Dido 'in the state of Pentheus when with mind deranged he saw the Furies advancing in ranks and two suns in the sky and two cities of Thebes, or of Agamemnon's tormented son Orestes . . .' See Virgil *Aeneid* 4 (translated by W.F. Jackson Knight), p. 111, Penguin Classic.

16 See Cantwell and Carlson (1983).

17 The picture a child builds up of death and dying is steeped with secret phantasies, from the early murderous attacks noted by Melanie Klein to the euphemisms mentioned at the start of this chapter. Unfortunately space does not allow for further elaboration here, but see Spinetta (1974).

18 See a review by Graham in Rutter and Herzov (1976) p. 771.

REFERENCES

Bowlby, J. (1969, 1973, 1980) *Attachment and Loss* vols 1, 2 and 3, London: Hogarth Press.

Cantwell, P. and Carlson, G.A. (1983) *Affective Disorders in Childhood and Adolescence: An Update*, Lancaster: MTP Press Ltd.

Jones, A. (1985) *Soul-making: The Desert Way of Spirituality*, London and New York: SCM Press Ltd.

Jung, C.G. and Kerenyi, C. (1963) *Essays on a Science of Mythology: the Myths of the Divine Child and the Divine Maiden*, New York and Evanston: Harper Torchbooks, Bollingen Library.

Knight, D., Hensley, V.R. and Waters, B. (1988) 'The validation of a Children's Depressive Inventory (DPI) and a Children's Depressive Scale (CDS), *Journal of Child Psychology and Psychiatry* 29: 853.

McKnew, D.H., Cytrun, L. and Yahraes, H. (1983) *Why Isn't Johnny Crying?*, London and New York: W.W. Norton.

Rilke, R.M. (1982) *Selected Poems*, ed. and trans. Stephen Mitchell, London: Picador Classics.

Rutter, M. and Herzov, L. (1976) *Child Psychiatry. Modern Approaches*, Oxford: Blackwell.

Rycroft, C.F. (1968) *A Critical Dictionary of Psychoanalysis*, London: Nelson.

——London (1985) *Psychoanalysis and Beyond*, London: Chatto & Windus.

Spinetta J. (1974) 'The dying child's awareness of death (a review)', *Psychological Bulletin* 81 (4): 256–60.

Waddell, M. (1989) 'Gender Identity: 50 years on from Freud', *British Journal of Psychotherapy* 5: 381.

Winnicott, D.W. (1965) *The Maturational Processes and the Facilitating Environment*, London: Hogarth Press.

2

THE SECRET LIFE
OF THE NEUROTIC CHILD[1]

Robin Higgins

> Childlike, I danced in a dream;
> Blessings emblazoned that day;
> Everything glowed with a gleam;
> Yet we were looking away!
>> Thomas Hardy[2]

THE SECRETS OF NEUROSIS

In chapter 1, we looked at some of the secrets that went with sadness, depression and their accompanying feelings, a sense of disparity, inequality or rejection, a sense of the inaccessibility of what one loves and longs for, a sense of thwarted desire and unrequited love. A distinction was made between secrets that were hidden from others and secrets that were hidden from oneself (unconscious secrets) and between the open expression of sadness and its more covert secret or masked expression in physical symptoms, or in hyper-excitability, mania and farce.

In this chapter, secrecy is implicit in the title. When we behave neurotically, by definition we keep hidden from ourselves and others the full force and motives of our actions. We do not know why we take a violent dislike to a seemingly innocuous person, or why we are stricken with panic at the sight of a spider or why we repeatedly have to check we turned off the stove. Fundamentally, in terms of the patterns which bring such 'unknowing' about, children do not differ from us any more than they do in their experience of sadness.[3]

Of course, this distinction of knowing and not knowing is not watertight. There are infinite degrees of insight we can enjoy into our neuroses before abandoning them and still more into the patterns which bring them about. So although the distinction still holds between secrets kept from others and those kept from ourselves, as in chapter 1, what is the known secret and what the hidden, what the conscious and what the unconscious, are often combined.

Indeed, the greater degree of implicit secrecy apart, the underlying patterns described in this chapter will be found to have many connections with those already met with in the previous one. Here the driving force for the emotions and their cover-up is anxiety rather than pain (though the two are frequently indistinguishable). But the source emotion for the secrets will again be love (and hate) and since anxiety is as universal as pain, an equivalent relation can be observed between, on the one hand, a normal state of anxiety as awareness or alertness and its more complex appearance in phobias and obsessions, and on the other hand, between a normal state of pain and sadness and the more complex state of (clinical) depression. As we come to look in more detail at the basic underlying patterns of splitting, displacement, projection and repetition in the secret life of the neurotic child, we will discover we have already met many instances of them when considering the secret life of the depressed child. The child who hides his depression under a cheerful *farceur* front is, for example, using (probably without knowing it) the splitting and denial pattern at the root of much neurotic behaviour. The move of denial, a theme which underlay the previous chapter, frequently accompanies the various moves described in this chapter.

These overlaps should serve to remind us of one further point about the term 'neurosis'. In the analysis of neurotic behaviour down the years, the emphasis has tended to be on the maladaptive qualities in the underlying patterns, on their excessive and distorted use. We have tended to lose sight of their potentially purposive and valuable properties. It is as though when inflammation gets out of hand and threatens to choke us (as it used to in diphtheria) we forget its profound curative force in other circumstances. Approaching these same patterns through the secret life of children, we cannot but be struck by the part the patterns play in creativity and in the defences often necessary for creativity to come about. Through the hidden meanings of their play and drawings, children prompt us to reassess our emphases and redress our imbalances.

SECRECY AND SPLITTING

Our habit of 'splitting', of dividing our experience into smaller and more encompassable units, of differentiating what we want from what we don't want, is fundamental to what we reveal and what we keep secret as it is, indeed, to our whole way of progressing.[4] Splitting entails separating units from Unity. If we don't split, we don't integrate. Yet once we split, we live in two worlds, one that is available and one that is hidden.

A key issue from early on is whether the world that is available to us feels like the one we chose or one that is imposed upon us. This distinction between what we experience as our choice and what as an imposition from without lies at the root of the distinction between the true and false self and how far we have defined these to ourselves or how far we expose them to others are among the basic issues of secrecy.

> Jonah was an only child. His birth followed the death of a sister. His parents dressed him as a girl till he went to school and continued to think of him as a girl until he reached puberty. He complained at times of feeling empty, a non-person, but for much of the time went around like someone in a dream, and was often in trouble because, as the teachers said, he was so easily led.

> Maria's mother Helen had been seduced by her own father, Maria's grandfather, when she, Helen, was a child. The seduction remained a family secret, and Helen grew into womanhood with confused ideas about men and her own sexuality. When she married Bob, all the old feelings surrounding her seduction surfaced. She conceived Maria but became frigid soon after the child's birth. When Bob, a warm and sensuous man, found himself excluded from his wife's bed, he first sought 'outlets' with other women. But this led to such outbursts of jealousy on Helen's part that he decided to 'keep it within the family'. That meant Maria and, to Bob's surprise, Helen secretly encouraged him. For a time, Maria went along with the secret. Outwardly, she appeared the quiet well-spoken girl, always pleased to help her parents and others. Inwardly (she was now 12 and passing through puberty) she was in turmoil. She felt betrayed by both her parents, who seemed to be in a joint conspiracy against her. In the end, she ran away to her Gran (Helen's mother) who at first pretended not to believe her, but before long relented and took her under her roof and helped her over the next three years to sort out some of the true from the false bits. Her Gran once said to her: 'I owe it to your mother.' Helen only understood years later what she meant by this remark.[5]

Another key split with obvious implications for secrecy is that between good and bad, in particular being a good or bad person with the good person as a rule being the one that is shown to the world and the bad person the one that is kept secret. A variation on the good/bad split is one between the 'well' and the 'ill'. In either case, the situation is rarely cut and dried.

Camille and Mary were inseparable sparring partners, attracted constantly by the principle of opposites. Mary's outward appearance was one of sweetness and light. With her strawberries and cream complexion, at 10 she was every male teacher's pet and she'd long since discovered how she could turn this power to great advantage. At home she could twist her father round her little finger as effectively as at school she twisted the teachers. Mary could do no wrong. She had few friends.

Camille followed a different course. As soon as she saw that most people tried to be good or, at least, like Mary put on a good front and kept the rest under wraps, she decided to invert, show the world her worst side and keep her best to herself. Taking her cue from her favourite pop-star Michael Jackson, she'd announce to anyone who happened to be around: I'M BAD, I'M BAD and promptly perform some outrageous act to prove her point. Unlike Mary she won many friends and so as the years passed, was slowly able to allow her good side to come out from hiding (at any rate, as she put it, in the early part of the week).

Estelle, aged 11, loved taking part in plays which she performed flamboyantly and with little regard for her fellow players. She'd throw herself wholly into the performance and as her self, which she always saw as Good, was vivid, colourful and larger than life, it spread over the *mise-en-scène* like a mist and an increasingly exasperated teacher was forever trying to rein her in and give someone else a say. Estelle's world was either all light or all darkness. Those who were IN assumed heroic proportions with no blemishes. Those who were OUT were monsters for whom no epithet was bad enough. Yet these alliances and antagonisms were apt to change kaleidoscopically and Estelle herself would be left in a whirl wondering who were her friends, whom could she confide in, and what sort of front she ought to show to this person or that. The ease with which she would make up to someone after an outburst and become friends with a recently hated enemy surprised even herself. 'It's as though I didn't belong to what I was saying,' she'd explain to them, 'as though it wasn't part of me.' More than once she claimed she was visited by a spirit.[6] 'It couldn't have been me that was so beastly,' she'd say, 'I'm a nice tolerant sort of girl whom everyone likes.'

Marcus was 8, the youngest of seven children. From early on he sensed his mother was worn out and that the only way he could get to her was by doing something stupendous. Mixed up with this secret wish to do something wonderful for her were all the feelings of fury that he couldn't get through to her. So the something wonderful he wanted to do for her was also something devastating.

He drew a picture of a boat loaded with nuclear warheads and labelled HYLY DANGERUS moving across the harbour bar and taking up its position deep inside the harbour. While waiting for the ship to explode, he drew himself as Jesus walking on the water. His great secret he said was that he was the new Jesus come to save the world and bound to be crucified when the bomb went up.

The secret world of make-believe, phantasy and experiment plays a central part in any child's exploration of the world. How great a part it plays will vary from child to child. The actress Estelle, relying heavily on hunch, impression and immediate emotion, could slip from role to role, game to game, with little urge to hamper her phantasy by any search for what others thought (unless it was about her). With moods that would intensify or fade with the suddeness of an April thunderstorm, she would spend little time debating what to exhibit and what to hide. In that sense, she was not self-conscious. In the continuous game that was her life, if penumbral happenings impinged on her (as they did on one occasion when a 14-year-old fellow actor made a half-hearted attempt to seduce her), she was surprised and shocked but immediately forgot about the whole incident.

Camille on the other hand was, from early on, much more aware of the limits of make-believe. She knew the secret fan club she shared with Michael Jackson was a pretend, a fiction she could soon smile at. But she had to learn the hard way. Once in being BAD, she smashed a bowl which her mother treasured. She'd thrown it in a fit of abandon with full force against the wall. At first she didn't believe what she'd done. 'You can put it together again,' she said, still locked in her make-believe. Then, hoping the whole sequence could somehow be erased, 'I never meant to break it.' Finally, overwhelmed at her mother's sorrow, she said, 'I'm really proud of you.' In this last remark she packed a crowd of responses: a wish to recompense her mother by giving her the good feelings this encouraging remark always prompted in herself; the relief that though her omnipotent world was shattered like the bowl, her mother survived and was permitting her to survive; a reversal along the lines that at the back of shame (which she undoubtedly felt), there must always be pride; an ironic dimension. From this moment on, there was never the same doubt in Camille's mind about the boundary between make-believe and for real. She could no longer believe that if she closed her eyes no one could see her. Secrecy and openness were never again to be as simple as that.

SECRECY AND DISPLACEMENT

In one sense, the very idea of displacement implies an element of the secret and hidden. Instead of an object (something out-there, hard, which we can hold in our hands), we have a symbol, a word, something that stands for the object. Instead of a word (a name) we have another word, a metaphor. A whole range of experience opens up along these lines, one event substituting for another, part for whole, whole for part, mobile metamorphoses as in Magritte's picture of *Rape* where the features of the female face are replaced by features of the female body, the eyes by the breasts, the nose by the belly-button and the mouth by the external genitalia (the familiar displacement from below upwards as in any *double entendre*).

> Tony, aged 7, had recently started at his prep school. He was finding the going hard, especially the homework which occupied most of his evenings. His form mistress was a large dark lady who was always telling him how much she wanted to understand him. She'd sit down beside him in class and ask him personal questions which made him blush. Then she'd go into a long explanation as to why he was embarrassed. She was called Mrs Klein. Tony kept a family of hamsters. Well, it would have been a family if the mother hadn't always gobbled up the children as soon as she bore them. Gazing at the lone parents one evening when he was meant to be doing his homework, Tony had the sudden inspiration to name that mother hamster Mrs Klein and immediately, as a result of this displacement, not only did he find himself more endeared to the hamster (and able to have long conversations with her) but the next day actually more able to stand up to the real Mrs Klein. She had only to open her mouth for him to think of his hamster and feel more at home.

As with splitting, when we displace we can move in two directions. Through substitutions we can reveal and expand meanings or contract and hide them in a solipsistic world. The question of whether a metaphor can be shared or remains part of a secret private world is one which taxes children (as it taxes poets) in varying ways and to different degrees.

> Lucy, aged 9, loved drawing maps of her house, her garden, the streets where she lived. These maps were substitutes for the real thing, but she felt at home with them. More at home, often, than with the real thing itself. The maps helped her to find her bearings in her own world, orientate herself in it. Also, in talking to other people, she found in the maps a frame for what could and couldn't

25

be talked about. They gave her a sense of security and control. If people tried to go beyond this frame before she was ready to accompany them, she saw them as trespassing and would turn away. Lucy had a nightmare which cropped up at turning-points in her life. She would be coming home into familiar territory from abroad only to find all the landmarks, the signposts, the bus-stops displaced, turned the wrong way round and muddled up. The maps were a means of coping with this nightmare, living with it and using it.

For Lucy, the map, a product of displacement, becomes in turn a means of controlling displacement. For a while, through her maps, her privacy was secured and she could communicate with the world in a way that, without them, she could not. Maps for Lucy, like his hamster for Tony, were Transitional Objects,[7] symbolic landmarks in a private personal space, paradoxically neither entirely hers nor entirely not-hers but something in-between, something which formed the basis for creative displacement.

In this connection, one aspect which has received particular attention in therapy, and which clearly takes a prominent place in secret communications, is what have come to be known as symptoms: a phobia, or a nightmare that can't be shaken off, or a paralysis where no neurological condition can be detected.

Eloise's parents always said they had two overriding concerns in life: their beautiful cultivated garden and Eloise herself. They vied with each other for the control of both these concerns.

Eloise had a recurrent nightmare from which she would wake screaming and drag a resentful mother in from her well-regulated sleep next door. The nightmare ran through variations but essentially it always had to do with a statue in the middle of the garden. The statue in the dream started out by looking like a combination of Venus and the Virgin Mary but before long it began to move and into the peaceful face of this pagan Christian amalgam crept first a sardonic grin and then the hole in the mouth grew larger and larger like a gargoyle. Eloise always woke when the mouth began to spew water and mud from the gutters all over the tidy lawn and topiaried box-hedges.

Peter, aged 6, overheard his mother say she was going into the same hospital his Grandad had died in two months ago. Peter was still mourning this Grandad and trying to sort out what death was all about. He found it impossible to believe his mother would be able to escape the fate that had met his Grandad if he went into the same place. Why else would she have tried to keep it a secret from him? For her part, she was sure if she mentioned having to go into Grandad's hospital, Peter would come to this false conclusion about her dying (she had to admit she herself had qualms about going into the wretched place) so she thought it best to avoid telling him. Her ploy of secrecy seemed to be working till a week before she was due to be admitted. Then he became agitated, wouldn't let her out of his sight and refused to go to school.

Terry's parents were always going to or having parties. He was an afterthought (he once heard them say) and now, at 7, he was thoroughly bored at being an afterthought. So he just walked out of the house and under a car. Both his legs were broken.

'You might have been killed,' his mother said.

'Would it have mattered?' he asked.

His mother looked at him stunned and walked away. From then on, they spent more time with him. But he had to do some other risky things to 'bring them back on the leash' as he said.

In this instance, Peter's 'school phobia' had nothing to do with school, but everything to do with his concern about his mother and his uncanny knack of tuning in to her secret anxieties. When they shared their secrets, he was sufficiently relieved to let her go. A child's tuning in to a secret incipient divorce, or bankruptcy may not be so easily resolved.

A phobia may indicate a child's need to regress from the excess pressures to an earlier time that was rushed over. A violent outburst or a 'paralysis' may be the only way to warn others about the threats which are around, without or within. In countless instances we can see how, in tracing back the displacement which occurs in a symptom, children come to discover the meanings already hidden in it, meanings whose depth and richness will often take them and others by surprise. With the resolution of a symptom, it is not only the child's world that is changed. The family may well have contributed to the shaping of a particular symptom in a particular child. When the symptom is dismantled in the chosen individual, the family may well find itself involved in a similar dismantling of its old secrets, its old social symptoms.

THE SECRET LANGUAGE OF THE BODY

One important area in the secret language of displacement involves the body or different parts of it. The displacement may occur in at least two ways. In one, the body is used as the metaphor. We speak freely of being 'hamstrung', 'paralysed', 'fainthearted' and often act out these and similar metaphors, treating them literally. When we feel hamstrung, we may actually lose the power in our legs; when fainthearted, panicked at the threatened stoppage of a vital organ.

Children's drawings are full of such body-metaphors.

> Timothy, aged 8, was always being put down by his father. Nothing he could do was ever good enough. He was too slow, too clumsy, would never learn. When he drew his right hand he always left off two fingers. 'That's a new way of doing a hand,' his teacher said, 'I've never seen one quite like that.' Timothy immediately apologised: 'O! I'm sorry. I know I'm no good at drawing.'
>
> 'No, I meant it,' the teacher said and, thinking about it that night, Tim began to believe her. It was a new way. His hand felt like that, grasping and deformed and he began to try out all sorts of different hands, adding and subtracting fingers and claws. At the same time, he tried out his own *hand*writing.

Displacing our experience into our body starts early in life and grows in complexity as we get older.[8] A headache, a belly-ache, a pain in the neck are just a few ways in which a child may mask, through a body symptom, an experience he's heard described in these terms.

But in childhood, when responses are still relatively undifferentiated, displacement often occurs in the opposite direction, from the body into our thoughts and feelings. The structure of a child's thinking may follow a bodily pattern, an oral, anal or phallic phase.

> Hugh, aged 14, had these times when ideas fell out of his head, unformed and unrelated to each other. 'My thinking diarrhoea,' he called it. When he was angry with someone he'd bomb them with his remarks (as a younger child he'd constantly be drawing scenes of bombs and bombing). But his attacks lacked focus and left him dissatisfied, with a sense of getting nowhere. It was only when he began going steady with Yvonne that his thoughts became, as he put it, more 'penetrating'.

This prominence of the body in a child's response often goes with a fusion of perceptual channels, sounds for example having shapes, colours, smells. The media are mixed, we say, though the point is, of course, that for a child they have not yet become unmixed. Our earliest experiences are synaesthesic, the images correspondingly vivid and eidetic. These embodied, synaesthesic experiences also go with a closer, more intense intimacy which we can only capture with difficulty in later years.[9] Like the gift of tears, this embodied experience is a secret dimension of childhood which we are apt to lose unless we cultivate it.

SECRECY AND THE PARANOID STYLE

Projection is a form of secret displacement, whereby we house in someone else thoughts, feelings, experiences which are our own but which we cannot, for some reason, acknowledge. The opposite of projection is introjection whereby we house in ourselves thoughts, feelings, experiences we have picked up from others. The cycle of projection and introjection is our way of relating to the world, expanding our experiences, learning in the broadest sense. For the most part, we operate the cycle without being fully aware of doing so. But through the cycle, and particularly through a move called projective identification,[10] we are more woven into the world than we often care to recognise.

> For a full hour, his parents unloaded on to me their anxiety about Ariel, their only child, now aged 7. At the end, 'he's all yours' they said and allowed themselves a smile of relief.
>
> In my first session with Ariel, I asked him why he'd come to see me. What did he think was the problem? 'That's for you to say,' he replied with a shrug. 'That's your job isn't it?'

His parents handed me their anxiety and child. Taking his cue from them, Ariel handed me the definition of his problem. Both parties imbued me with ambiguous feelings and equally ambiguous power. This waving of wands, the magical dismissal of what was theirs and the magical transferral of it on to me, occurs more commonly than is often recognised. Though in the example of Ariel and his parents the magic moves were quite explicit, their full implication took months to unravel. More often the wands are waved more secretly, without anyone noticing, but with the sense of a forcible bonding together being correspondingly heightened.

Several writers have noted the hidden conflict which goes on in boys and girls alike (especially at adolescence) between wanting to be thus bonded, woven into the world, intimate, loved and understood and wanting to be alone, left alone and not understood.[11]

The neurotic style which particularly reflects and distorts this projection/introjection cycle is the paranoid. Here we are in a world where, by definition, secrecy and suspicion stalk hand in glove, for the paranoid world is based on distrust and filled with aspects that have been deemed undesirable and split off, ghosts that refuse to be buried.[12] In this world secrecy and dissimulation become a mode of survival. Everyone is seen as looking over their shoulder, victimiser and victimised alike.

The secret life of a child in such a setting entails decisions on stark splits of loyalties. How realistic these decisions are depends on a hierarchy which always underpins paranoid states. At one level, there is a delusional system confined largely to the individual.

> Thaddeus, at 13, knew he had a chip on his shoulder and that there was no justifiable reason for his furtiveness, and apprehensiveness. He knew in his bones that others weren't really looking at him and that the world now wasn't the hostile place it had once been. There was no logic now in his sense of impending disaster. If it came about, he couldn't modify it. So why worry? Above all, why assume it was directed at him? He repeatedly asked himself why he should be so arrogant as to think they'd spend all that time looking at him and him only in Assembly. Of course, he admonished himself, if I go about in this stiff suspicious manner, starting up at any sudden noise, angry if people get in my way, of course they'll take the micky. He wished he could be more friendly, more genuinely friendly and not all the time be using his body as an instrument of detection. He wished he could change but he couldn't. And the more he stayed as he was, the more reasons he could accumulate for his suspicions. People undoubtedly did look at him at times as though he was peculiar, if not out and out bats. In his clearer moments, he didn't blame them.

Thaddeus and his father left the prison camp (where his mother had died) to come to England when he was 3 years old. His Polish father quickly found work and acclimatised to the new culture. Thaddeus was taking much longer. His acute scanning and searching attention, his intense empathy with his surroundings, operated without due detachment. He built up a highly slanted secret world in which selected facts became invested with a special quirky significance. He moved into and away from a paranoid state at one and the same time.

Thaddeus had one invaluable asset, his unparanoid father. That was why his delusion could be said to stop with him. Not so Achille whose childhood was spent in a paranoid atmosphere.

> As long as Achille could remember (and he was now 16) his father was fighting authorities, ostensibly on his son's behalf. Right now the old man was suing the school for some bruises the boy had sustained in gym. This was the third time his father had sued the school and all that ever happened was that Achille became increasingly unpopular among staff and boys alike. Given his father's disposition one might have expected Achille to become paranoid but, as it happened, the son's disposition was the reverse of the father's. Achille was of a gentle lethargic nature. He knew he ought to support his father in his battles for him, and he felt midly guilty for not being more enthusiastic, or voicing more *esprit de corps famille*.

30

Achille was the unparanoid child in a paranoid setting. A more common pattern was illustrated by Gary and Trev.

> These identical twins lived in a house that was boarded up like a castle. Their job, as soon as they could walk, was to amuse the Doberman-Alsatian mongrel and ensure that it scared off anyone approaching from half a mile away. As soon as they went to school they were in trouble, in accordance with the strict family tradition. Successive family members (and there eight in front of the twins) had engaged with the Law which, by the time Gary and Trev came along, was growing disinterested. The family was well known and more or less allowed to go its own way, united in its segregation. The twins had a relatively easy ride.

The third level in the paranoid hierarchy is where the paranoid atmosphere extends beyond the family into the neighbourhood and the children's secret lives are shaped by the gang world of the ghetto.

SECRET FORCES IN REPETITION [13]

Repetition in the form of rhythms punctuates our lives though for the most part we are quite unaware of their doing so. Some rhythms, like heartbeats, or breathing, or eating/eliminating, sleeping/waking, are obvious but pass unnoticed, built-in biological time-clocks that tick over and are taken for granted. Or are they?

> When Shauna's grandfather died, she became preoccupied with her breathing. How did she know the next breath was coming? Where did it come from? How does her body know to breathe? Who tells it? Suppose it just forgot? Or suppose whoever's supposed to tell it just forgot? Shauna was 5 and when she started to ask her mother these questions she got short shrift. These things just happen, her mother said. You don't need to worry about them. That's the best way to go mad. So Shauna stopped asking other people about these questions. But she couldn't stop worrying about them. How could she know it was safe to trust her body? Grandad trusted it and look what happened to him.

Some of the rhythms are not so apparent. They may crop up in dreams and only surface indirectly.

> Valerie was always dreaming but it was only after a time that I could begin to see in her dreams a cyclical pattern which was tenuously timed with her menstruation. The pattern took her regularly through the three phases of search and appeal, winning acceptance and being rejected. Valerie was 10 when she came to

see me. When she was two she was fostered for a year with 3 sets of foster-parents, before being returned to her own parents. Sometimes she enacted bits of these dreams in her waking life, particularly the bits about pushing people to their limits to see if they'll reject you.

These cyclical, repetitive and usually obscure patterns often represent attempts to resolve neurotic complexes and to move towards a new and better established position. On a larger scale, the patterns may be seen at work in a family, especially if the time-scale is expanded to include three or four generations. The compulsive repetition of secret physical abuse of a child by a parent (mother or father) through the generations illustrates this recurrent reminder of past mistakes and the persistent striving for change (however much it may seem at times a generational rut from which there is no escape).[14]

Much repetition is purposive and willed. We learn in large part through repeating. Our factual memories and the organisation of our cognitive data are based on this repetition of stimulus and checking. The secret shadow side to this careful advance lies in the compulsions where the repetition gets out of hand or goes wrong.[15] Wilhelm Reich described the compulsive character as a 'living machine'[16] a comment peculiarly relevant to the twentieth century if one bears in mind the work of the Futurists or Marcel Duchamp, or the horror of the Final Solution.

Werner had a wonderful memory for facts. He could reproduce pages of natural history classifications at the drop of a hat. He had a sharp preoccupation with detail. At 9, he knew the name of every plant in his garden, where it was planted and when. Also when it would blossom and die. He would get on to what he called 'a line' and pursue it like a homing missile. But often in the process, the line would get out of context. A central connection or a particular nuance would be missed. In the school pantomime, he was cast as an Ugly Sister. He recited his part perfectly, but never realised the play was about Cinderella.

His teachers either rhapsodised about his enthusiasm and the pains he took, or else found him dogmatic and opinionated. It all depended on whether he homed in on the subject they were offering.

Werner's movements were inclined to be inflexible and rigid. He spoke with tight precision. 'Be more spontaneous,' the PE master shouted at him and Werner tried. Every night he tried in front of the mirror. But it didn't come easily. He collected jokes and would re-tell them without regard for whether they were appropriate or whether anyone wanted to hear them. The jokes were distributed with the deliberateness of the slot-machine.

Werner was always trying to change. He found an article in one of his mother's magazines about Love and spent hours thinking about it. But he never discussed it with her or anyone. Indeed if anyone broached the subject, he would frown and walk away. One day he said to me: 'I think I know the Secret of Love.' But in the meantime, he said, he had to solve this 'problem about Change'.

I began to see a snag here. Werner's efforts to change were very comprehensively voiced but the effort and the voicing had become an end in itself. The effort stopped with the voicing and this compulsive act of re-telling the problem was designed (unconsciously) to avoid confronting and really changing the situation which gave rise to the problem in the first place. It was the same with his dreams which he'd write down carefully in a notebook, read out to me and do nothing more about.

One of the changes Werner wanted to bring about was a release from what he called sometimes (following his father) the 'pressure of work' and sometimes 'his internal driver'. This last often took the form of a voice setting up impossible tasks and impossible time-tables in which to carry them out. The voice, like Werner himself, expected great things of him, but partly because of the immensity of the demands and partly because it seemed to come from outside of him the voice paralysed rather than encouraged him. He felt distinctly uncomfortable at the pressure of this voice, at the same time as feeling secure and reassured by its commanding presence. He both wanted to be rid of it, and not be rid of it. He wanted it to be his voice, and he wanted it to be alien.

Actually Werner was terrified of change. One saw this at holiday time because with holidays external pressures were reduced. There was more room for his own space. But getting in touch with his own space was exactly what Werner feared. His compulsions, his superstitions (if he walked out of his house and saw a single magpie on a telegraph pole, he was convinced that however well the day had started it was bound to end in disaster), his 'internal driver' were all secret ways to bolster him against change where Change meant facing the unknown secrets of his own space.

Like Shauna, in the end Werner was up against the issue of trust. Can I trust myself as Other, this Other being my unknown feelings or You outside me whom I have to take in if I am to change and grow? The significance of compulsive repetitions is that they constantly bring a child up against this basic hidden trust, even though the forms they assume are apparently designed to hide this core of trust and have to be accepted as purposeful deceivers in the course of arriving at the core. 'Now I know I can have secret decoys,' Werner said, 'I can talk to people without having to work out all the time what I'm going to say.'

'I THINK I KNOW THE SECRET OF LOVE'

Among the root meanings of 'secret' is this idea that a secret contains the key to events. From these brief comments on the secret life of the depressed and neurotic child, an ironic paradox will have been observed: often in response to social pressures, what children keep secret (their sadness, their tears, their body-language, the roots of their symptoms) turns out to contain their most significant insights and gestures. It would seem that 'turning away', as Hardy put it in the verse quoted at the start of this chapter, can sometimes prove richly rewarding if we can summon the resources to turn back and glimpse what we were turning away from.

In depression and neurosis, as in the rest of life, the function of secrets reflects the ambiguity implicit in turning away. Do I have secrets to keep a space apart from You or to keep a space to share with You and only You? Is secrecy a mark of keeping apart and aloof, or keeping intimate?

If a relation is primarily a power struggle involving the 'murder' of one party or the other, then the air is bound to be full of secrets in the form of whispers, plots, rumours, confusions, and all that goes with paranoid states. If, on the other hand, the relation is primarily a duo, then the sharing of secrets, knowing what the Other wants before he or she has voiced it, is an essential part of the delight. In the suspicious paranoid atmosphere of power politics we have to play secret games[17] in order to survive. In the duo, such games are unnecessary. Secrets can be enjoyed for what they are. Our lot is to live with both types of relation.

NOTES

1 The word 'neurotic' is retained for this chapter because it is firmly entrenched in the language, having served over some two centuries to compress our reflections on some central aspects of human behaviour: as a disease of the nerves or of the nervous system unaccompanied by structural changes; through Freud's work on hysteria as a disorder of the personality rather than the nervous system; and as a set of styles or modes of coping based on such universal psychological patterns as denial, splitting, displacement, projection and repetition. See Shapiro (1965).
2 See Thomas Hardy, 'The Self-Unseeing', in *The Complete Poems*, Ed. James Gibson (1981) New Wessex Edition, Macmillan.
3 Questions have been raised as to how right Freud was to postulate that the forms of adult neuroses, where the structure of the mind is more settled and rigid, are comparable, let alone continuous, with those in childhood, where the mind is developing and so more fluid and plastic. In this chapter I have not attempted to address the issue directly but have focused on those

patterns which underlie neurosis and 'normal' development alike. Evidence from various quarters strongly suggests these patterns are in operation from before birth to the hour of death.

4 To mention some aspects of splitting: in perception or in memory the selection of certain events in a field and the exclusion of others; in creative expression, the choice and framing of units (motifs, movements in music); in maths, the nature and organisation of sets.

5 For a more detailed account of these secret assaults, on a a child's identity, see chapter 7 on the secret life of the sexually abused child. See also Welldon (1988).

6 As Agamemnon claimed in the *Illiad* to explain his behaviour towards Achilles (*Illiad* 19.86 ff). The influence of a shame- or a guilt-culture on what we keep secret and what we feel free to release raises fascinating questions which cannot be pursued here. See Dodds (1951).

7 See Winnicott (1978) *Through Paediatrics to Psychoanalysis*, chapter 18.

8 See Murphy (1989) on 'Somatisation: embodying the problem'.

9 The point was made by Plato in his myth of the Cave. It was taken up again by Traherne and the Metaphysical poets in the seventeenth century. Indirectly it is referred to in the Moments of Being (Virginia Woolf) and the Epiphanies (of Proust, Rilke, Yeats and others). See Jephcott (1972) and, more recently, Field (1989).

10 The concept is complicated. See Hinshelwood (1988) reviewing Sandler (1988).

11 See Glasser (1979).

12 Instances of this paranoid world crop up frequently in English literature. See, for example, Shakespeare's Richard III or Othello or Macbeth. More recent paradigms are Kafka's writings or Orwell's *1984* or the many accounts of life in closed societies and totalitarian states where a cunningly designed system of bribes and punishments sharpens the conflict for children and adults alike over loyalties such as those between family and state. See Faludy (1987).

13 Besides rhythm, the other close associate with repetition is variation which, in art as in life opens up endless possibilities. See Higgins (1987). These possibilities can only be hinted at in this chapter.

14 See Welldon (1988).

15 See Barton (1989) on 'Repetitive Strain Disorder'. Also various articles and correspondence on such disorders in musicians. See letter by Dickson (1989).

16 See Reich (1949).

17 See Berne (1966).

REFERENCES

Barton, N. (1989) 'Repetitive Strain Disorder', *British Medical Journal* 299: 405.

Berne, E. (1966) *Games People Play: The Psychology of Human Relationships*, London: Andre Deutsch.

Dickson, J. (1989) Letter, *British Medical Journal* 298: 1517.

Dodds, E.R. (1951), *The Greeks and the Irrational*, Berkeley and Los Angeles: University of California Press.

Faludy, G. (1987) *My Happy Days in Hell*; London: Corgi Books.

Field, N. (1989) 'Listening with the body', *British Journal of Psychotherapy* 5: 512.

Glasser, M. (1979) 'Some aspects of the role of aggression in the perversions', in I. Rosen (ed.) *Sexual Deviation*, Oxford: Oxford University Press.

Higgins, R. (1987) 'Variation form', unpublished MS.

Hinshelwood, B. (1988) 'Review of J. Sandler (ed.) *Projection, Identification, Projective Identification*', *British Journal of Psychotherapy* 5: 267.

Jephcott, E.F.N. (1972) *Proust and Rilke: The Literature of Expanded Consciousness*, London: Chatto & Windus.

Murphy, M. (1989) '*Somatisation: embodying the problem*', *British Medical Journal*' 298: 1331.

Reich, W. (1949) *Character Analysis*, New York: Orgone Institute Press, p. 199.

Sandler, J. (Ed.) (1988) *Projection, Identification, Projective Identification*, London: Karnac Books.

Shapiro, D. (1965) 'Neurotic styles', *Austen Riggs Center Monograph Series No.5*, New York, London: Basic Books.

Welldon, E.V. (1988) *Mother, Madonna, Whore: The Idealisation and Denigration of Motherhood*, London: Free Association Books.

Winnicott, D.W (1978) *Through Paediatrics to Psychoanalysis*, London: Hogarth Press.

3

THE SECRET LIFE OF AN EXCESSIVELY PASSIVE AUTISTIC BOY

Anne Alvarez

INTRODUCTION

My subject is a 17-year-old autistic boy whom I have been treating by the psychoanalytical method over a period of ten years. I will outline certain developments which have taken place in him during this period, but I should say from the start that these developments are limited. They are limited both by the nature of his illness, which seems designed to prevent innovation and change, and also by the considerable interruptions to which his treatment was exposed in his first six years at the Clinic.

I hope to show how he began his treatment with an effort at making contact with me as a way of overcoming intolerable anxieties about separation and separateness; how, to a large extent, he lost this link during the early interrupted years, and how he gradually came to find it again. I would also like to say something about two very different methods he now employs for achieving this contact. One of these seems to promote change and growth and life in him, while the other is death to development.

Referral

Bobbie was referred to a consultant at age 4 with a note from his GP that he was backward in speech and behaviour, and at times very withdrawn. He was psychologically tested then and several times since, and is estimated to be of at least average intelligence. Five times weekly treatment was recommended, but the parents could not manage it, and Bobbie started at the Clinic twice weekly with his first therapist. His mother was seen by a case worker, and they met most of the time in a foursome.

37

Bobbie spoke little, used to walk into ponds, run into the road, and would try desperately to stick fallen leaves back on to trees. He never used the word 'I' and once in nursery school said that a jigsaw was a 'broken mummy'. I used to see him on the stairs of the Clinic and he was an appealing, delicate looking child with a lost, floppy, rag-doll look about him.

History

Bobbie's parents, together with the maternal grandparents, came here from abroad a year before he was born. He is the middle child of intelligent parents in their late 40s, who have two other children, a boy aged 19 and a girl aged 9. He was born three-and-a-half weeks post-mature, and mother suffered considerable haemorrhaging. She was very depressed at the time of the birth and was left alone a good deal while in labour. She says that by the time Bobbie was born, she simply wanted to die.

He was breast-fed for three weeks, and for the first three months could not hold his food. He cried after almost every feed. He drank from a cup early, was saying words by 11 months, and stood at 1 year.

The event which seems to have precipitated his illness, or at least its obvious features, took place when he was 2. His mother became extremely preoccupied and upset while nursing her dying father, and sent Bobbie off to friends in the country for three days. He did not know the family, and became terrified of some dogs there. Then the grandfather died and eight days afterward, mother was rushed to hospital with pneumonia and in a state of shock. Bobbie was sent back to his dogs again. It seems that he became more and more withdrawn after this episode, and seemed, literally, to be frightened of everything. By the time he came to me he was attending a school for maladjusted children, in a class consisting mostly of psychotics.

Treatment

I have divided Bobbie's treatment with me into three phases. The first consists of a six-year period, from age 7 to 13, with once-weekly and once-monthly treatment. The second phase consists of the next two years, and the third of the last two years. In the last two phases he has been coming five times a week.

THE FIRST PHASE

This is the period during which Bobbie's treatment was exposed to considerable interference. I began seeing him on a once-weekly basis in November when he was 7, shortly after his previous therapist of two-and-a-half years had left the Clinic, and by which time his mother was four months pregnant. His baby sister was born in the following April and in the following December, I stopped seeing him for ten months because of the birth of my own child. Then in July two years later, his sessions were reduced from once a week to once a month, and the year after, he had another three-month break while my second child was born.

The first session – the longing to be stuck

Certain features of Bobbie's first session with me demonstrate his notion of the conditions under which psychological gaps could be bridged. It was only later that I learned something about the terrors that separation and separateness held for him, and the feelings they produced in him of being cast adrift, and falling through limitless space.

He was an attractive child, with an uncoordinated, floppy, boneless look about him. He came in to the playroom in a very lost and bewildered state, muttering 'gone' and looking frightened. However, after a few minutes in which he seemed to feel I had understood some of his anxieties about what had happened to his previous therapist, he picked up a little arched brick, saying 'bridge'.

Then he found a roll of string which he began to wind around himself and attach to my hand with growing delight and pleasure until finally he became entangled in it. He then said 'stuck' with obvious pleasure, and no trace of claustrophobic panic. I interpreted his hope that I would stay stuck to him and not leave him as his previous therapist had had to do.

A little later he resumed the string game, then let go his end of the string, while insisting I keep mine, and began to roll some plasticine. This was difficult for him, and he said, 'Mrs Alvarez make it soft.' Indeed this request, in various disguises, has been repeated endlessly by Bobbie over the years, and has involved many technical problems for me in just how soft to make 'it'. I took it at the time as his request for a malleable, soft mother-person in me who would fit in and around whatever demands he should make on her. This request had its correlate in the demand that nothing should be too hard in the sense of giving him an experience of its separateness and difference from him, or from his expectations.

The string game had somewhat touching connotations for me in terms of Bobbie's wish for contact, but I quickly learned with what devastating rapidity this contact could be lost. The string material seemed to represent Bobbie's need for a concrete, physical, almost bodily link between us. I learned that when he felt this type of link was missing, it seemed to provoke total collapse.

Falling

Bobbie's difficulties in retaining links of an imaginative and mental kind left him enormously affected by separations. He had already had a change of therapist, and his hopes of becoming stuck to an object were dreadfully disappointed by the births of, first, his mother's baby five months later, and then of mine, in the second year of treatment. He returned after the birth of his baby sister in a very desperate, wild, frantic state, giggling helplessly in a most hollow manner, falling about and expressing many suicidal fantasies which continued for some months. He drew pictures of trees – leafless, barren, stiff, forbidding things – (see Figure 3.1) which I felt conveyed his feeling that I, as his therapist, was really bearing no fruit for him and inviting no link with him. He had had a symptom at age 4 of trying to stick leaves back on the trees.

These sessions leading up to the birth of my child were marked by his falling much of the time into states where he seemed beyond loss and sadness, and even beyond the more active suicidal despair he showed at other times. He seemed to have given up. He clearly felt totally abandoned by me. He would simply crumple, or stare blankly into space. In later years, when he could get sufficiently outside such feelings to find words and verbal metaphors for them, he could describe having been 'down a dark well', or of having 'fallen down, down into the evening – like the rain – but it takes so long to fall'. He has shown me subsequently that a mother, or, on a more primitive level, a breast which separates itself from him in any way – externally or internally – is felt to be saying 'get lost', virtually peeling him off her and setting him adrift.

It is difficult to convey and painful for me to remember the dreadful feeling I often had of how *far* he had fallen or drifted. My attempts to try to show him that I understood how abandoned he felt seemed quite irrelevant. I was simply too far away.

Beginnings and endings of sessions involved particular agonies for him. He could not enter or leave the playroom without touching the walls all the way along the corridor leading to it. Sometimes he simply brushed the wall, at other times he touched his nose and then the wall, as though trying to link the two. In later years he agreed with my suggestion that he was saying to the wall something like 'Hello – are you still there?'

But even these pathetic attempts at linking failed. On one occasion near the end of a session he drew a picture of a caterpillar emerging from its skin, and when the session ended, he simply fell down three or four times as we made our way upstairs to the waiting-room. It was

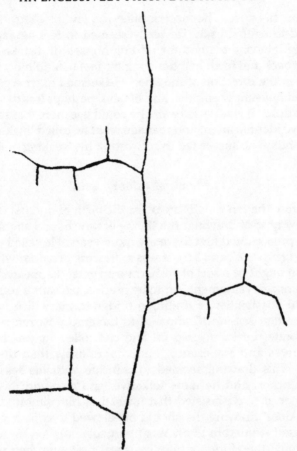

Figure 3.1 Tree

as though he had lost all his internal supports. He seemed to experience separations not as leaving him somewhere he did not wish to be, but as leaving him nowhere. This seemed to represent a well-nigh objectless state, which he later called 'a net with a hole in it'. He was, in his outside life, frequently overwhelmed by terror, of dogs barking, the thud of a taxi's engine, the sound of its windshield wipers, work on building sites. He often felt that bright lights hurt his eyes, and once, when a lorry thundered past he covered his whole head, not just his ears, saying 'it hurts my brain'. He used instead of eyes and ears, his nose as his main avenue of sensory investigation. He smelled literally everything.

He seemed to have practically no capacity for methods of projection and projective identification of bad feelings or objects or parts of the self in the sense first described by Melanie Klein (1963: 58). He suffered from constipation, and sometimes winter-long bouts of catarrh. He could not

41

bear to blow his nose. The more it filled up, and blocked, the more he felt he had to sniff it back. He really seemed to feel he daren't let go of anything. His one method for ridding himself of distressful feelings was to run back and forth half dragging his feet behind him, shaking his hands out in the direction of the floor. He seemed to emerge from this, not relieved but simply emptied and lifeless, perhaps less despairing but even more dead. It was years before he could use more focused methods of projective identification, and manage what he called 'making a mark'. In the meantime he succeeded in recovering his 'sticking' method.

The hook of a door – a link

Shortly before the ten-month break for the birth of my first child he did make a new type of drawing, the theme of which, and slight variations on which, preoccupied him for many more years. He called it 'the hook of a door' (Figures 3.2 and 3.3). It was a drawing of a door which looked as though it might be a sort of wrought-iron gate. It appeared to involve something of a development, or, to be precise, perhaps a recapturing of the hopeful possibilities of finding a bridge to me which had seemed to be in the first session. Compared to the empty barren trees, it was more elaborate, intricate, graceful and controlled. It was framed, yet with its curves and arabesques, much more lively than the trees had ever been. This drawing seemed to coincide with his sessions being somewhat richer, and he more talkative, and also with his making a new claim on me. He insisted that instead of him simply drawing his 'hook of a door' drawing, he should be allowed to copy my version of it. I, because I wanted to know what particular version he wanted in a session, would therefore ask him to draw it first, and then would copy his. But he simply pretended that this first half of the encounter had not taken place; he insisted that he had copied mine.

This seemed to be a way of ensuring that I was permanently stuck and tied to him in the sessions. He wished to hook or latch himself on to me, but he had little idea of a deeper, more extended, more living relationship. He simply looked blank if I asked what lay behind the door, and clearly he did not consider that there might be anything *inside* me. This method of holding himself and us together in fact positively interfered with my reaching him in a more alive way. I was kept simply too busy to think, while he, on his side, was totally preoccupied in getting a smooth unbroken line, particularly where the curve changed direction.

Still, this situation was a little less concrete than the piece of string, and he did also manage to find something to hold on to internally over the long break. He dealt with this problem in the following way. He had, around the time of the hook of a door drawing, begun to bring

Figure 3.2 Hook of a door

long, unused bus tickets to the sessions – the longer the better. The last session before the break, he left the ticket in my drawer as usual. To my astonishment, when the ten-month break was up, he simply came into the room, saying, 'Where's the ticket?' and found it.

At the time I was astounded at the ability in such an ill, lost and apparently mindless child to hold on to this long ticket of memory. It stopped him from forgetting me and must have helped him to feel, not exactly that I had *remembered* him, because it was a long time before he could understand such a notion as that of a person containing someone else in their mind, but that in my drawer – concretely – I did at least still keep his ticket.

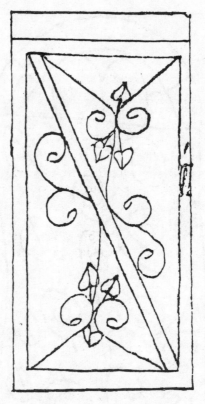

Figure 3.3 Hook of a door

He alternated subsequently between falling back into states of disillusionment and apathy, and recoveries of the copy-cat hooking type. Yet within this rigid, slow framework some progress was made. His parents switched him from his maladjusted school to a school for psychotic children, where he could have somewhat more individual attention and he began slowly to learn to read. In 1969 I had to reduce his sessions from once weekly to once monthly. He reacted with great depression to this situation, and even showed remorse and concern. He assumed it was because I was exhausted by him, and became considerably more helpful to his mother at home.

He did not collapse into the sort of suicidal flop I had seen before.

An object with an inside

The following year, we stopped for another three-month break while my second child was born. Bobbie returned from this break in the most animated and sane condition I had seen him. His grammar was improved, the phrases and occasional sentences were longer, and he began to make certain claims, no longer only for tickets, and soft plasticine, and copyings, but for my perfectly sustained attention. If I stopped talking, even for a minute, he demanded, 'Mrs Alvarez, talk'. This doesn't mean he was listening – for the most part he wasn't – it was more something for him to link up to, hook on to, and perhaps to an extent feel wrapped around by. But it meant that I had a slightly better opportunity of having interpretations occasionally heard.

Bobbie's parents had been pressing me now for some time to see Bobbie on a more regular basis, but I was still unable to manage it. They arranged speech therapy, with a woman who reported that his problem was not simply speech, but comprehension, causality and spatial disorientation. She continues to do extremely valuable work with him in these areas.

His last session before the summer break when he was 13, was a very moving one for me. I had been speaking to him about his difficulty in believing I could remember him over the holiday, and his difficulties in using his 13-year-old self to help him to think about me. When I knew he was in great distress, which he was sure to be about breaks, I had always to speak with considerable emphasis and, I would say, intensity. I was never sure if he was listening, or even hearing me, or if anything was sinking in. Anyway, I had an odd feeling talking to him about ideas like his mind, or time, since he did not seem to have such concepts.

While I was talking, he had been shaking and dispersing all his distress and anger out in the way described before, but he suddenly stopped, came over and examined my face with great tenderness, then the area of my breasts, and then said, slowly, 'Hello,' almost as though we'd been passing on a street and he'd just recognised an old friend he hadn't seen for ten years. For a moment he seemed really to be surfacing and regarding me as a separate person.

I did feel in this session that he had understood a little the difference between his hooking, sticking methods of bridging gaps, and the method I was talking about, which involved containing someone in the mind. But it was late in the session and late in the term and in spite of the help he was receiving at home from his devoted and by now more hopeful parents, there was a two-month break ahead.

On 18 July, Bobbie began a kind of breakdown at home. He was ill in bed with a cold and he suddenly sobbed and begged his mother not to go out to do some shopping. She told me that she had only planned to be gone for twenty minutes, but she decided not to go because she felt that something different was happening to Bobbie, and she should take it seriously. She and her husband literally sat at his bedside for a week while he sobbed and screamed. In the beginning he was terrified that the dogs he had feared for so many years were coming to kill him. Gradually, as the week progressed, he began to talk to his parents about the dreadful time when, at 2 years old, he was sent away to the dogs, and his belief that they *had* in fact killed him. He seemed to be describing something like the beginning of his autism.

When he returned in September, he began occasionally to replace the door drawings with pictures of conkers, with spiky outsides and one or two cosy chestnuts nestled within (Figure 3.4). He became interested in other children's drawers, and in trying to undo my smock, but very frightened by my requests that he should leave them alone. At these times I seem to have become a spiky cross father keeping him out of a desirable but forbidden place.

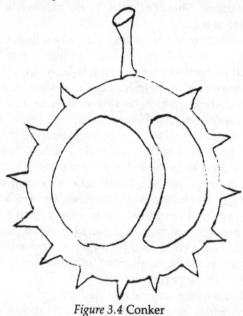

Figure 3.4 Conker

(Years later, when I was seeing him privately, he went to the lavatory, which is outdoors, just outside the playroom. Then for the first time, he plucked up courage to look up at the sitting room window, which he had spoken about but never dared look into. He had an immediate hallucination of a green spiky monster looking down at him.)

He did, however, manage to feel he occasionally attained to this desirable inside place himself. One of his ways of doing this was to lie on the couch, with his cheek on the pillow and his eyes gazing into mine, as though he felt he was right inside me. When this state was not achieved, however, a veritable avalanche of feeling was pouring from him, which by now the parents were unable to contain. His fears, his distress and anguish over any separation, from them or me, his sexual mischievousness with women friends of theirs, were overflowing even his parents' tolerant boundaries, and could certainly not be contained in once-a-month treatment. I arranged to start seeing him privately five times a week and have done so since that time.

THE SECOND PHASE

The long stocking

The change to five times weekly treatment did provide a much stronger and firmer holding situation. Bobbie's mother reported that, for the first time in his life, he was sleeping through the night, and not needing to be under about ten blankets.

He seemed to interpret this remarkable alteration in my behaviour in two ways. First, he saw it in a way bearing many resemblances to the old copy-cat 'make it soft' mother of the past, that is, as a gushy, guilty rescue operation on my part. Second, however, he did seem to see it as a genuine lifeline thrown out to him.

I would like to illustrate the two situations by material from two sessions, one in January and one in February, after the Christmas break, the first break under the new arrangement.

The spaghetti mother – getting unstuck

In Bobbie's very first session at my house, he had dramatised his mother's or sister's voice saying to him, 'Darling Bobbie, please forgive me, I'm so sorry I hurt you, let me bandage your knee.' She sounded all over him, while he lay back, the deserving but passive recipient of these frantic guilt-ridden attentions. In a later session close to Christmas, this cloying object grew even closer, became even more stuck to him in the form of a story about spaghetti stuck to a man's nose. The man could not get it off, as Bobbie could neither defecate easily, nor blow his nose, nor expel his outraged feelings about the coming break. The greater his distress, the more he sniffed it up. He seemed unable to let go.

He returned from the Christmas break, embittered, but finally able to put some of this feeling into me. He began the session by switching the light in the playroom on and off with a fast rocking motion, so it did literally almost hurt one's brain, agreeing heartily that he wished me to suffer as he had from the way I switched him on and off at Christmas, and each day. Then he plunged us into darkness and sat on the couch with his coat wrapped around him, saying 'Y-I' in a cruel old man's voice, which he agreed was meant to frighten me. It was, he said, his grandfather's voice. I spoke to him about his reluctance to come out in the light and be himself. He was hiding inside grandfather's voice, as under cover of darkness, but it was really he, Bobbie, who was furious with me, and was afraid to let us be a you and I. He then separated the two sounds a little more. 'Y-I'. He was silent. I asked what he was thinking a few times and he eventually said 'Prancelot' – 'Spaghetti'. I tried to show him how he tried to create a spaghetti mother in me – stuck together with him in the darkness; how I had to keep asking questions, making guesses, pulling replies from him as though blowing his nose for him, thinking about him every minute, always stuck to him.

He responded with great feeling to this, and said 'Throw spaghetti away – get it all off – gooey toffee everywhere – get it all off' – gesturing vigorously the while. He became very lively, but as so often in these moments of coming to life, he gave an impression of not knowing what to do with this unfocused, diffuse surge of feeling bubbling up. It was partly aggressive, partly loving, partly sexual. He came over to me, as though to hit me, then half patted my hair, then he tried to undo my smock. I stopped him, and he tried to open the door to the garden, and I prevented that. Then he stopped in his tracks, slumped a little, stared into space and said in a desolate voice 'Kisstone,' and then, 'not much mita in the water.'

This session seems to me to demonstrate two important developments: first, Bobbie's ability to expel into me in a focused, aimed way his suffering over the torturing switching on and off experience; second, his ability, for almost the first time, to shed the apparently good soft, but terribly cloying, suffocating object he tried to produce in me and inside himself. The session shows, too, the price he feels he pays each time he gives her up. He comes to life, his feelings and sensuality mount towards a more separate alive object, but any move she makes to limit his advances is taken as total rejection and he is paralysed again. A year later he could demonstrate how, if any aspect of him was rejected, he felt totally 'wiped out – no more Bobbie'.

On the other hand, his confidence was rising, his constipation and catarrh began to improve, and his realisation that a separate alive object could still reach out to him in an unsticky way was growing a little.

The long stocking – a lifeline

In a session in February, he reveals, I think, some belief in the possibility that there may be help at hand if he gives up his autistic methods of withdrawal.

He told of a game he had played with his sister where a boy and girl had been kept imprisoned down a dark well. A long long long stocking, or a long long long penis, or a long long long clitoris was thrown down, and each of them came flying up in the air, talking and shouting, landing on the other side of the street. So also did Bobbie's loved ones, parents and old teachers, some reproaching him, but all talking and terribly alive. As he described all this, his voice rose and fell and rose even higher in almost musical rhythms and waves. Normally he spoke in a flat, small voice – his words were mostly like little wisps of smoke or puffs of wind – you could easily feel they hadn't really been uttered by anyone, and he forgot them himself within seconds.

It is probably a fact that Bobbie's growing adolescent sexuality was helping enormously to rouse him out of the particular dead kind of withdrawal he was so habituated to down in his well; I think, however, he must also have interpreted the new five times a week arrangement as a genuine lifeline.

There is a third element in the long stocking material which has helped me enormously in subsequent years to understand the feeling Bobbie so often gave me, that my reach did in fact have to be very long. I felt at times and, I am certain, *showed* dreadful urgency and despair about what would happen if I could not reach him and help. I often had literally to move my head into his line of vision to remind him I was there. He seemed so dead, or at best, so in danger of psychic death, and yet so utterly incapable of taking any steps whatever to bring himself to life. It does seem probable that my urgency was absolutely essential to him at a certain point, as he could not feel it for himself. I have, unfortunately, come to learn something about the considerable degree to which he exploits this situation.

Bobbie's lack of grasp

Earlier I have described how Bobbie seemed to need to keep me talking and interested in him all the time. No breathing spaces were allowed; my silences seemed to mean to him that I had drifted off and left him to drift. This perpetual flow of speech from me was not, much of the time, used by him for purposes of understanding. The copy-cat spaghetti mother stuck eternally to him stimulated no feeling or curiosity. He seemed not to understand that he could follow my words. Nor did he appear to try, except when he was very desperate. Now that he had more or less what he wanted from me, he gave the impression of settling down for a life-long sleep on my couch.

I began to wonder where the ordinary forward-moving, life-giving, volitional impulses were in him, why for example he never grew bored and why he so seldom grasped the 'stocking' when it was there. Why did I have all the urgency, all the sense of time, impatience, concern about his lack of development, and at times unutterable boredom? Meltzer has suggested that these autistic children employ the maternal object as an extension of the self for the performance of ego functions, not only for purposes of omnipotent control, but also out of a special type of dependence (1975: 21).This, I believe, was true of Bobbie. It is also true that he exploits this situation of genuine need.

He resists effort of any kind because he is afraid, but also perhaps because of inertia due to a lifetime of immobility. His hands have hardly any knuckles; instead they are splayed out and boneless, as though they have never grasped at or clutched anything. He had, after all, been autistic for a very long time. His autism had become not only a reaction from the earlier horrors, but a positive life-style. He withdrew, or as he called it, 'drifted off', not just when he was in distress, but to avoid situations of really quite minor discomfort. He called this the 'lazy Bobbie'. It was simply easier, for example, for him to let go a thought or feeling that he had had two seconds before, and let it disappear forever, than to go back and pick it up. He lacked powers of recollection and memory and methods of integrating himself, but he was and is peculiarly reluctant to acquire them.

After much work on this, Bobbie did begin to experience some of his own impatience, then a growing preoccupation with time. His concept of time had been virtually non-existent. As we came to work on it, it began to take on very much the shape of the old flat closed-door situation of the 'hook of a door' days. As he began to dramatise this problem in sessions, it was clear that sessions had beginnings and endings but no middle. Both beginnings and endings squeezed him brutally out. The beginning produced a perpetual feeling that 'it's a bit too early' – I could never be ready for him; the ending was so dreadful that it invaded all the way back to the beginning. The agitation he experiences even now when I glance at my watch is indescribable. In his sleepy days, time did not seem to pass at all. Now it was so fleeting that it was as bad as the cruelly rocking light switch. Time was not something he could fill, nor could it fill him with anything of any interest or value. He could not seem to get hold of a period of time that he could experience as sufficiently long. His own attention was so fleeting and he drifted so frequently that he was in fact present only for a few seconds at a time. His experience of a substantial, reliable, permanent object was by definition very limited. Gradually, he did begin to talk about his hatred and dread of time, and this seemed to pave the way for him to take more active steps towards ensuring that he get the maximum amount of pleasure and security from the sessions and also from his life outside. He became able to plan a little.

THE THIRD PHASE

Movement – forward and back

Around the time of the summer break when he was 15, I gave up much of the previously 'soft' adapting to certain of Bobbie's obsessional rituals which slowed us down on our way to the playroom. Although irritated by this, he seemed struck by one remark I made. I said that although I wouldn't let him mess around at the top of the stairs, he should come to the session room and 'we could talk about it together down there'. He made me repeat this suggestion for weeks afterwards, especially the 'we'.

Early in the autumn, it suddenly occurred to him one day, as I persisted in my refusals, to ask me to join in a pretend game. In the game, we pretended that I had not denied him these rituals, but had permitted them all, and even made all the old interpretations relevant to them. He had played imaginative games before, but only rarely was I ever in them, and they were never organised like this.

These ramified and grew and were elaborated on until they soon included almost our whole history together since he started coming to the house. They described his journeys, his arrivals, his departures, his drawings, even his pretend games within pretend games. Part of this history was acted out in our play, and part of it was embodied in enormously long lists he made of subjects which had been talked about in his sessions.

A second type of game arose from a dramatisation of his parents' telling him that his sister and he were now too old to play sexual games, and he 'mustn't touch' her sexually any more. It seemed also to connect with the birth of a realisation that the 'we' I was constantly offering him to replace the old YI stuck together couple was not a promise of sexual intercourse. He dealt with this fleeting awareness of growth, frustration, change, separateness and sexual differences, by making his sister change into all sorts of boys of his own choosing. He even began to lay plans for one or two weeks ahead, concerning which day of the week these astonishing changes (which were to astonish his parents, but never him) should take place.

These games did, I think, involve genuine efforts to deal with matters which were of great moment to him – time, change, growth, separation from his objects, external and internal, but also separation from his own past self. They gave him enormous pleasure and I am certain did help, as all imaginative play does to an extent, to enlarge his internal world. He sometimes reminds me of someone who has been paralysed all his life and is flexing a muscle he did not know he had. He loved adding to his long lists, and checked the next day that I had remembered the whole list, together with its latest addition. He was delighted when I remembered, and always pretended not to notice if I left an item out. It was as though he had not previously realised that he could use his imagination for purposes of omnipotent control. These long lists, unlike the long stocking, were his creation.

The games did represent, I think, a considerable development in the direction of Bobbie's relinquishing external sticking techniques in favour of imaginative reconstruction; or rather, they began this way. Each game began with some meaning and function; it usually dealt with some anxiety past or current. After several days of repetition, he looked much less worried as we played the game, and could even sometimes smile at the him who was afraid a short while ago. But at the point where another child would have moved on to a new game, the process entered a third phase of glacialising, deadening, ritualistic, dreadfully boring rigidity. It would remain in this immutable form throughout all time if I did not refuse to play my part. He had got stuck – not simply to me but to his old self and his old way of doing something. (He has found over the years ever more subtle methods of avoiding thinking. He will do anything, for example, to get me to make an old interpretation rather than a new one.)

I have had to learn to resist the pressure to be the soft conforming object that plays in with this comfortable but sleepy inertia. While I was dutifully proving what a good remembering mother I was by reciting my lists or my lines, I was prevented from thinking, and from understanding whatever he was really feeling on a particular day; he was prevented from developing.

The difficulty is that while he appreciates this on one level, and friendly figures in his play often reassure him that it is safe to move forward, change and meet new situations, that it is 'OK to make mistakes', to 'stick up for himself', to 'come out of the deep freeze and learn to walk', he is at times still faced with another menacing figure, in human form now but extremely vicious, which warns him that to take any step forward toward grownupness, to observe, listen, talk, protest, carries enormous risk. He will be 'left to be dead forever and ever with no eyes, no ears, no mouth and no penis'.

More recently, as Bobbie has become more aware of his own need and wish to develop, to 'catch up' as he puts it, the brutal figure no longer plants itself so often in his path; instead it goads him on from behind, telling him he 'must talk to people', 'stop staring' and 'get in line'. This object seems to dog every step he takes, but its grip is loosening slightly. Out of the 'net with a hole in it', where Bobbie's persecutors were inhuman stray noises and lights and sensations, has crystallised a frightening, sometimes terrorising object whose human form is nevertheless beginning to take on manageable proportions. It has, however menacing, a location and a shape.

Postscript

Bobbie is a less frightened person now than when this paper was written. It is interesting to note how one unfortunate consequence of his more fearless attitude is that he now actively uses his autistic habit of withdrawal to avoid any situation he dislikes. In the early years of my work with him, it was often impossible for anyone to get him back from his withdrawn states. Then came a time when both his parents and I found that, with difficulty, we could. Then, as his awareness of time increased, and there was some ego development, he began to be able to pull himself back from these states, and even prevent their taking place. Now, however, it is increasingly obvious that he can go into these states almost at will for defensive purposes. He does this to avoid any situation he dislikes, or unpleasant fact of life: e.g. recognition of his illness, of what it has cost him, his inability as yet to earn a living, his 'baby brain', his jealousy of my other patients and my family, and his awareness that the 'make it soft' mother figure can be related to a husband and other objects, a hard fact of life for him at his age and level of sexual arousal to swallow. He simply announces threateningly when he dislikes the course a session is taking, 'Mrs Alvarez, I'm going to drift off', or 'Mrs Alvarez, I'm going to become Toby', a very ill autistic child whom Bobbie remembers. What was originally and still is at times a real dissolution and collapse is now put at the service of a more active and mischievous part of his personality. He is also correspondingly more actively helpful with the work of treatment, so it is extremely difficult to predict the course of the next few years.

SUMMARY AND DISCUSSION

Some tolerance of separateness and consequent ego development has been achieved in Bobbie. He travels about London and beyond by public transport, can make adaptive adjustments if things go wrong, can use telephones and restaurants, and carry on relatively normal conversations. He has joined a Boys' Club and is learning to box. He still has considerable learning difficulties, particularly in understanding why and how he knows something, but his comprehension is slowly beginning to move toward the level of his reading and arithmetic skills. He is 17, however, and his social life with normal boys of his own age at school is still very limited, and his capacity to earn a living minimal. When frustrated, he no longer always flops; he can show genuine, sustained, but almost overwhelming anger. He is more alive and awake to his own realities, and this occasionally persuades him, albeit reluctantly, to think about his experience.

I have tried to show some of the developments which have led up to this state: first, how Bobbie found briefly but then lost a link to his object, with consequences very like psychic dissolution or death; second, how he found this link again, but how it was and is an extremely inadequate one; third, I have hoped to show how the inadequate sticking link is at times replaced by a more living one, and the moves he and I have both had to make in strengthening this situation.

Discussion of Bobbie's longing to be stuck

It is possible, I think, to view Bobbie's static relationship both to his object and to his own past experience in the light of Frances Tustin's theory of Normal Primary Autism. She describes this condition as a normal state in the very young infant in which 'his whole experience seems to be in terms of his own body stuff to which an end or boundary is not conceived'. This condition is prior to the realisation that he has a skin, that his body and self has boundaries and that 'the flow of his body stuff can come to an end' (1972: p. 60). She agrees with Winnicott's insistence on the value of this illusion in earliest infancy. In Winnicott's words, the mother

> affords the infant the opportunity for the illusion that her breast is part of the infant. Omnipotence is nearly a fact of experience. The mother's eventual task is gradually to disillusion the infant, but she has no hope of success unless at first she has been able to give sufficient opportunity for illusion.
>
> (1958: p. 238)

Tustin too stresses the danger of premature impingement of separateness and consequent premature loss of the illusion.

Partly because I was Bobbie's second therapist, many details of the early years have never been available to me. I do know a little; that his mother was very depressed when he was born, that he had difficulty holding his food for the first three months, and that he had two traumatic separations from his parents at age 2. I do not know whether he entered these separation experiences in a state that was less than robust emotionally. Any attempt, therefore, I make to link Bobbie's material with theories of infantile development must be purely speculative. What I do know is that his material has involved a perpetual attempt to preserve a static undifferentiated situation between himself and me, and between himself and his own previous experience. He will not go forward out of himself, neither toward his object nor forward in time, unless what he is meeting is absolute familiarity,

54

continuity and sameness. His string play, his copying, the endless touching rituals, the spaghetti mother, the repetitive games and the more recent verbal trickery to produce repetitive interpretations are all bent against awareness of boundaries and of what lies beyond them – novelty and the unknown. The interference with opportunities for mental growth is incalculable.

He has, nonetheless, made certain cautious and difficult moves outwards. Recently he represented these by a dramatisation of himself being released from a deep freeze where he had been 'left to be dead forever and ever with no eyes, no ears, no mouth and no penis'. He demonstrated a person struggling forward in thick ice, beginning to use his legs, and gradually moving and walking more freely as he gets further out. The difficulty is that what he seeks is a setting not far removed from the chestnut material of earlier days: a country cottage where everyone does absolutely everything together all day long. Unlike the chestnuts, the inhabitants move, but in perfect unison. It is a kind of half-way house between his autism and being really alive; it permits some contact and some development but under rigid and jealously defined conditions.

Discussion of the withdrawn states

It is evident, I think, from the differences between the dark well, the falling material and the cosy chestnuts, that Bobbie's states of apparent withdrawal were not always of the same order. Some seemed to involve a real helpless dissolution, a total disappearance and drifting off, others seemed more like a lazy letting go. Some seemed more hostile and negativistic, others had a dreamy sensual quality. Sometimes, in fact, Bobbie is simply pretending to be withdrawn, while he keeps a very watchful eye on my every response. Silence and immobility are common to all of these states, and it has often been extremely difficult to distinguish one from the other, especially as one state may follow another with great rapidity throughout a totally silent and immobile session in a week of silent immobile sessions. Despite this, on many occasions I have been relatively certain that Bobbie's drifting off was not defensively motivated or even motivated at all in the proper sense of that word. Several writers seem to me to be in accord on the need to make some sort of distinction here. Esther Bick, for example, distinguishes very carefully between 'unintegration as a passive experience of total helplessness, and disintegration through splitting processes as an active defensive operation in the service of development', and considers that the former situation is conducive to anxieties which are of a catastrophic rather than a more limited persecutory or depressive character (1968: 484). Tustin, too, says of the logic-less child, 'It is a mistake at these levels to bring in the notion of intent on the part of the child'(1972: 51).

Meltzer and his co-authors make a similar, but much more elaborated point. They state that although these autistic children do project their ego into the maternal object for purposes of control, they also do so out of dependence. These authors find that when the projection is out of dependence, interference with it by refusal on the part of the therapist to perform the ego function results in flop rather than anger, with subsequent withdrawal into a state which they term the 'Autistic State Proper'. This is described as a static-like interruption in the transference of autistic patients, which is viewed as a suspension of ongoing mental life, and results in a temporary state of true mindlessness (1975: 8). This state is not, Meltzer insists, a defence against anxiety, but is brought about by the 'bombardment of sensa in the face of inadequate equipment and failure of dependence' (1975: 19). He believes that the depersonalisation and confusion which result far outstrip in complexity that produced by massive projective identification; the children are said to suffer rather from a *failure* to achieve projective identification.

Meltzer's definition of the inadequate equipment is of an inadequate internalised maternal object, but another way of putting it would be to consider the inadequacy of the child's ego, and the vulnerability and exposure which result. Changes in routine, a decision on my part to cease performing some function for Bobbie, the setting of any type of boundary or limit, could produce dreadful bewilderment and depersonalisation. He did not seem to feel the bit of routine was missing, he felt he had disappeared along with it; in his words, 'wiped out – no more Bobbie'. He seemed to have no membrane to place between some central self and experience. He was simply bombarded. Loud sounds 'hurt his brain', and he winced in apparent pain whenever I switched on the light. Every experience was, literally, 'a bit too early' for him. He was either totally exposed and present, or completely absent in his drifting state. He has often made me think of the metaphor of 'backbone', he was so lacking in it. Even now, when in fact his standing and walking posture is much more erect and firm, and his dress neat and no longer hobo-like, he can slump and crumple on the couch so that his form becomes astonishingly boneless and shapeless.

Tustin cites many examples of cases of infantile material where the experience of separateness was not that the infant had lost not only the breast, but also its own mouth. She describes the infinite depression which results (1972: 12) She, like Meltzer, describes the flop type of depression, and suggests that the autistic children who have a protective shell against psychotic depression are more possible to help than the 'amoebas', the passive, inert children, like Bobbie, whose self-protective behaviour seems to be solely on the pattern of a reactive psychological response – that is, in terms of immediate convulsive expulsion. She suggests that the 'crustaceans' who have a shell have interposed a developed piece of behaviour between a stimulus and their reaction to it: they can blot out awareness of a shock to which the more flaccid child has succumbed (1972: 54). It may be that it is the unfortunate coexistence of extreme depression with excessive passivity which compounds the problem so terribly both for this type of child and for the therapist who tries to reach him.

A feature of the counter transference

I want now to consider a possible relation between an element of the counter-transference and Meltzer's concept of the autistic child's 'inadequate equipment'. Meltzer is here conceiving of an internalised maternal object which is only two-dimensional, paper-thin, and inadequate as a container for the reception of the infant's projective identifications. He posits a possible experience of maternal attention of the in-one-ear-and-out-the-other type, and suggests that certain personality features in the child, or severe depression in the mother in the autistic child's infancy might provide this type of two-dimensional experience (1975: 19). His theory is that where the child comes to lack an internal object which provides sufficient opportunity for projective identification, and there is in addition insufficient opportunity for dependence on the external object for what Esther Bick has called adhesive identification (a type of clinging dependence in which the separate existence of the object is unrecognised), the child's only recourse when in great distress or terror is to the mindless autistic state (1975: 228).

According to the theory, a more three-dimensional object would be experienced as having space and room inside it for the child, and on the mental level, attention, thought, memory and time for the child. It is possible, I think, to view Bobbie's material as moving from the more dissolved, well-nigh objectless state where his object was little more than a 'net with a hole in it', to the two-dimensional 'hook of door' adhesive situation, and eventually, to something offering greater security in the chestnut material and the drawer which contained his ticket.

To a limited degree, there has also been some move toward a perception of an object with a mind which can receive the impact of his emotional projections, remember him and think about him, as instanced by his glaring at me while vengefully switching the light on and off, and by the memory games. There has also been some corresponding but equally limited development of his ability to use his own mind for these purposes, for example in the long lists and imaginative games which are his creation, and in his new-found ability to plan.

I would like now to describe a particular feature of my counter-transference to Bobbie when he was in his most fallen drifted states. My suggestion as to its possible therapeutic usefulness, and its possible theoretical implications must be taken, however, as purely speculative. Meltzer and his co-workers lay great stress on the importance of mobilising the scattered attention of their autistic patients. They describe certain modifications in analytic technique that seemed necessary to this purpose, e.g. they permitted greater physical contact than would normally be the case, and found fairly continuous interpretation to be important to their patients (1975: 15). I would go slightly further and say that there were times when I seemed to almost literally have to pursue Bobbie, by calling his name, by speaking with greater loudness, emphasis and even intensity than usual to make him aware of my presence; sometimes I had to move my head into his line of vision. It seemed necessary to search for him, not because he was hiding, but because he was lost. His own image of the long long stocking which was thrown down the well to release him and his loved ones, while having specific reference to the change to five times a week treatment, also exactly corresponds to my experience that at times my reach had to be very long. This may have something to do with the length of time he had been autistic, and the fairly little impact the infrequent sessions in the early years had on this situation. He was a long way off and he had been there a long time. It often seems, even nowadays, that the only thing that matters to him in a session is my aliveness, not any specific attribute of it. Tustin has drawn attention to the risk for the mother of autistic children in becoming a 'prodder', and the consequent danger that the child may become even more over-reactive to stimuli (1972: 63).This has been a constant technical difficulty: for me to be aware of what seems to be Bobbie's genuine need to be sought, to be rounded up and called back, while knowing that in his by now well-established and life-long immobility, he has a million ways of exploiting this, and even at times, as the spaghetti material shows, just enough ego of his own to resent it.

Yet it is my impression, and it can only be an impression, that some of these interventions of mine did help to bring him more to life, at moments when he seemed quite dead psychologically. The theoretical explanation is difficult. Tustin and Winnicott lay great stress on the infant's need for the illusion of continuity and for containment when the illusion fails. It is my impression that both these concepts involve an assumption of some aliveness on the part of the infant. Winnicott suggests that the mother affords the baby the illusion by an almost 100 per cent adaptation to his or her needs. The mother provides the breast just at the point where the infant is ready to create it, and at the right moment. The significant phrase, as I see it, is this: 'where the infant is ready to create it' (1958: 238). In Bion's terms, a pre-conception meets with a realisation (1962: 91). I believe I had such experiences with Bobbie of a meeting in the 'hook of a door'-type sessions and during the memory games, but not when I had literally to go after him in his dissolved states.

O'Shaughnessy has followed Bion's thinking in outlining for us the importance of the absent object as a stimulus for thought. She points out that the object when present is prima facie a good object, but when absent and therefore frustrating, it can be, unless thinking eventuates, felt as a bad object present rather than a good object absent. If the crucial step in development takes place, the absent breast is thought about, recognised as missing, and awareness of its existence as a separate object grows (1964: 34).

The theory is that if the mother can bear, contain and return in a modified form the anxieties the infant projects about such frustration, the stage is set for thinking to develop. As I see it, this aspect of the theory again assumes some aliveness and some capacity for projective identification on the part of the child. Bion himself stresses that his concepts of container and contained are only models, abstract representations, and in fact sheds his own metaphor by going on to describe the relationship by means of certain abstract signs (1962: 90). Nevertheless, as I understand it, the theory, stripped as it is, involves some directional flow from infant to mother.

A perpetual problem in my work with Bobbie was that in his most dissolved states, he seemed to have drifted so far that he was presenting neither a need for the illusion, nor, as far as I am able to tell, was he projecting into me his fear of, say, dying. Yet I was terribly afraid that he *would* suffer permanent psychic dissolution. Bion does suggest that certain patients may evacuate virtually their whole personality, along with their fear of dying. 'The seriousness is best conveyed by saying that the will to live, that is necessary before there can be a fear of dying, is a part of the goodness that the envious breast has removed' (1962: 97). I do not know whether Bobbie had evacuated all this in this manner (there is some material to suggest he felt peeled off and cast away vengefully), or whether he had lost it or let it go under more helpless 'bombarded' conditions. He seemed, at any rate, not to know or care that he or I were there, and I believe he sometimes benefited from my reminders that we both existed.

This raises a further question of how the infant may come to learn about the separate existence of its object. Bobbie's material could suggest that such awareness is called forth not only through the balance between illusion and absence, but also to cope with the object's uncalled-for, uncreated, surprising *presence*. The object may come to be recognised as separate, and, most important of all, as alive, not only by its mobility and freedom to be absent when called, but also by its mobility and freedom to be present when not called – to make the first move, as it were. This must surely be one of the ways in which introjection of and identification with a living object takes place – through the perception of its self-generating mobility, away from or toward the infant. The dangers of intrusion are obvious but so are those from too great an impingement of absence.

Finally, I would like to say a word more about the technical dilemma. Tustin has pointed to the risk for the mother of autistic children in becoming a prodder. Betty Joseph has drawn attention to a similar risk in the analysis of very passive patients. She writes, 'one can often find that the patient appears to have projected the active interested or concerned part of the self into the analyst, who is then supposed to act out, feeling the pressure, the need to be active and the desire to get something achieved.' She describes a particular patient who frequently made her feel that he would be able to move and to make contact and use his insight if only she would take the initiative. Her view is that if she did push at such a moment she would confirm that 'no object is good or desirable enough to attract him sufficiently for him to seek it out and involve himself with it, and therefore that part of the self that can take initiative remains unreachable' (1975: 212). She warns,

> the kind of acting-out and the projective identification of parts of the ego that I am discussing can very easily pass unnoticed and bring a very subtle type of pressure on the analyst to live out a part of the patient's self instead of analysing it.
>
> (1975: 215)

This is a warning clearly to be heeded, yet the theoretical and technical question and issue for Bobbie concerns whether he, in his most drifted states, had such a part of the self that could take initiative.

It is my impression that, in spite of all the subtle pressures and misuse and projective identifications that at times accompanied these states, there were other moments when he did not have such a part of the self. It was missing, but not necessarily projected. As the Lack of Grasp and Postscript sections show, Bobbie's withdrawn states do much of the time have a motive and purpose and involve the type of projective identification of his own capacity for awareness of time and for activity that Betty Joseph describes. When he announces threateningly, 'Mrs Alvarez, I'm going to drift off,' there is no question of his doing anything but practically inviting me to chase him, and this has to be interpreted to him. Fortunately, nowadays his drifted states are more frequently of this character than of the helpless type. I do think, however, that some of these states were of a different order and may have involved a condition which was either prior to the use of processes of projective identification, or involved a giving up of such processes. In any case, at certain moments it did seem important for me to feel an urgency he could not feel for himself. Whether this is anything more than a feature of my counter-transference to Bobbie's devastating passivity, or has any relation to the theoretical issues I have discussed, must remain an open question.

NOTE

1   This chapter was first published in 1977 in the *Journal of Child Psychotherapy* 4 (3).

REFERENCES

Bick, E. (1968) 'The experience of the skin in early object-relations', *International Journal of Psychanalysis* 49: 484.

Bion, W. R. (1962) *Learning from Experience*, London: Heinemann.

Joseph, B. (1975) 'The patient who is difficult to reach', in P. L. Giovaccini, *Tactics and Techniques in Psychoanalytic Therapy*, vol. II, New York: Aronson.

Klein, M. (1963) 'On Identification', in *Our Adult World and Other Essays*, London: Heinemann.

Meltzer, D. *et al.* (1975) *Explorations in Autism*, Strath Tay: Clunie Press.

O'Shaughnessy, E. (1964) 'The absent object', *Journal of Child Psychotherapy* 1 (2): 34.

Tustin, F. (1972) *Autism and Childhood Psychosis*, London: Hogarth.

Winnicott, D. W. (1958) *Collected Papers*, London: Tavistock.

—— (1965) *The Maturational Processes and the Facilitating Environment*, London: Hogarth.

4

THE SECRET WORLD OF BEREAVED CHILDREN

Susan Wallbank

'Give sorrow words: the grief that does not speak
Whispers the o'er-fraught heart, and bids it break.'
(Macbeth iv.iii)

Dependent for their very survival on the adults around them, children are essentially vulnerable. If they are to live – to manage to grow up into adults themselves – they need to be provided with shelter, food and warmth. The list of ideal conditions for growth and development would also include love, security and continuity of care.

Unfortunately, not all children will grow up in ideal conditions; for one reason or another – illness, parental separation or divorce, poverty and, for many children in the world, even famine and war – their lives may be interrupted by events which threaten their security and disturb that precious system of personal care and attention. The loss by death of one of the important people in a child's life may seriously affect the stability of the system on which the child is dependent for nurturing and sustenance.

Bereavement increases vulnerability. Bereavement is a high-stress, high-affect, life-changing event. Anyone, adult or child, who loses someone they love, is potentially vulnerable in several different ways. Bereavement increases one's physical vulnerability; the impact of loss disturbs sleep and eating patterns, the ability to concentrate and remember is diminished, and the likelihood of periods of ill health increases, especially in the early days of bereavement. Many deaths create the necessity for practical life changes and these expose the bereaved to further stressful situations. The emotional effects of losing someone much loved and needed can seem overwhelming at times. There can be a sense of being out of control of oneself and of the world around one. Many people, at one time or another in the first year of loss, describe themselves as feeling almost mad with grief. Bereaved children are particularly vulnerable. The death of someone very close to a child emphasises their helplessness – the lack of control they have over the events taking place in their life, and their dependence on others for the fulfilment of their needs. It also exposes them to the threat of possible further loss.

The world of bereavement can be an intensely lonely place. So much of the painful work of grief must take place deep inside the bereaved person. How much greater this aloneness will be for the small child who has not yet found the words to express their sadness; for the grieving 8-year-old who has no place to expose his feelings; or for the confused teenager who is expected instantly to become the man-of-the-house on the death of his father.

Most children are adaptable, and adjust to the new circumstances in which they find themselves. They discover a way of living with one carer instead of two. They learn to exist in a home suddenly devoid of laughter because the whole family is suffering a major bereavement. They learn to live alongside a severely depressed adult. They survive. The creation of a hidden, secret world may be a necessary part of the techniques and strategies they instinctively employ in order to ensure that survival.

A major bereavement can threaten the physical security of a child. If a child loses its only parent, or both parents at the same time, there will be an urgent need to find alternative parent-type figures. Children need to be cared for. A young child may have little or no say in the plans made for its future. Hopefully, there may possibly be an older sibling, grandparent or aunt able to move in with the child and care for him or her in the family home. Often, however, such a loss will result in the child having to move in with relatives – if he or she is fortunate enough to have relatives willing and able to take on responsibility for his or her long-term care.

Not only does such a child lose parents, but he or she will also lose most of those things giving life order, continuity and purpose. The child may lose friends, school, community activities, the people next door, the family doctor, the lady in the corner-shop, or the bedroom he or she has always known. Perhaps even the family pets will have to be found new homes or, worse, destroyed.

In a relatively short space of time the child finds him or herself living a new life in a new world. A separation has taken place between the past and the present. A young child may have little understanding of why his or her world has suddenly fallen apart. Those who have taken on the caring role may themselves be grieving the loss of a dearly loved sister or brother, daughter or son. In their pain, they may be unable to talk with the child about the events surrounding the death; particularly if it was violent or complicated. Or, they may feel it wiser not to discuss the past with the child – better to move briskly on towards the future.

Little children soon stop asking questions when they receive no answers; and older children learn not to 'rock the boat' – possibly the only vessel capable of ferrying them safely across those years which lie between their present vulnerability and the freedom of adulthood.

For such children, the past can become a secret world; one that is rarely, if ever, mentioned. They may grow up knowing very little about their mother or their father. When they go to school, they become aware that other children have a sense of personal history and talk openly of mothers and fathers, of babyhood and infancy. They become aware that they are slightly different from other children; theirs is a past clouded in secrecy.

In a two-parent family, the death of one parent will disrupt the organisation and structure of a child's life. Year by year, in England and Wales, about 180,000 children under 16 are growing up in families which have suffered the loss of a parent through death. Four out of five of those children will have lost a father.

For a while, a child's fragile security may be threatened as it confronts the repercussions and need for change that such a loss may bring. The family may be financially poorer because of the loss of a wage earner; the surviving parent may decide to move home, preferring to be nearer relatives or friends; a parent may need to stop work to care for children or take on a new job to supplement the family income. At a time when the family is shocked, disoriented and under great pressure there may be the need for major life-changing decisions to be made. Now that there is only one parent in the family to care for home and children, the work load will have to be redistributed. Even quite young children may find that more is expected of them. Children may find their daily routines considerably changed; they may have to take on tasks previously done by their dead parent or give up activities because there is no longer anyone to take them to the match on Saturday, to drive them to the swimming pool or to pay for their dancing lessons.

A bereaved parent's patterns of social contact may also change. Often single parents have fewer opportunities to mix socially. Even such a simple task as getting out of the house may prove a daunting prospect with baby-sitters to be found and paid for. Familiar family friends may disappear, being replaced by new friends; people who have a greater affinity with the remaining parent's new single status but little knowledge of the past. Contact between the child and the family of the parent who has died may decrease – a child can all too easily lose access to grandparents, aunts and uncles.

The closure of each of these familiar pathways to a child's past will tend to seal off the memories and events contained in that section of their history. Many children find it hard to recall people or things happening before the age of 5 unless their reservoir of memories is stimulated and reinforced by the adults around them. Children taken into care are especially underprivileged in this respect; often they have no-one truly capable of helping them rediscover and explore their past histories. If there is no-one willing or able to take on this task the child's past becomes locked away – a secret even from it's owner.

A parent's wish to create a new partnership may provide children with a substitute father or mother figure, but such relationships bring with them the potential for further disruption. Children may be asked to adapt rapidly to new routines, rules and roles within the home. Obviously, it requires much concentration on the present and the future to ensure the success of these new beginnings. All too easily, the essential work of the grieving process, which, inevitably, involves looking back at painful memories, can be hindered; and all that was good (and bad) from the past allowed to slip away in a desire to move rapidly forward, away from the sadness.

All major practical life-changes will affect the children in the family. They will have to learn to adjust to a new way of life. There is little the child can do to moderate or influence such important happenings. Although some parents bring their children into decision-making discussions, many do not. Ultimately, it is the adults who will make the decisions and children will be expected to fit in and adapt to the changing circumstances created by those decisions.

Recognising the necessity for the construction of a new future, children may have to subjugate their private wants and wishes; relegate them to a hidden place where they can do no harm. Any attempt to express personal needs which are counter to a parent's plans may bring parent and child into a confrontational situation. Confrontation can be hard when it takes place in a family wounded by grief and bereavement.

Alongside the necessity to restructure one's life after a death, there exists the need to mourn for the lost person; and, through the work of grief, to reach an understanding of what has gone from life for ever, why it has gone, and to eventually achieve acceptance of the loss.

All grieving people – be they adult or child – find themselves, to some extent, in a 'secret' world after a major bereavement. Our society does not easily tolerate the outward expression of too much pain and sadness. If relationships are to survive, the grieving person rapidly learns to adapt their behaviour when in company, and let the tears flow in private. Like an iceberg, grief rarely exposes more than its tip.

The death of an important family member will affect each person in the group, and each will grieve in their own way for their own unique loss. The importance of the loss which a child has suffered may not be fully recognised. As one girl said after the death of her brother, 'Everybody was sorry for Mum – but I lost a brother. Mum's still a mother. She's got me, but I'll never, ever be anyone's sister again.'

Few children receive letters and cards of condolence highlighting the special loss they have suffered. They are rarely perceived as the 'main griever', their loss appearing secondary to that suffered by their parents. Older children may even be expected to take on the responsibility for the care of a grieving parent. Not only do their needs go unacknowledged, but a burden is placed on their shoulders when they are feeling most vulnerable.

Many people find it hard to talk to someone who is grieving, and this reluctance is increased if the bereaved person happens to be child. There may be considerable hesitation because an adult does not know quite how much the child knows about the death, or the circumstances surrounding it. They may fear that their words might distress the child, make them cry. If the child is further upset, this might have the effect of placing yet another burden on a grieving parent.

Even when a child permits an opening into its private world of loss, it may be hard for the adult to follow it up. The child who, weeks after losing his mother, greeted a neighbour picking him up from school with the words, 'Hello, you're not my mother, are you?' was possibly offering an opportunity for dialogue; but the suddenness of such a statement can leave an adult confused. The moment passes and is gone.

Children rarely inherit objects or money. To be left something by someone is to be seen as having been important to the dead person. A Will is a public acknowledgement of the importance and worth of a relationship, and to be included in one can create a sense of private personal satisfaction. Given the opportunity, dying children will go to great lengths to ensure that their personal property is fairly distributed amongst their friends and family. They recognise the importance of possessions. Sadly, few families take similar care in ensuring that a child will benefit from the death of a beloved grandfather or a favourite aunt. Objects can be more valuable than money: a pair of glasses, a pipe or lighter, a pen or the picture that used to hang above the chair by the fire. It is through such mementoes that links are forged between the present and all that was valuable and good in the past.

Children are not automatically included in the funeral rites following the death of a family member. Older children may be discouraged from viewing the body, even if they express a firm wish to do so. Visiting the grave or the place where the death occurred may be seen as morbid and unhealthy behaviour in a young person.

A death in a family will disturb the delicate connections which exist between family members. The death of a child will leave the parents deeply grieving; remaining children not only lose a brother or a sister but, for a while, they are also in danger of losing the security of the familiar relationship they have had with their parents. In the parent's absolute focus on what has been lost from their life for ever, the remaining children's need for love and care may be seen as unimportant. Children can so easily feel themselves to be a burden at such a time. A dead child instantly becomes the special child, the most loved, valued and wanted child in the family. In the same way, a dead parent can suddenly become the perfect partner to the grieving widow or widower. How can a child cope with such idealisation? How can he or she compete with a perfect but dead sibling? How can he or she reconcile the imperfect past it remembers – albeit imperfectly – with this new edited version offered by adults? Where have all the quarrels gone, the angry scenes, the fights?

Death, particularly sudden death, undermines the security of the adult's world. If death can strike once, it may do so again. Some parents become terrified of further loss in the early months of their bereavement and cling to their children, not wanting them out of their sight.

Death changes the patterns of family life. It destroys routines. It creates disruption and disturbance which can be threatening to young people. The business of the young is to get on with the work of growing up. The business of adults is to provide a secure background for that work to be accomplished. Death disturbs these natural patterns.

The practical implications of a major loss will gradually become clear to a child in the days, weeks and months of bereavement. New routines are developed, fresh patterns of behaviour begin to be established. However, the emotional implications are harder to assess.

Can little children understand the concept of death?

'There was an old woman who swallowed a horse – she's dead of course.'

The writer of this old nursery rhyme believed so, and research indicates that many quite young children are able to accept the finality of death. Children have considerable exposure to a 'natural world' where death is a common occurrence – everyday life brings dead animals, and insects and flowers. It is a rare child that has not held a 'funeral' for a pet that has died. The reflected world on the TV screen portrays variations on the theme of death and loss. Both sources enable the growing child to gradually build up a working knowledge of death which can then be tapped into when necessary.

If children have some understanding about death, does it then follow that they will be able to grieve for the loss of someone close to them? All the adult responses associated with grief may also be experienced by a child. Like adults, after learning of a death, a child may deny the loss. They may be numbed with shock, confused and afraid. They may search for the person they have lost long after they have acknowledged the fact that he or she will not be coming back. They may cry, or may not cry. They may be subject to rapidly changing moods. Like an adult, they may feel intense irritation, anger or a sense of guilt that something they did, or failed to do, contributed to the death. They may feel that their life has little meaning without the person they have lost. They may feel that they are going mad. They may be surprised at how little they feel. Like a grieving adult, they will have days when the loss is uppermost in their thoughts, and days when it seems unimportant and they are able to concentrate on the business of the moment.

However, children may face particular problems in grieving simply because they are children. One of the first needs an adult has, in order to set in motion the process of grief and rehabilitation, is the need to acquire knowledge. There is a desire to know how, when and why the death happened. The first major part of the work of grief involves the exploration of the events leading up to, and surrounding, the death. These are then replayed time and again, a private personal video running in one's mind. The evidence is searched and researched, until, through increased understanding, a way is found of accepting what has happened. Children may not have ready access to that kind of knowledge – they are often completely dependent for information on the adults around them – not only might they be denied the facts surrounding the death, but some younger ones may not even be told that the person is dead.

How can a child begin to grieve if they are told that a dead father has just gone away? How can a child understand what is happening if they are excluded from the funeral and all family gatherings associated with the death? How can a child grieve if they live surrounded by the pretence that everything is just the same as it used to be? Certainly, the fact that someone who was once so much a part of their life and is now no longer there will become apparent to a child. They will, of course, recognise that something is missing from their lives. They will sense the feelings associated with this change in the adults around them. Responding to this awareness they will grieve in accordance to how much this loss affects their life – a little or a great deal.

The gateway to knowledge is language. Very small children have an insufficient grasp of language to obtain information or verbalise their feelings and thoughts. They will respond physically to any threat or disturbance to their security; crying, clinging, refusing to eat. Their behaviour will convey their needs, and these can be met by sensitive care from those around them. They may need a lot more cuddling and attention for quite a while.

Slightly older children may have to learn a new kind of language to accommodate the new situation of death and bereavement. They are likely to be at a stage in their life when, every day, something new is learned. They want to learn; and will experiment by placing new-found words alongside the relevant event, action or feeling. If they are to learn successfully – with the minimum amount of disturbance – they do need the help of the adults around them. And they do need to be given the vocabulary of bereavement and exposed to the emotions and events of death.

Perhaps the adult wish to protect a child from exposure to the two taboo subjects of sexuality and death is a natural one. It is natural to want children to be happy, to allow them a period of innocence before they take on the cares of adulthood. The vocabulary of death does seem harsh, too brutal to offer to a little child. It involves using words like death – and dying – and grave – and funeral – and body – and burning – and burying. Perhaps also, few adults have reached a full understanding and acceptance of their own mortality and that of those they love. The bereaved child will be dependent for knowledge on bereaved adults who may well be confronting a new learning situation themselves; adults who are intensely vulnerable and protecting themselves from exposure to any fresh source of pain – including that generated from their own children's pain and confusion.

The pragmatism of the child can be unbearable to the grieving adult,

'But you said daddy was dead and isn't coming back, so why don't you get me a new daddy?'

'But why did they have to burn mummy's body?'

'Why can't I have her books and toys? She doesn't want them anymore!'

Innocence of death is destroyed the moment the child confronts a personal major bereavement. No amount of pretence will convince a child that everyone is happy that mummy has joined the angels in heaven when they can see with their own eyes the pain and the sadness her going has created in the rest of the family.

Alongside lack of information the child may be subject to incorrect information.

'Daddy has gone to sleep.'

But you wake up from sleep. Why doesn't Daddy wake up? If I go to sleep then, perhaps one day, I might never wake up, either.

'Your little sister was so good, that God wanted her with Him in Heaven.'

If I'm good will He want me too? Will I disappear one day, as well?

Adults who believe in a life after death will be comforted by those beliefs and perhaps be able to pass that sense of comfort on to their children. Resorting to religious clichés simply as a means of avoiding using words such as 'dead' only creates greater confusion in the child.

The more complicated and distressing the circumstances surrounding the death, the more likely it is that the child will tend to be protected from the truth. In protecting the child, adults also protect themselves from the child's reactions to that knowledge. Thus, the suicide becomes an accident, cancer becomes 'something the matter with mummy'. However, the more unusual and complicated the circumstances of the death are, the greater the chance of it being spoken of outside the home. Some such deaths acquire a high news value in local communities. Perfectly sane adults seem to believe that children become blind and deaf after a bereavement. The child sits in the corner of the room as the weeping adults discuss the death, but it is presumed that child has no knowledge of how it happened. As a result of this adult desire for protective behaviour, children may find themselves coping with several differing stories. There will be the story their friends relate in the playground – news travels fast. Then there will be the version from the immediate family, followed by the story as told by the more distant relatives. An older child may well read about the death in the local newspaper. In such cases, children model their behaviour on that of the adults around them. They rapidly discover the need for secrecy. They work out what is required of them, what is acceptable behaviour, and what questions must be avoided at all costs.

If a child is denied access to knowledge – if he or she is not encouraged to ask questions – or if they have a limited grasp of language, there is then a danger that wrong ideas and incorrect interpretations will develop and flourish. How is a heart actually attacked? How can something as gentle as a stroke kill you?

> 'Mummy always said I would be the death of her. She was right. I was.'

> 'Stress kills people. Dad was angry with me. If I had been better he would still be alive.'

Children create an inner world which contains all the fears and confusions, the doubts and inaccuracies they are unable to express. They may find themselves trapped inside a world of horrific anger, fearful guilt and dreadful recrimination, and have no obvious outlet for those feelings. Unable to communicate verbally, their thoughts and feelings are translated into actions which may well be similarly misinterpreted. The child who cries at night is more likely to be understood than the one who begins, once again, to wet his bed; or the teenager who gets in trouble with the police.

In extreme cases of multiple bereavement and dramatic life disturbance, children have been known to stop speaking completely – simply cease to use language as a means of communication. It can take great patience and skill to learn how to reach into the secret world of suffering that exists inside these deeply distressed children. Sometimes, a child's paintings can portray memories too frightening to be expressed verbally. Art and play therapists can help create a safe place where the child is gradually enabled to explore the terror of the past. These same techniques can be useful in less traumatic loss situations. Many children find it helpful to put their memories and thoughts down on paper in the form of a story or a picture.

Once past the age of 5, only part of a child's life will be focused on the home. The older a child grows the greater the importance of their peer-group relationships. The world of school and of friends takes on an added and increasing significance. Hand in hand with the experiential development offered by these new worlds is the need to comply with a different set of rules – often the password to success within these closed groups is conformity. To be bereaved breaks down that sense of sameness. Children are aware that, if they express their grief and sadness, there is a danger they will become separated from those vitally important relationships. Sadly, it is not uncommon for bereaved children to become increasingly isolated and alone. To avoid such a fate, children may be forced to lie, to pretend that they are fine. They become adept at making up excuses, skilled at explaining why patterns are changing in their daily existence – why the holiday is cancelled this year, why they don't take a packed lunch to school anymore, or have a clean shirt to wear. It might seem better to plead overwork in turning down an offer to go home after school with a friend, rather than accept and lay oneself open to having to return the gesture – to invite them into a home which is full of sadness and unpredictable behaviour, one chaotically organised in the early days following a loss.

Maintaining an image can be important to a child. Admitting one is now too poor to go on the school-trip may bring a few sympathetic words from one's friends but the price for that sympathy may be paid for later in isolation as friends find it hard to deal with this new development – an unequal situation which contains elements of embarrassment, plus the potential for high emotional outbursts; something many children in their teens find particularly hard to cope with.

Because they are 'different', bereaved children may even find themselves ridiculed or bullied at school. Kids are very adept at spotting the vulnerability in one another. Not all friends and acquaintances will be unkind, however. Many will do their best to be helpful and supportive, but this being a friend to a bereaved person is such a new situation to them too, that they will often not know quite what to say or do: whether it is best to mention the death or pretend it never happened; whether someone will be too sad to be asked to the disco, or feel neglected if left out. The basic principle seems to be – when in doubt, do nothing. And so, usually, good friends provide a safe but silent space for their friend's grief.

The sheer normality of school life can be a relief from the pressure of an intensely emotional and distressed home. Day after day, the child travels between these two separate worlds. Some children behave well at home but use their time at school to be difficult, angry or aggressive. Others behave perfectly at school, burying themselves in their studies, but engage in confrontation and attack within their family circle.

A grieving child may not be able to deal with the same pressure of school-work and homework expected of a child who is not grieving. The loss of the ability to concentrate and to remember facts may seriously interfere with their studies for a while.

It is essential that there is good communication between parent and school for quite a long period of time. All too often, after the initial passing on of information that the child's parent or sister or brother has died, when the kind words have been said and the offers of support and understanding given, then – quickly then, is the matter forgotten. On the one hand, the child may feel relief – wishing more than anything for things to be 'normal' once again. Enjoying the fact that life flows on as if nothing has happened, at school at least. Homework still has to be in on time, exams sat, sports days participated in. On the other hand, the child remains acutely aware that things can never be the same again.

Ill-considered jokes and humorous comments gain fresh significance and may deeply affect a grieving child. If it is a mother who has died, then mothers suddenly seem to be the butt of all jokes. If the death was due to a heart attack then the word heart – however light-heartedly mentioned – jumps out of every conversation. A completely innocent remark can bring an embarrassing rush of tears. A class discussion about the elderly can be an ordeal for a child who has just lost a dearly loved grandmother.

At school, many teachers will be able to deal sensitively with a bereaved child's feelings. Understanding teachers will be capable of recognising a child's need for privacy. They will comprehend the importance of not isolating a child – in not making them seem too special – enabling them to keep a position in the peer group. Alongside this, however, teachers must also offer support at those times when it might become necessary, a very difficult task.

The primary school child with only one or two teachers has a better chance of being cared for than the older child attending secondary school who will come in contact with many teachers during the week and across the curriculum.

Children, particularly vulnerable children, operate on a system of maximum self-protection. It may seem better to accept punishment for forgetting one's games kit than admit that there's no one to get it washed and dried overnight since mum died – thereby providing protection from the necessity of opening up a painful subject. It has the additional advantage of maybe protecting one's parent from a possible accusation of bad parenting. It can be easier to answer in the affirmative when someone asks how you're getting on, rather than to tell the truth and admit that one is feeling lousy.

Sometimes it can be very hard to know exactly what the truth is. Sometimes the truth, if spoken, might seem shocking and unpalatable. The truth might include anger at the dead person for dying and creating all this pain and upset. It might mean being absolutely fed up with living with seemingly selfish grieving adults who go on and on about how sad they are feeling. It might mean being most upset over the fact that the school trip had to be cancelled because it coincided with the funeral. Children know that such truths are not what adults want, or expect, to hear when they ask a child how they are feeling. Such truths belong, more appropriately, to that secret world of the grieving child.

People develop their own time-scale and unique pattern of personal grieving. These rarely match anyone else's pattern of grief. When the child wishes to talk and ask questions, adults may find this too painful. And when the child needs to remain silent, adults may wish to encourage speech. If the child is unable to respond in 'the right way' they can be thought of as unfeeling, heartless, or as having 'got over it rather nicely'.

Individual adult patterns also differ. A wife may accuse her husband of being uncaring after the death of one of their children because, unlike her, he does not want to talk about the loss he has suffered. His need for silence conflicts with hers for speech. Dealing with a major bereavement, such as the death of a child, can place an enormous burden of grief on a couple's relationship. Sadly, this strain is reflected in increased separation and divorce rate figures for bereaved parents. The necessity for the creation of even more 'secret worlds' in the surviving children of such torn-apart families is great. Not only may they be dealing with the containment of their feelings and fears following the loss of a sibling, but the subsequent war between their parents may require that they take sides in the battles raging around them. Still trying to understand the devastating effects of a death which has split their world into the two distinct parts of past and the present, they confront a further schism between the world of their mother and the world of their father.

Children can and do adapt to the major losses and changes that interrupt and disrupt their lives. Most families do try their very best to help children come to terms with the loss they have suffered, and most adults attempt to find a way of exploring with sensitivity and understanding the fears and thoughts a child may have after such a loss. Some families find that they grow even closer after a major bereavement through sharing their feelings and acknowledging their differences. They gain a new and increased respect for one another in the process, and insight into human behaviour not readily available to those whose lives have not contained such life-disturbing events.

Reaching an understanding of a death and its full implications can take months, or even years. In some ways, the after-effects of a major bereavement will continue for the rest of one's life.

The young girl who has no father to give her away on her wedding day may experience a fresh sense of loss and sadness, even though his death occurred many years ago.

After the birth of a first child, the loss of a mother seems, once again, to matter so much.

A change in life or a period of personal vulnerability can allow a death in the past to rise to the surface of one's thoughts. For a while there may be the need to grieve again for the one who died – to investigate the meaning of that loss in the past and its effects on the present.

In such an investigation grieving adults look back through time to see themselves as the grieving child: to watch that child as it struggles to cope with events beyond its control; to observe, as it experiences emotions which take it out of reach of friends and family.

For the first time for many years it becomes possible to look into that secret world containing the shock, the pain, the fears and fantasies too dangerous for expression when a child. And to remember that other secret world which provided places of safety and escape – small oases of private comfort, long, long ago, at a time when they were so desperately needed.

5

THE SECRET LIFE OF CHILDREN WHO HAVE EXPERIENCED EMOTIONAL ABUSE[1]

Sheila Melzak

INTRODUCTION

What is emotional abuse?

Emotional abuse occurs when adults responsible for taking care of children are, over a prolonged period, unable to be aware of and meet their children's emotional and developmental needs.

Damage to particular areas of a child's personality at one stage of development can make the child vulnerable to further damage later on. The emotionally abused child keeps her[2] experiences secret from both herself and from the external world. It is in part the internalisation of this secrecy that leads to distortions in the child's perception and thinking and hence in her capacity to learn and have relationships.

Contrary to the evidence, most children want to believe that emotionally abusive adults are acting in their best interests. They have difficulty in acknowledging or speaking about their experiences of emotional abuse. They fear the consequences of revelation: more abuse, pain, confusion and the loss of the frail relationship with the main care-giver.

Professionals and neighbours, may not see the signs of emotional abuse and may be reluctant to intervene between parent and child. Emotionally abusive relationships may thus continue for a long time before becoming apparent, if acknowledged at all. Severe damage to the child's personality and progressive development may have occurred before the meaning of a child's difficult behaviour and concerns become clear. This damage may not be amenable to therapeutic help. Each child must be assessed in her own right.

Emotionally abused children may or may not present symptoms or behaviour that are obviously linked to their abuse. The response to

75

emotional abuse may be a general under-functioning in all areas of development and serious psychological or physical symptoms (Berger and Kennedy 1975). Alternatively these children may show developmental difficulties in specific areas such as delinquency, social withdrawal or under-achievement rather than general immaturity. Their development may be seriously disturbed and distorted in their efforts to raise and maintain their low self-esteem.

Children are impressive in their flexibility in the face of family trauma and can withstand enormous external stress with the protection of supportive parents. Emotional abuse involves more than one or two traumatic exchanges between parent and child. There are certain chronically negative parent–child interactions that severely limit a child's capacity for healthy development.

Emotional abuse in children may lead them to feel emotionally damaged in adulthood or to repeat the style of parenting they themselves experienced. As adults they survive, but may unconsciously either repeat primary abusive relationships or compensate for past deprivations and distortions via present relationships – both strategies being unsatisfactory (Barocas and Barocas 1979; Shengold 1979; Miller 1981).

In Selma Fraiberg's articles 'Ghosts in the Nursery' and 'Muse in the Kitchen' (Fraiberg 1987), she demonstrated the way in which some adults bring unconscious fantasies and fears from their past to the task of child care and are unable to see children in their care as they are. This leads to serious difficulties both in managing children and in being sensitive to their needs as separate individuals.

The effects of emotional abuse depend upon the stage of emotional development when it is inflicted. Masud Khan (1963) used the concept of 'cumulative trauma' to describe the development of children who experience insidious emotional abuse throughout their childhood, the effects of early abuse linking up with, and sometimes even causing later abuse.

Garbarino (1989) points to five basic types of psychological maltreatment of children.

1 *Rejection*. Children need emotional acceptance, validation, attention and celebration at all stages of their development (see also Covitz 1986).
2 *Isolation*. To practise social skills, children need relationships with adults, special parenting adults, peers and children of other ages. Over-protective and possessive parents can seriously impede a child's development.
3 *Terrorising*. Some parents use fear, humiliation, verbal abuse and threats of violence to manage their children. This can build an internal world of distrust in others. These children are not bound

by the normal rules of negotiation with the outside world. They may be withdrawn or bullies. A parent may find ways of terrorising that are effective in forcing the desired behaviour – which makes children particularly vulnerable to this form of abuse. Terrorising may take the form of humiliation or double bind. It may have cultural support in teasing and bullying. It is sometimes used to 'educate' children into the adult's ways of thinking and behaving.

4 *Ignoring*. Parents under stress may be more likely to ignore their children. This may occur in situations of separation and divorce (Wallerstein 1989). Parents in mourning for present or past losses may ignore their children's needs, e.g. refugee parents mourning home, family and country (Barocas and Barocas 1979, Melzak 1989). Unemployed parents having to adjust to new lifestyles and poverty, isolated parents, mentally ill parents all may ignore their children's emotional developmental needs.

5 *Corruption*. A parent may overwhelm a child with their own unmet needs in the form of sexual corruption, substance abuse and aggression – all resulting in the child's mis-socialisation into the role of the victim or perpetrator of corruption.

The internal and developmental consequences of abuse for a child may be those intended by the parent figure. However our focus needs to be on the *child's* experience of these five varieties of parenting style during development.

It is a paradox that children can be very attached to emotionally abusive parents. This is highlighted in this extract from the writings of Adrienne Rich where she deals with the long process in which she came to understand her complicated feelings towards her father.

> For years I struggled with you: your categories, your theories, your will, the cruelty which came inextricable from your love.
>
> (Rich 1986)

We need to consider why one child is very attached to her abusive parent while another may detach herself and search for a less abusive parent. This raises many questions about the community and society's responsibilities towards children. Complex attachments have to be considered when children are separated from their parents. Children may need to go through a protracted and intricate mourning process before they can form real new relationships and meaningful healthy attachments.

Adults and children have a different internal model of the world of human relationships as a result of their different experiences and the differences between childish and adult ways of thinking. Children can only develop a realistic model of the world via relationships with adults that are emotionally validating and developmentally challenging. The child, in order to develop an internal world that is adaptive, realistic, positive and healthy needs a special relationship with one particular adult in the early years. Adoption research (Lambert 1981; Hodges and Tizard 1989) shows that even children brought up in institutional care in their earliest years can become especially attached later to one new adult and make use of this relationship to build upon in order to develop emotionally in a healthy way.

How society deals with emotional abuse

There is no clear consensus about the definitions of emotional abuse, its short- and long-term consequences, the efficacy of various styles of parenting and the rights of parents. This has enormous implications for prevention and treatment (Graham-Hall and Martin 1987).

Emotional abuse is not easy to recognise let alone ameliorate, unlike physical abuse, where the effects are observable, and where there is some consensus in the law and amongst caring adults about the consequences for children. Ideas about standards of parenting are social phenomena involving social judgements (Garbarino and Gilliam 1980). Minimal notions of good enough parenting are continuously negotiable.

The dilemma of many emotionally abused children is not noticed by family, friends, the community, by school or social services. It is also true that the parents of some emotionally abused children attempt to change their style of parenting without social services knowing anything of the situation.

While statistics are available on emotional abuse cases recorded in social services child protection registers, many professionals who work with children know that these figures are a huge under-estimation.

In 1988, the NSPCC recorded 1,684 cases in England, Wales and Northern Ireland. The figure is about a third of cases of physical abuse and of neglect recorded, and about two-thirds of recorded cases of sexual abuse. Very few children are separated from their families as a result of emotional abuse.

Clearly, not all emotionally abused children come to the attention of social services. Many parents do have some insight into their own difficulties and ask for help. Not all emotional abuse is carried out by parents and only parental abuse is officially registered. Most emotionally abused children fall into a statutory grey area where neither the law nor social services can effectively protect them.

This may be one of the damaging effects of a culture that has abandoned most of its former respect for parenting. Parents or adults *in loco parentis* are often unaware of the consequences of their own actions. Sometimes they are discouraged by economic, practical and political constraints from considering the complexity of children's emotional needs, feeling forced to focus on only one aspect of the child's needs, jeopardising the child's long-term development in all areas.

Adults often find a fine line between what is considered to be abusive and what is not. This is complicated further where very good physical care may be provided while carers fail to meet the child's less observable needs for affection, attention and stimulation (Graham-Hall and Martin 1987).

The current statutory context

According to the present child care legislation, emotional abuse can be defined as follows:

> The severe adverse effect on the behaviour and emotional develop-ment of a child caused by persistent or severe emotional ill-treatment or rejection. All abuse involves some emotional ill-treatment. This category should be used where it is the main or sole form of abuse.
>
> (DHSS and Welsh Office 1988)

Social services departments all over the country are delegated by local authorities to hold responsibilities for protecting the children in their area. Where there is concern, suspicion or evidence of abuse, conferences of professionals and concerned adults can be called, where plans to protect the child's interests can be made. Professionals of different disciplines and lay people are supposed to work closely together in identifying, monitoring, assessing, helping families to change their style of parenting and if necessary, making plans for the child's future (Department of Health 1988). In reality, limitations of resources, coupled with serious difficulties of multi-disciplinary working prevent adequate child protection.

While legislation for children does change slowly, it characteristically lags behind advances in psychiatry, psychology and medicine in identifying and treating mental health difficulties, including treatment of emotional problems generated in abusive families. At present it is difficult for the law to look at consequences of parental styles on children's development unless these are observable. Our law accrues evidence over time, by which point severe damage may have been done to the child's emotional development.

Discussion needs to be focused on standards and quality of care, rather than on observable consequences. It is, at present, often impossible to protect children who will be the adults and parents of the next generation, and to prevent a repetition of the cycle of emotional abuse.

I will now try to illustrate the effect of emotional abuse by describing the story of one child and the process of her treatment.

SHARON'S HISTORY, ASSESSMENT AND TREATMENT

Sharon was referred for psychotherapy assessment at 8 years of age. Only a few months previously she had left her mother, Mrs A, and was living with a foster family the Bs. She had been taken into care, at her mother's request, after her family's long-term involvement with social services. Long-established emotional abuse towards Sharon within her family appeared to be irredeemable. There had been periodic case conferences and Sharon's name was on the Child Abuse Register, but there were never sufficient grounds to take Sharon legally into care via a Care Order.

Ironically, while emotional abuse within her family during her first eight years was the cause of severe emotional problems, this continued once she was separated from her family and placed in the local authority's care. The abuse experienced in care was of a different kind from the original abuse, but in no way was the care sensitive to her developmental needs. After she left her parents' home, primary caretakers were chosen for Sharon who had great difficulty acknowledging and dealing with the serious problems caused by the original abuse. These environments were thus emotionally harmful to her and built on the original abuse instead of ameliorating its effects (Kahn 1963).

Inadequacies (including meagre resources) in the childcare system prevented professionals connected with Sharon from co-operating productively.

History

Sharon's mother, a middle-class, emotionally deprived white woman, had been beyond the control of her parents, delinquent and consequently placed in care. She gave birth to Sharon in late adolescence, the father being a black man with whom she had been involved for three years but who left before Sharon was born.

While in a Mother and Baby Home, she met Mr A, a young white man, who had spent much of his life in care. He had been brought up in a children's home and was later adopted by his foster parents. He was hard-working and deeply insecure. When Sharon was 2, they moved into his mother's home in a multi-cultural inner city area. He projected his considerable deprivation, anger and anxiety on to black people whom he feared and felt hostile towards, being particularly jealous of Mrs A's relationship with Sharon.

The poor relationship between Sharon's mother and Mr A deteriorated when they moved to council accommodation in a mainly white suburb where they felt victimised. Sharon had by now begun school and had problems settling into group life. Mr and Mrs A suspected that she was singled out as the only non-white girl in her class. These suspicions of racism indeed had some foundation. In the city neither her behaviour nor her colour had been conspicuous and had not been commented on.

Ironically, before she attended nursery school, her mother and step-father had many pleasant memories of Sharon as a beautiful golden-brown baby and toddler, and of their honeymoon with her by the sea, where many holidaymakers admired her beauty and sweet nature.

Meanwhile, the A's had two sons of their own. Both parents were overwhelmed with pessimism, deriving no pleasure from each other or their children. They asked social services for help with housing, marital difficulties, and parenting Sharon.

They had a physically violent relationship but, when separation was suggested, they retreated from the marital therapist. Mrs A was explosive and violent in efforts to control and discipline Sharon, towards whom she often expressed ambivalence. She told workers that she herself was unloved and unsatisfied – she cried easily when offered sympathy. At the same time, she dressed Sharon immaculately for school.

Mr A often hid Sharon in cupboards when his workmates or neighbours called at the home and on the rare family outings he hid her under the car seat. In contrast, when Mrs A periodically left home for a few days at a time, workers suspected that he abused Sharon in some way. There was no clear evidence of this.

Sharon was punished with equal severity for naughty behaviour, accidents, her parents' negative moods, normal childishness and un-changeable aspects of her appearance. This left her confused about rules of negotiation in conflicts with others.

Showing disruptive, disturbed behaviour on beginning school, she was moved from her first primary school at the age of 7 to a small educational unit in which ten children, two teachers and one helper worked together to deal with socialisation and learning difficulties. All the workers felt, however, that the family problem was essentially marital and that Sharon had many strengths. Sharon had certainly experienced some positive parenting either from her grandparents or her parents.

From the start I noticed the separate effects on Sharon of Mr A's consistent but disturbed racist behaviour and Mrs A's inconsistent, explosive behaviour. Mrs A was alarmed that she hated touching Sharon saying, 'Sometimes she sits very close to me and I see her hand creeping out nearer and nearer towards me . . . I move away.' She always needed to criticise Sharon and label her every action 'bad'.

These aspects of Sharon's history had significant negative effects on her development, being intimately connected with the problems that she presented at home, her foster home, at school, and those shared with me. This sharing was both verbal and non-verbal, via fantasy play and the transference.

The team at the Family Consultation Centre, being aware of the importance of continuity of care, had repeatedly tried working with the As, hoping to change the family structures and dynamics to enable the family to refrain from making Sharon the scapegoat for its problems.

The workers were continually trying to balance continuity of care against the traumas of separation. This dilemma was compounded by the feeling that they would not obtain the resources for finding an adequate placement for Sharon. All agreed that any break in the continuity of her care meant a threat to Sharon's emotional security. There was no guarantee that a good enough placement for Sharon would be found quickly, if at all.

All children removed from their families, no matter how resilient, experience severe separation anxiety, self-doubt and an enormous loss, and may not be able to mourn at this time. Only rarely will children experience relief at separation. They are more likely to be less trusting of adults or themselves in the future. All this compounds any pre-existing difficulties a child may have.

It is obviously necessary sometimes to separate children from their biological parents. The decision to place Sharon into local authority care at this point can be supported without underestimating the fact that, at the age of 8½, Sharon had already internalised her parents' ways, attitudes and style of relating.

In her years with them she had experienced much pain and confusion. She could not bear to experience these contradictory emotions and feelings towards her family and the world. As a result of not really dealing with these feelings, Sharon could not cope with the normal social demands made on an 8-year-old girl to socialise, develop and learn in school.

Once in care, Sharon was placed immediately with a short-term foster family. The Bs were chosen because Sharon was a mixed race child and this white couple had previously successfully adopted a black child.

All workers recognised that Sharon needed to be placed in an adoptive family quickly. Social services wanted also to allow her to deal with her complicated negative feelings about herself as black, rejected and naughty, as well as her feelings about other people, about leaving her family and about finding a new family who could truly accept her.

Diagnostic Assessment

The difficulties Sharon showed in the foster home were the following: she took no responsibility for her actions, always blaming any bad situation on the fact that she was black and using this to absolve herself of all responsibility. She told lies. She copied her foster brother mercilessly, e.g. if offered a drink, she would ask for orange juice and if the foster brother asked for Ribena she would change her mind. She valued neither her possessions nor herself. She was unable to concentrate on intellectual activity, work or TV. She had excessive nervous energy. She fought with her foster sibling.

At school Sharon showed further difficulties. She was in a small class with a caring teacher who reported since her coming into care: increased distress; spitefulness and jealousy of other children; difficulty in concentrating; issues around colour and feelings of discrimination.

The assessment was suggested because simply removing her to a new environment would not change her into a well-balanced child. After meeting Sharon, certain parts of her history, outlined earlier, stood out as significantly abusive: the immaturity of her biological parents who had themselves experienced emotional deprivation in their own childhoods; any change in their external circumstances caused them considerable stress; Sharon's experience of severe emotional cruelty and inconsistent parenting from the age of 4; the externalisation onto Sharon by her biological parents of their personal difficulties, neither being able to acknowledge their own emotional problems let alone work them through.

At the diagnostic stage I met Sharon twice. I tried to assess her need for psychotherapy and the implications of our clinical assessment in helping social services to make plans for her care. They questioned whether she was adoptable.

Sharon presented as a child generally emotionally immature for her age but with extraordinary self-awareness and awareness of reality. Considering the degree of deprivation, both emotional and material, I was surprised at this quality of self-awareness, her rich, vital personality and her wide range of emotions – from pleasure to sadness, to humour to desperation, to murderous anger to delight, to fear.

Sharon was an extremely attractive, energetic child. Physically she was agile and very much in touch with her slim, flexible body. She had brown curly hair and brown skin. Her eyes were black and tended, with her expressive face, to reflect her mood.

Sharon achieved her self-awareness and hold on reality at the cost of her intellectual attainment within school. Her mind dwelt on her muddled identity. She articulately expressed the longing for a home where she could be valued and accepted as herself.

She expressed also confusions about whether she had been taken into care because she was black or because she was naughty – while she acknowledged her parents' difficulties and their inability to care for her, she also expressed a wish to go back to the familiar. She was able to express her conflict-ridden feelings of anger towards both her parents and I felt that she would benefit from being able to work these through.

Sharon's main difficulties were: negative feelings about herself and her low sense of her own worth; denying aspects of her own self including her blackness; denying conscious negative feelings towards her mother (these emerged indirectly in her dramatic play and drawing but seemed to be projected onto her biological father and her step-father); serious difficulties in relating to her peers and to adults – basic trust, the capacity for concern and sharing; problems in managing her aggressive feelings; problems in learning.

She also showed extreme deprivation. She talked about her parents' cruelty and violence but also about not being fed. She was extremely envious of other children, wanting anything they had, and suffering when she could not get what she wanted. She found it hard to talk about fights at school, her spitefulness and stealing, and she tended to blame and feel attacked by the unfairness and injustice of the external world. Initially she was alarmed that I might visit her school and talk with her foster parents.

The Centre team felt that psychotherapy was necessary to help Sharon to adjust to a new permanent family. We agreed that it would be necessary to continue the therapy at least through the early stages of her adoption to help her to settle.

We emphasised that beginning therapy should not be seen as an alternative to finding a potential adoptive family quickly. We stressed that the length of her stay with 'short-term' foster parents should not be protracted.

Initially the psychotherapy would contain and hold some of her anxieties, but working through these would take at least two years.

History (after being taken into care)

Only after a whole year with the Bs, who were intended to be the short-term foster family, did the local authority grant permission for Sharon to be adopted and for money to be released to look countrywide for this placement.

The Bs were very clear that they could not adopt Sharon but they were very attached to her and wanted the best for her. They became increasingly aware of the lack of social services resources, and felt increasingly bad about Sharon's situation. The boundaries of their commitment to Sharon were changed several times for reasons totally beyond their control. They felt increasing pressure to adopt Sharon themselves.

Decisions on Sharon's placement may have been hindered by dis-agreements within social services at several levels: How damaged was Sharon? How adoptable was she? Could adoptive parents be found locally? Could finance be released to advertise nationally? The cheapest, easiest solution and some hopes that the Bs would adopt Sharon, were over a long time balanced against long-term planning for Sharon's future.

This cautiousness did not match with Sharon's sense of time and her need for continuity of care. Sharon's extreme confusion and insecurity, which originated from her earliest experiences had by now been compounded within the foster placement.

It was after eighteen months with the B family that the prospective adoptive family, Mr and Mrs C came forward through an adoption agency specialising in finding parents for black and mixed-race children. Mrs C was black and Mr C was white. Again the workers were divided, some being pleased to find a mixed-race couple, others having grave doubts about this family being right for Sharon.

On a whim, and in the excitement of moving, Sharon had decided to revert to the name on her birth certificate, Emily. Mrs A had chosen this name for her, but Mr A changed it when she was 2. Both names had complex meanings for Sharon, representing different aspects of herself. After a few weeks she wanted to be called Sharon again, but the Cs insisted that she was called Emily at home and at school.

This was worrying given Sharon's obvious confusion. They claimed to anticipate and understand that Sharon inevitably would have many difficulties, but their understanding seemed cerebral and not heartfelt. Inevitably as a result of the quality of her relationship with her own mother and internalisation of her parents' racism, and institutionalised racism, Sharon would have particular difficulties with Mrs C, even though the fact that Mrs C was black may also have been a potential strength. In practice, the Cs could neither tolerate Sharon's hostility towards Mrs C nor her easy contact with Mr C. The Cs agreed verbally to Sharon continuing her therapy for a few months after the placement, but were unable to support it, a fact of which Sharon was very aware.

The week after her therapy ended, Sharon, on her first school holiday away from home, stole a cake from another child and then hid for some hours, knowing that the teachers were searching for her. The Cs found this kind of behaviour not only incomprehensible but also intolerable. After only a few months they suddenly asked for Sharon to be removed, saying that they could not tolerate her behaviour and the fact that she seemed to 'hate' Mrs C. Sharon's behaviour was directly connected with the central theme apparent from her therapy. It was not surprising that she stole a cake in a week when she was adapting to terminating therapy, and soon after leaving her foster parents, something we had anticipated in our preparative discussion with the C family, but which they were unable to hear. The Cs seemed uninterested in *understanding* Sharon's behaviour in any area except that of her overt racism and its roots. They wanted Sharon to adapt to their standards and priorities and could not give any credit to her years of life before meeting them. It seemed that the Cs, in spite of impressing social services as being good, professional, articulate, potential adoptive parents, were, in fact, quite unable to recognise and meet Sharon's developmental needs.

In locum social services had placed Sharon with the C family. They had felt that this was the least detrimental alternative for Sharon – the alternative being a local authority children's home. When the placement finally broke down, some workers felt that too many professionals had been involved in Sharon's case, whilst others claimed that Sharon was much more disturbed than had been realised. Sharon was placed back in a children's home.

Sharon had to deal with the many adult figures who shared the various legal, statutory, emotional and practical aspects of her present and future parenting. The general institutionalised racism in society was another factor militating against her needs as a mixed race child being met.

Sharon's treatment

The therapy revealed the extent of the damage to her self-esteem and the confusing representations of adult figures in her internal world. These were acknowledged and the early stages of working through began. These representations of self and others came alive via the transference. There she directed me to play the role of various negative and positive and idealised aspects of the personalities of her (first) parents as they must have been experienced by her at different stages of her development.

There follows a small part of the psychotherapeutic work. It gives some idea about the problems that Sharon was left with at the end of her treatment, those that she resolved and worked through on her own, and those for which she may need more help in the future.

She worked well in her sessions. Sometimes, as would be expected with a girl of her age, she was very resistant to talking or to sharing her deeper feelings, whereas she chatted easily about present concerns. At other times, in keeping with her lively personality, she was able to bring her concerns via dramatic play. Slowly the following themes emerged:

1 What was her mother really like? Sharon explored both aspects of her conflicting feelings about her mother. For a long time she held on to the conscious fantasy that her mother was wonderful but a victim of terrible men. At the same time increasingly her anger at, and fear of, her mother's malevolence emerged. Hopefully our work integrated the contradictory feelings towards her biological parents. Sharon brought material in several ways but usually around this theme: the battle in her mind between the idea of the mother she wished she had, and her fluctuating awareness of her real mother. This process of becoming aware of the reality of her situation was the aim of the treatment. This painful, slow process had to proceed at her speed.

2 What was her biological father really like? Slowly, over many months, her conviction that he was an abandoning, evil, black monster transformed into explorations that some black men were good people. There was even a possibility in her mind that he might be a popular musician (she met Afro-Caribbean men for the first time only when she moved to the Cs). As time went on she allowed herself to think about what he was like and why he had left her mother.

3 What was good quality care? This was linked to Sharon's complicated feelings and explorations about her own worth – physical, moral and emotional. The over-determined theme of food reflected not only her mother's neglect and witholding, but the unpredictable emotional food. Real food and emotional food were inextricably linked in Sharon's mind.

4 What had happened at the various points in her history? Were the rejections and punishments her fault or caused by people and situations beyond her control?

5 Her strong anger, envy and jealousy of her peers, especially in relation to important adults.

In an early session she told the following story and we wrote it together.

Sharon's story

Kermit is a little girl. She doesn't like school but she does like her food, sweets, chocolate and ice-cream. She doesn't like fatty meat or liver but she does like steak and chicken and turkey.

Kermit has two brothers who are human. She is a little cuddly animal. She is good and they are good but everyone calls her names like Blackie.

Inside, Kermit feels human too, just like them. She doesn't understand why they call her Blackie and Chocolate in a nasty way. Kermit calls them Whitey back but she doesn't understand why she does. She would like to understand.

More than anything Kermit would like to go home. She half would and half would not like to understand why she can't go home. She wants what she wishes to happen now, without lots of grown-ups explaining things to her in ways that she can only half understand . . .

She loves her mum and her dad. She loves her dog Leo and her brothers Elton and Shane. She loves her cousins and her aunties and nans and grandpa . . . she thinks they must like her because they send her money and things like toys at Christmas . . . BUT Kermit is very sad still, because presents aren't enough. They don't want to be with her and she does . . .

They say they don't want to live with her. They give Elton and Shane more than they give to Kermit . . . They have rows all the time, sometimes about her and sometimes about each other.

They thought Kermit was very naughty, because she wound them up . . . but Kermit thought that all little girls were naughty . . . so she feels muddled . . . because she doesn't think she is that different from other little girls . . . she did wonder if they didn't like being mum and dad for Kermit . . . they didn't seem to like her beautiful brown skin and beautiful dark curls and Kermit didn't really understand why . . .

Maybe they were the ones who were muddled . . . Can grown-ups have muddles . . .???

Kermit knows Elton and Shane like her . . . they like girls with brown skin and dark curly hair . . .

Kermit feels very muddled about her skin and her hair. She doesn't expect people to like her, even though some people say they do. At the moment Kermit doesn't really trust people . . . she thinks they have cheated her . . .

Sometimes she tries to trick them and that is good fun . . .

Sharon understood that we met in order to sort out and discuss her worries and problems. We characteristically lurched into a frenzied dramatisation. These were of events in the A household, particular aspects of which continued to trouble her, or else of events in the present that were on her mind, or issues connected with her present uncertainties about who and where she was and would be.

She also shared the pleasures and achievements of her new life and new experiences with a shy, mature and controlled pride. When she was troubled by anxieties from the past or the present, she became more disorganised and speedy, and found concentration impossible. She did respond to firm, clear communication and verbalisation of her fears and concerns. She could be warm and loving but was sensitive to any sign of potential rejection. She could be overwhelmed by despair at her present situation and her wishes to 'return home', although it was positive that she could express and share these feelings.

A typical session began with Sharon rushing into my room, sitting down and showing me some homework. On the odd days when she arrived before her session time, she was to be found apparently concentrating deeply on a page of a comic or school work and ignored me until this was finished. She agreed that she was very cross that I was not immediately available for her.

Once she rushed into the treatment room. She furiously emptied out my handbag and stuffed most of the contents back in the few seconds between her entry into the room and mine. She at first denied what was obvious, and then said that she had done this because I was seeing another child. For weeks she was convinced that I was seeing another child from her class, despite several adults assuring her that this was not true – this other child was being seen by another therapist. This demonstrates Sharon's strong wish for a special person of her own, and the depth of her envy and rage.

Often she would clearly illustrate her extreme guilt, fear of punishment and difficulties in assessing the boundaries of situations. One day she spilled some paint on my skirt and muttered to herself (as if I was not in the room): 'Oh God! Sheila is going to kill me.' She was astonished when I did not hit her and she kept saying over and over: 'You really aren't? I don't believe you.'

On another occasion, when she noticed a pane of glass in my room had been broken, she stepped back in fear saying, 'It wasn't me, really it wasn't' and agreed that she had often been punished for incidents in which she had not taken part, and so at times when she felt anxious she really was not sure what she had done, or if she might be punished. Her conscience must have become especially severe in this situation.

Sharon had clearly been traumatised and had experienced excessive anxiety, shame and guilt as well as emotional and physical pain.

Our initial chats often evolved into a fantasy game in which she acted her mother and she asked me to act her social worker or herself. She sometimes acted her wish that her mother's nice days were more typical and that she was at home; I would put into words that it was her wish. At other times she acted the reality of her inconsistent, wild, screaming, primitively authoritarian mother. These plays then evolved into plays about school, or happy couples who might adopt her.

Another typical play was one in which Sharon acted a shouting, intense, authoritarian boss and she cast me as an abused worker. I linked up the reality of her parents' behaviour with her inadequate feelings when living with them. This work was in stages: first putting the feeling of the abused worker into words, then relating these to a child living with an inconsistent mother and finally to her specific experience. She could not easily sort out if they were too bossy or if they were incompetent.

Most sessions ended with a game of hide and seek, Sharon always hiding and her therapist always having to be the seeker. She agreed that she never quite believed I would bother to find her, that I cared enough to find her or that I cared enough to spend an hour playing with an ugly, naughty brown girl. We did a lot of work on her colour and her negative feelings about her colour and her appearance.

The final theme was that of food. Sharon often initiated fantasy games in which she was a cook, a restaurant owner or a take-away chef. The importance of food had many roots for Sharon. The short-term foster parents had taken her, for the first time in her life, to restaurants, parties, etc. and she was entranced by every outing, telling me in great detail what happened. In the past food had been important in her parents' home. Sometimes pleasant experiences such as birthday parties were recalled but also times when she was deprived of food as a punishment. She often talked about poisoning people, in particular her mother, or drew a great fish biting her mother to death. She frequently made plasticine poison cakes, in the pretend restaurant.

As a result of her particular experiences, she could be difficult and taxing to the most experienced parent, with a rich fantasy life and strong energetic personality which made her both a joy to be with and an exhausting companion. She had been deeply instilled with the idea that she was to blame for any incident, and liable to be randomly punished by exclusion, rejection or physical abuse. This could result in her testing out adults and peers by behaving wildly and uncontrolledly and being very demanding. She could also be delinquent, lying and prone to distort the truth, either wilfully, or because her strong wishes and fantasy life sometimes made the separation of fantasy and reality difficult.

We worked on these issues from her past concerning her biological mother and father, her stepfather, who is, in fact, her psychological father, and her siblings Elton and Shane. In our games we often reversed roles, where she asked me to be Sharon and and she acted her mother, her stepfather or her real father. We also explored her position within her foster family, who obviously became more and more significant to her.

Over time, Sharon's image of herself and of anybody who was not white began to change in more positive directions. I considered Sharon's concern with her colour only part, albeit an important part, of our work. The more fundamental theme was Sharon's position within her psychological family, and her relationships with her parents whose confused images were firmly embedded in her internal world.

Whenever things did not go exactly as she wanted within or outside her sessions, she was reminded of her rejection by her parents and could not sort out whether this was to do with her colour, her behaviour or her thoughts. It rarely occurred to her that difficulties may have had nothing to do with her.

She connected any situation where she was at odds with others with her experiences within the family. She needed repeated clarification about the irrational nature of the system of rules within her biological home, which was not necessarily what went on in other places.

Then, abruptly, we became concerned with Sharon leaving our area, saying goodbye to various people, including myself, and moving to her prospective adoptive family.

We did some good work during the termination phase, but Sharon was still a very vulnerable child. I feared that our lack of working through all these aforementioned issues would militate against Sharon's settling in to her new family. An example of this was the incident when, away on a school trip, she caused much anxiety for her teachers by running away and hiding, something that she did during therapy when she felt low and needed to be reassured about her worth. I assume she felt low on the trip and wanted reassurance but the teachers could not have known this and assumed that she wanted to provoke them.

When we realised that Sharon's treatment was going to be ended quite abruptly, we decided to use the final few sessions to explore issues of separation and loss, and work on a book which was our record of her history and work in her psychotherapy, the themes we had explored and the ways in which she changed her view of herself during the time I had known her.

In her final sessions Sharon constantly said she did not want to be adopted by this family. She wrote on the clinic blackboard, 'I love the Bs', at the end of most sessions, scurrying to the back of my room and writing on the reverse side of the board a message that I would inevitably find when she had left.

In these last sessions, although struggling, she was trying hard to make emotional contact with the adoptive family at her own level. We had made a collection of books about black children and families. There were many pictures of individuals and groups. Sharon picked out a photograph of a mother and daughter and asked if she could mount this and take it for her prospective mother.

In these sessions, we talked again about her grief at her own first parents' actions and her anger and fluctuating self-esteem resulting from her rejection. We explored her difficulty in believing that grown-ups could be really different from her own mother and father. We also talked about the difference between their actions which made her feel that she was a horrible girl, and the fact that she was not a horrible person even if she sometimes did naughty things.

In our final session, Sharon enacted her own feelings of helplessness and vulnerability by curling up on my lap (something she had not done before) with her thumb in her mouth, allowing herself to regress, feel sad and cry. She felt depleted, unloveable and full of trepidation about her move. I was powerless to do anything except acknowledge her feelings and my own, and put them into words that she could hear and understand and indicate that she could contact me at any time by letter or telephone.

Aftermath

I did not hear from her again for many years though I heard about her from residential workers. She had lived in one children's home when she left the C family, for nearly a year. She began to succeed in primary school and adapted well to secondary school. She developed skills in drama and dance. She returned to the B family and lived there until their marriage began to break down, she was then removed. This was puzzling, and a further abuse to Sharon. She was placed in a different children's home, again for nearly a year.

Adults who met her seemed to continue to be divided between those who saw her struggle and vulnerability and felt that it would benefit from therapeutic help and those who saw her extroversion, warmth, humour and health as a sign of strength.

One day, when Sharon was 14, I met her in the street. She grabbed my arm and hugged me very hard. She pulled me over to a group of black teenagers who were dancing to the sound of a large sound system. She was excited and happy. 'Look, look at me I'm black, these are my friends, aren't you pleased? We do black dancing, we listen to black music. I'm going to be a dancer . . .'.

We talked in the street for more than half an hour. She hoped to be fostered soon by a white woman who had two black children, one of whom attended her school. She felt that they all fitted together. It was her own idea to be fostered in this family.

I felt that she had integrated this aspect of herself over the years on the basis of the work we had done. It was also clear from our meeting and from a brief contact with the children's home staff that though she had much strength, humour and emotional energy and ability to survive against enormous odds, she still also had self-esteem which fluctuated and many confusions about herself.

The day before she was due to move to her new family, not the family she had found herself but another chosen by social services, she took an overdose and was found by another child. She still turned aggression that belonged with the external world into aspects of herself. There was still some psychotherapeutic work to be done.

Summary

In Sharon's treatment, I tried to explore her particular inner experience of various emotionally abusive external events, and ways in which these have permeated and affected each normal stage of her development and the normal developmental conflicts.

She brought many pre-Oedipal issues to her treatment, issues concerned with the one-to-one relationship between parent and child, or jealousies between parent, child and sibling.

Though her biological mother, Mrs A, complained about Sharon's rejection by her stepfather, I felt that Mrs A must have felt threatened by any warmth between Mr A and Sharon, and let Sharon know her feelings. Sharon also may have been abused by Mr A.

At the end of our clinic contact, I felt that I had an incomplete understanding of Sharon's perspective about relationships between men and women. She certainly had an idealised wish for perfectly happy married parents, but I felt that her thoughts were dominated by a wish for a committed validating parent. The sex of the parent was less important than his or her capacity to parent. I understood Sharon's teasing behaviour with her foster father and later with her adoptive father to signify this tentative search for a 'good enough' parent (Winnicott 1960), rather than an Oedipal wish to have her own husband and get rid of female rivals.

It is clear that many adults had failed this child but, above all, the child care system was demonstrated to be inadequate to meet the needs of some children who are separated from their families.

Conclusions from Sharon's case

Sharon's story illustrates the deep-seated persistent effects of long-term emotional abuse in all of the five varieties described by Garbarino (1989). While in her mother's home, and when taken into 'care', she experienced isolation, rejection and being ignored. Her interests and intelligence were not validated, stimulated or developed.

In the foster and adoptive homes and in the local authority children's home, her rich personality, potential, talents and mixed racial origins were not developed or celebrated. In her foster home she had no access to the black community. In her adoptive home her impulsive behaviour, her difficulty in being alone and her lack of intellectual interests led to further rejection. In the children's home she could not fulfil her need to develop special deep relationships with one or two adults.

The cumulative effect of emotional abuse on Sharon becomes clearer if we analyse the different abusive elements of the external world and emphasise that *they interacted with each other during her development*. The primary abuse experienced with her biological parents was not ameliorated within either her first foster family or the adoptive family, as neither could make a serious commitment to her. The longer Sharon stayed with the foster family the less it became possible to prepare her for a new family as the temporary nature of the placement became progressively obscured.

Social services could not find a suitable match between *Sharon's developmental needs* (both to work through the effects of the primary abuse and to move forward in her development) and *a new family* which could take on these needs. They opted for the 'least detrimental alternative' rather than find placements in Sharon's 'best interests' (Goldstein *et al.* 1973, 1979). Thus they failed to find a good enough adoptive family for Sharon. Further emotional harm to her development resulted from a series of attachments, raised hopes, separations and losses.

This was the result of lack of adequate resources in social services to enable good practice to be carried out. For Sharon, the cumulative failures to meet her needs were a force that broke down her self-esteem – something she tried to maintain at some cost to her relationships with her peers and adults, and to her ability to learn in school. This force was undoubtedly internalised by Sharon during her time 'in care'. This, I would term 'secondary emotional abuse'.

As Blom-Cooper (1985) emphasises in his report of the enquiry into the Jasmine Beckford case, many of the problems in the systems of professionals responsibie for protecting children and keeping them safe are the result of difficulties in keeping in mind the complicated needs of the developing child.

SOME SOCIAL PERSPECTIVES ON EMOTIONAL ABUSE

Psychological therapeutic help to individuals and families (Minuchin *et al.* 1967; Minuchin 1974, 1984, 1989; Fraiberg 1987; Asen *et al.* 1989) is not the only way of treating and preventing abuse. Sharon's case clearly shows that sociological and political frames of reference are also needed to understand the relationship between children and adults. These important perspectives go beyond the scope of this chapter, but it is essential to highlight key issues where legal or social change is needed.

Privacy and the Family

In considering the complicated issue of the privacy of the family, civil liberties have to be weighed up against the issues involved in protecting children. At issue are the rights and privacy of the family versus the concerns and care of the community and the rights of the children. How can these best be balanced in such a way that children's developmental needs are most effectively met?

> We have a preference for privacy, to safeguard the right of parents to raise their children as they see fit . . . free of government intrusion *except in cases of neglect or abandonment*. [We can assume here also abuse]. The aim of this privacy is to safeguard each child's need for continuity. The preference for minimum state intervention and for leaving well enough alone is reinforced by our recognition that the law is incapable of managing – except in a very gross sense – so delicate and complex a relationship as that between parent and child.
>
> (Goldstein *et al.* 1979)

The balance of these polarities relates also to protecting children against abuse by adults outside the family. Social workers and lawyers often have the difficult task of balancing continuity of care for children against their physical and emotional safety. Research also shows that the more care breakdowns a child experiences, the less likely it is that a permanent placement will be found (Lambert 1981; Bean 1984; Rushton *et al.* 1988).

It is important to remember here that emotional abuse by adults towards children is not only committed by parents. It is often legitimised in many institutions in which children dwell, such as child care institutions, schools, etc. (Millham *et al.* 1980) and carried out by many adults responsible for the care of children.

Children in care

There are many successful placements with adoptive families of children at Sharon's age or even older (Lambert 1981; Bean 1984; Hodges and Tizard 1989). It is also unusual for biological parents to give up their child for adoption, as in Sharon's case.

Sadly, however, children who are taken into 'care' have many developmental problems, some of which can be worked through in foster homes, children's homes and adoptive families. Long-term difficulties caused by years of emotional abuse and neglect need understanding, skilled handling, and sometimes the help of informed professionals.

Families taking on emotionally damaged children need many strengths and often much support. It is tragic for children that many place-ments fail because the new families cannot deal with the effects of primary abuse. Inadequate care is given to choosing families or matching families and children; sometimes families are not adequately supported.

All through my work with Sharon, the difficulty in finding a family where she fitted well puzzled me. Perhaps the lack of general commitment to a child-centred philosophy leads to confusions in parents as to their responsibilities, and to confusions amongst professionals working within the child care and protection system.

> First we take the view that the law must make the child's needs paramount. This preference reflects more than our professional commitment. It is in society's best interests. Each time the cycle of grossly inadequate parent – child relationships is broken, society stands to gain a person capable of becoming an adequate parent for children of the future.
>
> (Goldstein *et al.* 1979)

Adults and children have quite different needs and adults are responsible for children. To use Goldstein *et al.*'s terminology, it is puzzling that adults do not always act in children's 'best interests', and that when biological families break down, decisions are made according to the 'least detrimental alternative'.

The attempted professionalisation of child protection and placement has caused a dehumanisation of the child care process. Attributes of 'good enough parents' (Winnicott 1960) acting 'in the child's best interests' (Goldstein *et al.* 1973) have been split up between the caring humane aspects of parenting and its more objective, careful planning aspects. There is less sensitivity to the needs of children – something that may not occur in less professionalised communities where there is more attention paid to the child's attachments and concept of time.

The most recent abuse trends published by the NSPCC show that much abuse occurs where children are not living with their biological parents and have been with their care-giver for less than two years. Though it is clear that emotional abuse occurs in all social classes and cultural groups, children most likely to be registered, and hence possibly taken into care, are children from poor families, where both parents are out of work and where it is likely that previous abuse has been recorded. These social factors, along with marital problems and internal dilemmas resulting from their personal history, may all interact to interfere with their capacity to parent.

Sharon's case is, in many respects, quite typical. Her family was under severe social, economic and family stress. We all wondered whether solutions to this stress, in addition to further therapeutic work with the family, would have removed the need for Sharon to start her career as a 'child in care'.

96

Young people who come into care are drawn almost exclusively from the ranks of the poor and disadvantaged and, though many reasons are given for the move, it is frequently the inability of the family to cope with illness, bereavement, divorce and remarriage.

(Carlen 1988)

Any life event, for example new children, loss of work, moving home, could be added here.

Not all emotionally abused children come to the attention of social services, and certainly not all come from poor families but perhaps there is a link between the inadequacies of the child care system and the poverty of its clients.

Many children are separated from their families with the implicit assumption that 'in care' their developmental needs will be met more effectively: deprived, damaged children will be enriched and healed, and delinquent children will be disciplined and socialised. There are, however, often insufficient resources for this task.

Extensive amounts of very respectable recent research in the field of children's experience of local authority care seems to have changed neither policy nor practice.

Well-documented research (Millham *et al.* 1980) on social work training was carried out in the 1960s and 1970s with sound recommendations. They quoted various studies demonstrating the tremendous impact of residential care on children. They recommended to the DHSS that training courses for senior staff should emphasise good residential care of children as a high priority for social services departments. They also noted that good research work carried out in the 1950s, along with recommendations on the care of children, was repeated thirty years later; the recommendations still had not been put into practice.

It is possible to prevent children coming into care, and to support and help children once they are separated from their families (Department of Health 1988). This work includes good quality assessments and plans for finding new families, in addition to individual psychotherapeutic work. However many locally based social workers find their teams are insufficiently resourced for this task.

Projects designed to prevent admission into care include those organised by the Rainer Foundation and CARLI (Care Alternatives Liaison Information) (*Guardian* 1989).

These resources are not available in every area and paradoxically are often organised by voluntary agencies. Sometimes developing children would have to be separated from their families even if preventative interventions were optimal and readily available.

Children and the Community

It is important to keep challenging the inadequacy of local authority 'care'. Whilst certain families are criticised and punished by the state for emotional abuse, neglect and deprivation of their children, the state does not necessarily offer a better quality of care.

Social workers involved with children's futures often are not supported in making developmentally sensitive, child-centred decisions. Well before social services might become involved, parents who find parenting difficult cannot obtain the sort of sustained support they need. Some parents need community support that respects their privacy and that is long-term.

In the final analysis, it is our community that is responsible for its children. If the community cared, it would have adequate structures to protect children, would ensure that good plans were made for those who need to be separated from their families, and would provide families with every practical, material and therapeutic possibility to change.

Good child care policies need money, and in times of financial shortage, the needs of children are often not made a priority, however short-sighted this way of thinking may be. These are political decisions.

It seems that our community does not adequately value and support the role of the parent. We can ask what are the implications of this? The implications affect both biological parents and those professionals who act *in loco parentis*.

> If all social workers, both residential and field workers, were adequately trained, and if their value to the community was reflected in their salaries, they would, as a profession, impose an enormous management problem, making reasonable demands for themselves and their clients that could not, in fact be met.
>
> (Millham *et al*. 1980)

As a child psychotherapist I can only ask: Why not?

NOTES

1 I would like to thank the team at the centre where this work was carried out for all that we have learned together about multi-professional team work and change within different therapeutic models. Also special thanks to Peter Rosner for all his time spent with the computer and for one or two discussions about emotional abuse!

2 For brevity, I shall use 'she' and 'her' throughout this chapter when making general points. All these points are, of course, equally applicable to male and female children.

REFERENCES

Asen, K., Evan, G., Piper, R. and Stevens, A. (1989) 'A systems approach to child abuse management and treatment issues', *Child Abuse and Neglect* 13: 45–57.

Barocas, H.A. and Barocas, C.B. (1979) 'Wounds of the fathers: the next generation of holocaust victims', *International Review of Psychoanalysis* 6: 331–40.

Bean, P. (1984) *Adoption – Essays in Social Policy, Law and Sociology*, London: Tavistock.

Berger, M., Kennedy, H., Campbell, D., Lindberg, S. and Markowitz, R. (1975) 'Pseudobackwardness in children – maternal attitudes as an etiological factor', *Psychoanalytic Study of the Child* 30.

Blom-Cooper, L. (1985) *A Child in Trust: The report of the panel of enquiry into the circumstances surrounding the death of Jasmine Beckford*, London Borough of Brent.

Carlen, P. (1988) *Women, Crime and Poverty.*

Covitz, J. (1986) *Emotional Child Abuse, the Family Curse*, Boston, Mass: Sigo Press.

DHSS and Welsh Office (1988) *Working Together*, HMSO.

Department of Health (1988) *Protecting Children, a Guide for Social Workers Undertaking Comprehensive Assessment*, London: HMSO.

Fraiberg, S. (1959) *The Magic Years, Understanding and Handling the Problems of Early Childhood*, New York: Scribners.

——(1987), *Selected Writings of Selma Fraiberg*, edited by L. Fraiberg, Ohio State University Press, pp. 65–99, 100–36.

Garbarino, J. (1989) 'Emotional abuse', unpublished talk given at Haifa University, Department of Education and Psychology, January.

Garbarino, J. and Gilliam, G. (1980) *Understanding Abusive Families*, Lexington MA: Lexington Books.

Goldstein, J., Freud, A. and Solnit, A. (1973) *Beyond the Best Interests of the Child*, New York: Free Press.

——(1979) *Before the Best Interests of the child*, New York: Free Press.

——(1986) *In the Best Interests of the Child*, New York: Free Press.

Graham-Hall, J. and Martin, D.F. (1987) *Child Abuse Procedure and Evidence in Juvenile Courts*, London: Barry Rose Books.

Guardian (1989) 'Home from Home', Women's page, 20 Dec.

Hodges, J. and Tizard, B. (1989) 'I.Q. and behavioural adjustment of ex-institutional adolescents', and 'Social and family relationships of ex-institutional adolescents', *Journal of Child Psychology and Psychiatry* 30 (1): 53–76, 77–98.

Lambert L. (1981) 'Adopted from care by the age of seven', *Adoption and Fostering* 105 (3): 28–36.

Khan, M. (1963) 'The concept of cumulative trauma', *The Psychoanalytic Study of the Child* 18.

Melzak, S. (1989) 'What do you do when your parents are crying?', paper given at the 2nd International Conference of Centres, Institutions and Individuals Concerned with the Care of Victims of Organised Violence, 27 Nov. – 2 Dec., San José, Costa Rica.

Millham, S., Bullock, R. and Hosie, K. (1980) *Learning How to Care, the Training of Staff for Residential Social Work with Young People*, Farnborough: Gower.

Miller, A. (1987) *For Your Own Good – The Roots of Violence in Child Rearing*, London: Virago.

Minuchin, S. (1974) *Families and Family Therapy*, London: Tavistock.

Minuchin, S. (1984) *Family Kaleidoscope*, Cambridge, MA and London: Harvard University Press.

Minuchin, S. (1989) Unpublished paper presented at the Day Conference on Child Abuse and Family Systems Theory, The Institute of Family Therapy, London.

Minuchin, S., Montalvo, B., Guerney, B.G., Rosman, B.L. and Schumer, H. (1967) *Families of the Slums*, New York: Basic Books.

NSPCC (1989) *Child Abuse Trends in England and Wales 1983–1987*, London: NSPCC.

Rich, A. (1986) *Your Native Land, Your Life*, New York, London: WW. Norton & Co.

Rushton, A., Treseder, J. and Quinton, D. (1988) '*New parents* for older children', British Agencies for Adoption and fostering, Discussion series 10.

Shengold, L.C. (1979) 'Soul murder – child abuse and deprivation', *Journal of the American Psychoanalytic Association* 27 (3): 533–59.

Wallerstein, J. (1989) *Second Chances – Men, Women and Children a Decade after the Divorce*, London: Bantam.

Winnicott, D.W. (1960) 'The good enough parent', in *The Maturational Process and the Facilitating Environment*, 1976, London: Hogarth.

6

THE SECRET LIFE OF CHILDREN WHO HAVE EXPERIENCED PHYSICAL AGGRESSION AND VIOLENCE[1]

Sheila Melzak

INTRODUCTION

Between 1983 and 1987 the numbers of children on Social Services, Child Abuse, at risk registers more than doubled. In 1988 there were 4,519 cases of physical abuse in England, Wales and Northern Ireland (NSPCC 1989). The majority of recorded abuse occurs to children under the age of 5. These statistics reflect only a fraction of the incidents of physical violence towards children.

Although some children are separated from abusive parents and some families become involved in therapeutic change, such is the nature and privacy of family life that many children who have considerable stresses in their development – and experience considerable suffering – go unnoticed by adults.

An act of physical aggression performed by an adult towards a child may not have the same meaning for the child as that intended by the adult (Ferenczi 1933). The adult may intend to communicate to the child that her[2] behaviour is wrong or undesirable and in such a case, the physical aggression is intended as a punishment. The adult, however, may also use physical aggression to express his own distress, rage, frustration, pain, irritation or powerlessness: essentially the various stresses in his life that are not necessarily caused by the child, but which the adult cannot easily articulate. Often physical punishment follows the parent's feeling that verbal constraints are ignored (Epstein 1987). Sometimes the content of the adult's communication may not be intended for the child.

The particular effect of acts of physical aggression on a child's development will depend on many factors including the age of the

101

child, the level of her emotional development and the circumstances of the experience. It is important, for example, whether or not the child has access to adults or peers with whom she can share her feelings and who would validate her painful experiences and offer less confusing relationships. From the child's point of view, the experience of physical aggression by adults can produce a variety of contradictory negative feelings, e.g. fear, anger, helplessness, humiliation, unhappiness, worthlessness and confusion. The child can feel that she must be monstrous to deserve such frequent unpleasant treatment; she can also feel that she is the cause of her parents' distress, rage and misery (Evert and Irne 1987).

Even if the child can change her behaviour the physical aggression may actively discourage this or cause her so much anxiety that she is no longer able to think about anything in the short, or even the longer term. This can be the result of the adult's behaviour. The adult's unconscious communication is also received by the child, who can be aware of the adult's feelings of helplessness and frustration, as well as her inability to express her feelings. Such difficulties between an adult and a child are not confined to any particular social class, race, sex or nationality.

The child will use every faculty at her disposal to make sense of and alleviate her painful situation. She may try to protect the adult by taking care of the vulnerable parent or by making the parent perfect in her mind, at some cost to her capacity to evaluate reality, or deal with her own needs.

In contrast, the child may identify with the parent's style of managing feelings and communications. At different points in her development the child will use fantasy in various ways, both to understand and to defend against the relationship between the particular struggles of her stage of development and her particular external reality.

I am a child psychotherapist, not a social worker or an academic researcher, and my professional perspective affects the way in which I think about the subject of child abuse. Child psychotherapists are trained to look carefully at the dynamic changes in the internal world of children, and to reach an understanding with each child of their psychological reality, which may be different from external reality. We work with conflicts, delays and distortions in the structure of the developing personality, with fantasies and irrational fears, with the struggle of the child's mind to comprehend the world, and with the compelling tendency to distort painful reality. We work with feelings which may be difficult for the child to acknowledge and experience consciously, for example, guilt, anxiety, rage, loss, despair, helplessness, unbearable conflict and emptiness.

The inability to express and work through feelings can lead to serious behavioural, bodily or emotional symptoms. At all times we assume that the symptoms which manifest themselves are connected with latent, often unconscious feelings and past traumas that are difficult to identify, let alone express. This is the work of the psychotherapy session, and this is why children may seem to attend for a long time, even for years. We try to discover creative ways for the child to work through internal difficulties, thereby enhancing her capacity to cope with life.

I am often puzzled by the arbitrary line drawn by our society between on the one hand physical abuse of children that is manifested in a gross, visible way, and on the other, the physical abuse that inflicts pain but leaves few outward signs or physical symptoms. The invisible emotional damage and psychological cost of all forms of physical abuse in the continuum from controlled beating as a form of punishment, to gross, uncontrolled physical abuse in which a child's bones are broken, is painfully clear to anyone who is aware of the emotional needs of children. It is this abuse that confuses the child.

For a child psychotherapist to be asked to write about physical violence separately from emotional violence, is a contradiction in terms. In every situation where physical violence occurs, there is also, by definition, emotional violence. This abuse can interfere with every area of the child's personality, her thinking, her relationships, her self-esteem and her conscience.

Anna Freud wrote about the relationship in child development between environmental conditions and the rate of internal structuralisation of the personality (A. Freud 1982). She emphasised that the harmful impact of abnormal environmental conditions on development has always been recognised, even without the additional evidence from child analyses:

> What needs emphasis, though, is the fact that there is no one-to-one, invariable relationship between the fact of parents being absent, neglecting, indifferent, punitive, cruel, seductive, over-protective, delinquent or psychotic and the resultant distortions in the personality picture of the child.
>
> Cruel treatment can produce either an aggressive, violent being, or a timid, crushed, passive one; parental seduction can result either in the complete inability to control sexual impulses ever after, or in severe inhibition and abhorrence of any form of sexuality. In short, the developmental outcome is determined not by the environmental interference per se, but by its interaction with the inborn and acquired resources of the child.
>
> (A. Freud 1982)

I will illustrate this chapter with the detailed experiences of one child, but I hope that some general points about the effects of physical aggression can be drawn out in the context of the above quotation.

103

The context in which children experience physical aggression and violence

It is clear from debates about the punishment of children that there is no universal view as to what constitutes physical abuse. Not all adults hold a child-centred perspective. Various professionals and parents have differing and contradictory priorities in relation to children and their care.

Physical abuse is thus set within a particular social context in terms of relationships between the families, the community and the state; the relationships between adults and children and the priority accorded to children by society.

It is clearly contradictory that some physical aggression towards children is permitted by the adult world whilst some is defined as problematic, illegal and therefore punishable. Some physical aggression towards children is dealt with as an educational issue, some as a social problem, some as a mental health problem and some as a political problem. These differences reflect fundamentally different philosophical positions. We need to ask *when* physical aggression towards children becomes a problem, and *who* in the adult world experiences the problem.

Contradictory attitudes resulting from two separate philosophical traditions were discussed in Valerie Sinason's article 'Spare the rod and a thought' (*Weekend Guardian*, 13 Aug. 1989). She identifies the Greek tradition: Plutarch wrote:

> children ought to be led to honourable practices by means of encouragement and reasoning and most certainly not by blows . . . for so they grow numb and shudder at their tasks, partly from the pain of blows, partly from degradation.

By contrast we can find in the New World translation of the Hebrew Scriptures (a version of the Bible),

> The one holding back the rod is hating his son, but the one loving him is he that does look for him with discipline.
>
> (Proverbs 13: 24)

These two broad philosophical traditions about the nature of child development are reflected in educational and psychological theory, in culture, literature and religion.

I assume that there is a continuum between the kind of physical aggression generally 'permitted' within child-rearing (and which some would call abusive), and the child abuse recognised by the law.

Who defines physical aggression towards children as a problem?

The legislative (DHSS and Welsh Office 1988) and professional (Department of Health 1988) frameworks surrounding child abuse uphold the contradictions so far considered and, as a consequence, children can still experience physical aggression of an abusive nature in their upbringing. Whilst little is known, for example, of how Jasmine Beckford, Tyra Henry and Kimberly Carlisle (Child Abuse Enquiry Report 1985, 1987a, 1987b) experienced their short lives, we do know that professionals were unable to co-operate in order to protect them (Child Abuse Enquiry Report 1988).

Professionals can easily become confused between the *intention* of adults who physically abuse children and the *consequences* of that physical aggression for the child.

The contradictions within and between the two philosophical systems, between the educational philosophies with their varying assumptions about child rearing, and the social philosophies about the relationship between the family and the state, are still present in the legislation. They are also present in the minds of adults professionally responsible for the care of children. The painful secrets of these children's lives are thus maintained.

Who is responsible for physical abuse and aggression?

Here is another complicated question. Is the individual parent responsible for physical abuse and aggression as a result of their social and psychological history? Does the responsibility lie with male parents rather than female (Gordon 1988) the couple, the state, society, class position or economic status? Research considering various variables has been reviewed by Nigel Parton (1985). The accountability for child abuse has been settled in various places at various points in time (Gordon 1988).

We can ask many questions such as: Why do some families end up making links with Social Services whilst others do not? How are statistics collected? Is there more physical aggression in families in lower social classes, or in families from minority cultures? How much is physical aggression linked with feelings of increased social stress and powerlessness?

Working in North America but with a similar statistical framework to Britain (where NSPCC statistics show more recorded physical abuse in poor families) Giovannoni and Becarra (1979), in a study attempting to test the idea that people of lower socio-economic status and members of minority cultures were 'more tolerant of mistreatment and likely to have a higher threshold for considering actions as mistreatment', found quite the opposite. It is likely that the differences in recorded behaviour may be due to social conditions and the balance of social stress and support (see Garbarino and Gilliam 1980).

A child is emotionally dependent on adults, certainly dependent on adults for physical care and mostly dependent on adults for education and socialisation. It is in the area where physical and emotional care of children overlaps with their education and socialisation that much violence, aggression and fear can be seen. Children, parents and families cannot be separated from the social context in which they live. Parents have other pressures in their lives in addition to the tasks of being parents. For example, maintaining marriages, friendships and family ties, finding work and homes, and establishing an adequate income. In this society different families clearly have different freedoms and choices.

Power relationships within families, between the dominant establishment culture and the culture of individual families, racism and classism all have an effect on relationships and need to be taken into account when considering the causes and effects of physical aggression on children. When all these are considered, a necessarily complicated framework emerges within which responses to our unanswered questions about physical abuse can be rigorously approached (Korbin 1981).

What are the options for offering therapeutic help to families?

There are various ways of looking at acts of physical aggression and violence in families. Whilst 'medical' models will focus on the pathology within the individual and within families, thus reducing the complexity of the presenting problem, other therapeutic models will examine the context in which families live: family networks, communities, social issues of status, power and opportunity. The former models may result in punitive interventions in which children and parents are separated without adequately planned or resourced therapeutic support to change patterns of interaction within families. More effective interventions consider the social context and elicit support from familiar community networks even if a temporary separation of child and family is necessary (Parton 1985; Minuchin 1984, 1989). Effective therapeutic work is carried out in some community-based clinics by psychiatrists, psychotherapists, psychologists and social workers. Thus, change in parenting style for these children could come about through a combination of social change and individual change. Intervention that combines work on feelings, with education for parenting and acknowledgement of the social stresses on families requires considerable resources that society may not find worth prioritising.

When the level of violence in society and the stresses on some families are so high it is not surprising that we also see physical violence within families. Under stress, adults may become extremely irritated by the 'childishness' of children and use physical means to stop childish behaviour, instead of finding ways to remove themselves from the intolerable or irritating situation. In the more serious acts of non-intentional physical violence and abuse of children, it is likely that, in the adults' minds, the child ceases to be a child and the relationship between adult and child is obliterated even if momentarily. The child comes to represent a negative figure from the adult's past, a figure who made this adult feel helpless, humiliated and devalued during childhood. These problems may not be amenable to treatment.

Various writers have concluded that abusive parents are inaccurate in their interpretation of their child's signals because they have a limited range of responses to their children. Abusive parents have difficulty in empathising with their children and, therefore, are less likely to respond to subtle signs of suffering. They are also likely to misjudge the child's developmental abilities (Herzberger 1983). Such a parent may interpret his child's failure to perform some activity as a deliberate attack on the parent, who may take physical revenge. Epstein (1987) emphasised the complexity of the process of identification of a parent with a child. For this task it is important that parents can achieve a realistic recollection of their own childhood. Epstein helped a group of parents to develop insight into their children's behaviour, to see children's needs and experiences as separate from their own, to increase their range of responses to their children and to separate internal and external sources of stress.

Parents who experienced physical violence in their own childhoods will not necessarily identify with that style of parenting. As mentioned earlier social stress factors such as change, loss, concerns about money, etc. can be crucial. Research on violent families suggests that they need a great deal of support in order to become more child-centred.

From the child's point of view

For a child who experiences physical aggression and violence within the family, it is irrelevant whether or not the adult intends to punish the child. Equally it is irrelevant whether the adult wishes to deter certain behaviour or to express their own distress.

At each stage of development the child has certain tasks which must be completed. Unresolved difficulties at one stage may be carried forward to the next stage as a result of the progressive forces of development.

The capacity of young children to think and to solve problems changes as they develop. Piaget made numerous observations of children and invented ingenious experiments to demonstrate the way in which the thinking of children is different from that of adults (Flavell 1963).

Similarly, emotional development takes place in stages at each of which children will have characteristic fantasies, wishes, desires and feelings (Sandler 1975). The child who survives physical violence in the course of her development is able to resort to many possible mental strategies to prevent herself from acknowledging the reality of her parents' actions and the mixture of feelings they have towards her. It is a reflection of the child's mental strength if she can talk about the actions and the complicated, contradictory behaviour of her parents and other adults. We would not expect most children to be strong enough to cope with the effects of abuse except at some considerable cost to their mental health. This cost may include the development of pathological defences such as identification with the violent adult, denial, withdrawal into fantasy, severe repression or externalisation and splitting. There may also be restrictions on ego functioning, arrested emotional development and delinquent behaviour. Shengold (1979), Schreber (1903) and S. Freud (1910) provide useful insights on this subject.

It is difficult to offer therapy intensive enough for very damaged children in a Local Authority Family Consultation Centre as such children need intensive and well-timed treatment. Any delay after the damaging, traumatic events of such abuse makes the consequences even more difficult to work through.

Therapists working with children intensively in therapeutic hospital settings or boarding schools, describe their work with children separated from their families (Boston and Szur 1983) or in situations where their parents receive therapeutic help simultaneously (Flynn 1988).

Referrals to Local Authority clinics include many children such as the boy whose 'secret life' and treatment will be described here.

The various referral symptoms mentioned earlier are signs that a child is under stress and may well indicate that she is experiencing physical aggression from adults. Only careful observation and assessment will reveal the nature and extent of the child's emotional injuries.

A CASE HISTORY

While children are affected in a variety of ways by the physical aggression of adults, there are certain characteristic signs of aggressive abuse. These signs are as much connected to the content of what the child shares with the therapist as they are with the quality of the contact between child and therapist. Writers on the subject often state that physically abused children are so traumatised by the first abuse that they will try, unconsciously, to repeat the behaviour that led to the abuse, out of a kind of astonishment that their parents could cause them so much pain and confusion. This style of relating can appear in the relationship with the therapist.

The boy discussed here was not physically abused according to the criteria of the Social Services department, technically having experienced no observable serious injury, but certainly having experienced physical violence which has both frightened him and affected his development in his formative years. Amos is typical of a large group of disturbed children who are seen as problematic in families and schools and who are referred for treatment.

Amos was a tall sturdy boy, with brown complexion and a charming, expressive face. When I first met him he was 5 years and 9 months old. Even the most superficial of observations revealed this boy's enormous difficulty in managing his anxiety and controlling his behaviour, as well as his immaturity in relation to his chronological age – his babyish way of talking and the large number of grey hairs on his head. (The latter may or may not be stress-related.) Amos's experiences of the world and his developmental difficulties illustrate well some of the current theoretical and practical problems in trying to understand the effect of physical violence on children and the provision of treatment to ameliorate these effects.

Amos was smacked, mostly by his mother, from the age of 18 months. This was sometimes a response to her difficulty in managing his behaviour, and sometimes a response to her own low moods. When he began school, his teacher could not manage his behaviour and wanted to suspend him; he was beaten at home with a belt and sent to his room. This was how the parents were punished as children. The parents were fundamentalist in their religious beliefs, bringing from their family network and religion and culture ideas about good and evil spirits. During treatment, the way in which these beliefs had affected their parenting of Amos emerged. As is usually the case, the developmental history of the child emerges during treatment and cannot easily be collected at the diagnostic stage of meeting with the child and his family.

Amos's grandparents on both sides had come to England looking for work opportunities that had been advertised in the separate countries from which they originated. They brought to England not only their capacity to work, but also their culture and parenting style. In England, to their surprise, they were faced with a hostile, racist society in which they did not feel accepted. Their strong wish to achieve, and to keep their own culture and religion and values, was continually thwarted. They felt apart and different. Amos's mother was raised in England and his father by his extended family abroad.

Amos was described by his parents as being especially active. They described his tormented sleep in which he would toss and turn. They had noticed this from the time he began school. On a few occasions he woke up and went into his parents' room, but appeared not to recognise them, looking at them with horror and saying 'Why have you changed?' Amos's parents would watch him asleep and felt there was a strange atmosphere in the room. They did not immediately think that he might be troubled and that this was causing his distress. Instead they thought the room and Amos himself were possessed and called in a priest. The priest told them that Amos was not possessed but, over time, some ceremonies were performed on the house. The considerable anxieties these ideas created in Amos became a focal theme of his treatment. Clearly these ideas had affected many aspects of his developing internal world, in particular both his view of himself and of his relationships, and his capacity to move his thinking from the concrete to the abstract, from primary to secondary process.

Faced with a sensitive, impulsive, energetic little boy, however lovable, the parenting skills of many adults would be sorely stressed. In their efforts to help Amos control his behaviour, his parents brought not only their family's parenting style, but also their enormous anxiety, as members of a minority culture, that their child should fit in. They were desperate that he should not be noticed at school for his difficulties. Their efforts to manage his behaviour served to exacerbate his problems rather than moderate them. This dynamic evolved in a situation where a further factor was operating: Amos's parents felt, albeit uncertainly, that he was being picked on at school because he was noticeable as a child from a minority culture. At 5 he was moved from one infants' school to another.

Amos's father, basically a gentle, quiet man, often denigrated by his wife, was distraught after he hit Amos with a belt in an ashamed and helpless outburst after complaints by his son's school. Amos's mother was an insecure, very intelligent woman, the child of separated parents (a subject with which she had not come to terms before Amos's treatment began); she did not trust men. She regretted giving up her studies and planned to take them up again. She loved her children intensely but found Amos especially difficult and was often impatient with his periodic uncertainty and need for persistent reassurance, as well as the fact that sometimes he totally ignored her (see Epstein 1987)! She felt that there had been a marked difference between her two pregnancies, and that Amos had been unmanageable and out of control even in the womb. These facts emerged well into the treatment process. We were able to explore how she had projected these feelings onto the unborn child. At the diagnostic stage, she had described with bewilderment how Amos had been such a quiet baby and that her problems only began when he became a toddler. Amos's grandmother took a significant part in his pre-nursery care as his mother returned to work soon after his birth. She had a 'traditional' style of parenting and smacked Amos for any misdemeanours.

At the time of conception, pregnancy, birth and the first year of Amos's life, his mother was very preoccupied, not only with the new relationship with Amos's father, but also with her eldest son, Tom, whose father (not the same man as Amos's father) was battling for access, and who had snatched Tom from school on a few occasions and taken him to his home for several hours. Amos's mother was anxious about the whole process which, after a long time, was legally clarified and became manageable. It was a very long time before Amos's mother could acknowledge the effect this had had on her during Amos's earliest months. She said he was very wanted and loved. It slowly emerged that he had always been difficult, and that she was preoccupied for many months. It was clear that he had been hit around the head, smacked on his legs, as well as being beaten with a belt.

Amos's mother often expressed her astonishment that Amos did not respond to her as his older brother, Tom did. Tom, at the age of 12, was a model of maturity, obedience, self-control, and a success at school. As Tom was not in treatment we can only speculate about why he was so competent. The family remembered Tom as a child who had not needed any smacks; he was always compliant and co-operative. It is possible that Tom's mother was much calmer and more attuned to his developmental needs in his early years than she was to those of Amos. It is also possible that Tom was temperamentally less like his mother than Amos and more placid.

The Assessment

At the time of his assessment, Amos's mother was in the last days of a third pregnancy. By the time I met Amos he already had a special teacher in his second school who gave him individual help. The school found his aggressive, attention-seeking behaviour very hard to manage in a situation where children must survive in groups. He would kick his peers, spit at the dinner ladies and continually ask his teacher for support, help and encouragement, oblivious to the other children in his class. In addition to his aggressive, egocentric and immature presentation at school, however, the school were more concerned about his high level of anxiety and his sometimes being out of touch with reality. He would talk about imagined presences as if they were real, and about accidents to members of his family with tears and pain. In retrospect it is clear that these represented his imagined fears and the persistence of magical thinking. Some of these were events from his distant past. He talked about two Amoses and made a picture of the two for his headmistress one day. He was described as pointing vaguely behind him and saying: 'Stop telling me to do this.' He often blamed other children for initiating conflict situations.

111

There were concerns that he was psychotic, had some serious emotional disorder and would only be educable in a therapeutic school. School staff reported that his parents hit him in school in front of the teachers. The staff described Amos as being unable to listen to any reprimand at the time of his admission to school, but after some months his listening began to improve. However, the school felt he could not manage and wanted him to be assessed for special education. The school psychologist felt sure that Amos's problems could be ameliorated within mainstream school.

In the first sessions Amos made pictures of his family and reassured me over and over again that he was a good boy. He asked many questions to establish whether I was a good person. If I was I would give him all he wanted! He was very agitated and I could not fathom all the sources of his agitation. He mentioned that he had a new baby sister at home. He was understandably preoccupied with babies among other themes. On referral, the school had reported his continuing expressed wish to be a baby again. We discussed the fact that I had pinkish skin and that his skin was brown.

Amos showed no physical aggression and behaviour that was out of touch with reality. He felt (predictably) unsure of me and I needed to be very careful in communicating clearly with him. Most of all I was struck by his very strong fantasy life and concrete thinking, characteristic of children two or three years younger. His tremendous struggle to 'behave properly and be good' was evident. He made a great deal out of passionate hugging and kissing his mother goodbye in the waiting room, as if he was terrified she would forget him. He also hugged other female staff in the clinic, not in a seductive way, but rather as if to say 'I'm Amos, like me please.' Once in the treatment room after an initial explanation he acknowledged that he visited me to play and so that I could help him with his worries, muddles and problems. He was particularly confused between good and bad thoughts and actions and the way people he knew seemed to change from good to bad and back again. He could acknowledge his immense fear of punishment. He was clearly flooded with a mixture of earlier anxieties. He needed a lot of calming to settle him down at the beginning of the session and, when it was time to stop, he felt rejected and wanted to continue. This pattern went on for months. During the first sessions I had to reassure him that I would not smack him; he had not come to me as punishment. Our only rule was that I would not let him hurt himself, or me, or mess up the room.

At the end of his assessment for psychotherapy, I felt that Amos needed and could use treatment. His development seemed to be stuck along two particular developmental lines:

112

1 The line concerned with fantasy and reality, primary and secondary process thought.
2 The line towards anxiety management.

I felt that Amos's ego development was stuck, leading him to function in an immature, disorganised way and inhibiting his healthy forward development. The development of his conscience seemed to have become stuck in its earliest stages leaving him with a very primitive and punitive conscience with which he often came into conflict. He knew he was naughty sometimes! It was difficult for him to control or take responsibility for his feelings or actions. Paradoxically he was terrified of the consequences of his actions.

By the age of 5, in order to manage in school, children need to be able to think about and concentrate on school work, which presents tasks for which sustained secondary process thought is essential. They need to be preoccupied with play and with working out internal problems. They also need to be able to share with other children and accept the authority of the adults in the school. Finally, they need to have some understanding of the rules of the school and of what others are feeling. Psychoanalysts call this phase of development latency. Amos seemed totally unable to manage any of the stresses of school life unless he had the one-to-one support of an adult or a child more mature than him. In these circumstances his achievements in school work were well above average and his play was creative and complicated. Without this support he swiftly became anxious and lost control, appearing to become like a much younger child with temper tantrums. He became flooded with anxiety and various other affects, hitting other children and becoming chaotic in this thinking, usually experiencing others as having caused his actions.

Anna Freud describes stations along the route of development from infancy to maturity, at which the different parts of the personality combine in particular and characteristic ways (A. Freud 1963). Normal development is uneven and children will not necessarily move evenly along all lines at the same time. We would expect infants to be overwhelmed by feelings and to cry and wriggle when in distress. From the general physical experience of infant discomfort a child gradually acquires the capacity to experience tension, worry and anxiety mentally. Yorke and Wiseberg (1976) discuss the development of the mental signal anxiety: 'measures of containment and the increasing capacity for mastery of overwhelming mental excitation will increase as the mental apparatus becomes more sophisticated'. They describe how the ability to restrict anxiety to sample proportions slowly develops alongside language, secondary process thinking and the capacity to repress. In order to develop signal anxiety a child must have some ability for affective control; children usually have temper tantrums at the stage when speech is developing and cannot have established signal anxiety at this stage.

Amos, with his immature speech and tendency to have temper tantrums, showed many of the developmental characteristics of a much younger child. One aim of treatment would be to help him move along the developmental line for anxiety management towards the age-appropriate point. At 6 we could expect Amos to be in the latency phase. Sarnoff writes:

> the latency phase is characterised by an instability which is manifested by shifts between normal latency and regressed states. There is no intimation of serious pathology when one of these shifts occurs unless the shift is characteristic, chronic and results in behaviour that interferes with the progress and growth of the child.
>
> (Sarnoff 1971)

At the start of his treatment it was obvious that Amos was often smacked but he was also loved by his parents. It was also clear at this time that Amos loved to sleep in his parents' bed. This may have been very over-exciting for a small boy. In general, the picture that emerged was, from Amos's point of view, confusing. His parents were inconsistent with him, sometimes humiliating and sometimes over-exciting him. This may explain why he had such a hard time managing his feelings and fantasies and behaving in an age-appropriate way. This style of parenting not only failed to contain his infantile feelings, but also interrupted the flow of progressive, onward development, and served to prevent Amos from managing his feelings as he matured. By the time I met him he had already internalised part of his parents' style of relating to him. He felt confused and incompetent. As I understood it, Amos suffered from a developmental disorder, and I felt that psychotherapy would help him to disentangle his muddled and confusing internal world so that he could move forward developmentally.

The Treatment

The extent to which Amos had been abused only emerged in the course of his treatment. The themes guiding his treatment took some time to become clear. In the early sessions he was very anxious to please me but seemed positive towards me and towards the opportunity of spending special time with me. It was important to establish a treatment alliance, that is, a relationship based not just on his liking me or wanting to see me, but on my using my experience and training to find ways to work with him so that we could help him to acknowledge his feelings and work through those feelings from the past that were interfering with his life in the present, and thus change.

In his early sessions he made some happy, age-appropriate pictures of his family in bright colours, and assured me that everything was fine at home and that he was a good boy. His level of anxiety, however, belied his statements – as did his behaviour. He always took a long time to travel from the waiting room to my room upstairs. After a few compliant sessions, Amos began to indicate via his play the sometime chaos of his internal world. He would rush from one topic to another and from one game, fantasy, play, etc. to another. It was hard for him to focus even when I tried to support this aim. Later, after a few months, this became a theme of his treatment. He could alternate between being calm and organised (showing the contents of his thoughts verbally or through play) and at other times he would arrive restless and unsettled, a clear sign of anxiety, of some initially hidden cause. As I got to know Amos, it became possible to help him to manage himself by a simple comment such as 'You are all over the place today. I wonder what you are worried about. Let's be detectives and find out together, just like Batman and Robin.' Increasingly the current anxiety would emerge via dramatised play or the quality and emotional tone of his contact with me.

Our previously positive relationship changed one day when he noticed some new toys through an open door of another room in the clinic. Ignoring my protests he ran in and became very cross and defiant with me when I said that the toys belonged to someone else; that it was not our room. I had to take his hand and lead him back to my room. He was defiant and anxious on this and other occasions, clearly waiting for me to hit him. When I assured him that I would not hit him, or tell his mother, or let him have toys from other rooms, he began to sulk and say he did not like me.

It was clear that he not only feared being hit, he also wished to be hit. He would actually have experienced my hitting him with some relief, but such relief would only have been partial because it would have been unequal to the amount of his imagined badness. This is a characteristic of aggressively abused children, described by many writers (see for example Furman 1986).

After months of treatment he began to oscillate less in his behaviour between chaotic and organised behaviour. For a long time his negative relationship with me was based solely on my withholding something he wanted to do or play with. Gradually the negative transference became more complicated, and expressing these feelings and worries, and my acknowledgement and interpretation of them, brought Amos relief. Slowly his difficulty in assessing the difference between acceptable and unacceptable behaviour, thoughts and feelings, seemed to lessen. From making happy family pictures, he began to act, being able to transform into super heroes such as Superman, the Incredible Hulk, terrifying monsters or giants covered in layers of armour. At the same time, when he made pictures from my squiggles or made his own pictures, he drew birds and expressed his wish to fly away. He agreed to my suggestion that maybe he was very frightened and that he felt safe when he pretended he could change into the super heroes with layers of armour to protect him. I asked him what was so frightening and he replied 'Sometimes Mummy is bad. I've got two Mummys, a good one and a bad one.' I replied that it seemed as if his one Mummy could change from being good to bad and back again and he did not understand what made her change, but we would find out. There was only one Mummy though. I reminded him also of his feeling that there were two Amoses, a good one and a bad one.

Especially relieved at the end of this meeting, Amos stood close by me, but without flinging himself at me. He said quietly, 'I am very frightened sometimes – I feel like a little bird inside.' Although this was the first real acknowledgement of his deeper feelings, it needed a long time and the continuity of sessions for Amos to integrate his own various feelings and express them in a way that was socially acceptable. He also needed a long time to modify his punitive conscience. At the time of his assessment, Amos had some unhealthy defences such as denial, repression, confusion and withdrawal into fantasy. In other ways Amos was too open, vulnerable and inadequately defended to cope with the intellectual and social pressures of school and home life. Amos needed a long period of therapeutic involvement to rid himself of his unhelpful defences and acquire useful ones.

The super heroes were one of Amos's unconscious defences against his anxieties about real and imaginary monsters in his life. It is part of normal development that small children at certain stages deal with anxieties via play and dreams. For Amos the monsters and super heroes in his imagination had several meanings. They were his way of experiencing his parents when they were not sensitive to his needs and level of understanding, and when they traumatically overwhelmed and hit him. They also represented his own aggressive impulses towards his parents which he could not accept. By playing monsters and super heroes he identified with his parents' aggression and also learned to master his own.

According to psychoanalytic theory of normal development, the small child becomes aware that there are two sexes, and of the physical differences between them. Slowly the child changes the infantile attachment to adults and becomes specifically and possessively attached to familiar adults of the opposite sex, usually the parent. During this time the parent of the same sex, or close adults of this sex become dangerous rivals in the child's imagination. The child eventually comes to identify with the parent or close adult of the same sex. This period of intense emotions and wishes is repressed, forgotten, pushed into the back of the mind and the child leaves this Oedipal phase of development and enters latency. During latency the child is less concerned with intense loving or antagonistic feelings towards parents and more able to concentrate on school and to explore and develop through play, fantasy, imagination, stories and friendships with peers. Amos had the difficult task of identifying with his father in an atmosphere where his mother's ambivalence towards men was all-pervasive.

Two fundamental themes emerged in Amos's sessions. One was his conflict between omnipotence and helplessness, both equally frightening states for a small boy. The second was a deep narcissistic hurt, a feeling of his own worthlessness which seemed to have been built up through the various phases of his development to date from a combination of his own misunderstandings and the confusing style of parenting. It seemed that the combination of unrealistic expectations, inconsistency and confusion in Amos's external world, together with his parents' beliefs about good and bad spirits, mirrored his age-appropriate developmental fantasies and thus prevented him from moving forward developmentally towards a more solid hold on secondary process thinking in all contexts, including school. During his therapy sessions Amos had an opportunity to explore his fantasies and I, as therapist, was able to carry out what has been called ego strengthening therapy (Sherrick *et al.* 1978). As therapy proceeded Amos improved his use of secondary process thinking and managed his anxiety in a better way.

One of my tasks as therapist was to put into words for Amos the difference between his wishes, his fantasy exploration of the dilemmas in his life and his pretend games. He found it helpful when I said that outside the door of the therapy room he was a small boy, not Peter Pan the boy who never grew up, or a fish or a bird or a hero with super powers or a robot or a fast rocket or a terrible monster. Within the therapy room we could pretend and talk about all sorts of feelings. This had the effect of giving Amos a more solid sense of his own self-esteem, which, at the start of treatment, was very frail. He would characteristically pretend to be a robot, super strong, who could fly and jump and was frightened of nothing. After a few minutes he would look desolate, realising that not only did he not have super powers, but neither could he do what was expected at home or at school. He would say that the robot felt all wrong; it had the wrong batteries and that he was sure that the mother robot had made him all wrong with the wrong wires in the wrong places. I had to introduce the possibility that he could change his feelings about himself.

Amos's fears that he was no good, or that alternatively he was an omnipotent monster had been confirmed over and over again by his parents' inconsistent withdrawal and abusive punishment, neither of which he could understand. While his fears often came true, for example his experience of physical aggression, he was confused and deflated that in reality his omnipotent wishes were not confirmed. He could not manage to do what he wanted at school; he felt frequently misunderstood; not only was he not a super hero, but he was not even as big as his father and he could never have his mother to himself. By pretending to be a robot and asking me to programme him in various ways, he showed me how unsure he was about what to do in social situations with adults and children. Sarnoff (1971) describes how one of the requirements of latency is to give up magical thinking. At the start of his treatment, Amos could not do this as he did not have the ego strengths to manage in other ·ways. It took some time working with Amos to consolidate the various aspects of his self and help him to enjoy the qualities and potential of being a small boy, and to develop some pleasurable anticipation of the future and of growing up. During the treatment at different stages we explored his wish to stay a baby, to be Peter Pan, the boy who never grew up, to be various animals or machines.

As we explored the idea of change and transformation, Amos struggled with a magical view of this as represented in cartoons. Deep inside he felt fragile, helpless, useless and puzzled. As he began to trust me, the negative feelings emerged that were a transference of feelings from different stages of development. He felt useless and robbed; I was a useless person and could not understand him as I could not fulfil his wishes to feel good, to have whatever he wanted – toys, super powers, the ability to fly (to fly away when life was too painful) and in particular his father's body. At this time his pictures were of powerful, magical phallic symbols, rockets going to planets, snake charmers teasing snakes out of baskets; even his cars were in the shape of triangles with the apex of the roof pointing towards the sky. He both wished for and feared powers of magical transformation and change.

All these themes were expressed in various ways. One day he told me a story about an alien boy in a rocket ship. He was looking for money that a robber had stolen from his mother. He would succeed in protecting his mother and retrieving whatever had been stolen because he had a gun and a telescope (both phallic symbols). In the transference, separation and loss were also strong themes. He often asked me questions indicating his doubt that I was with him emotionally, saying: Are you there? Are you feeling sad? Are you cross with me? Where are you? – when I was neither sad, nor cross, nor preoccupied. I could reply that maybe when he was little the grown-ups who looked after him seemed busy, cross and sad, and behaved in a muddling way. He dealt with the stress of this by wanting to remain the hero of his fantasy world, to stay a small child just like Peter Pan. It was also clear from our sessions that adults had sometimes overestimated and sometimes underestimated his abilities.

Thus through play and through the transference, Amos communicated the mixture of his concerns from all levels of his development, including infantile discomfort, his difficulties in sharing, his feeling of being unloved and criticised. Material from the past and from the present was mingled together. In the transference I had alternated between being good and bad early parental figures, but I suddenly became a competitor, the Oedipal father. One day he tried to draw a picture of a dinosaur and asked me to draw my own. He became more and more distressed that the picture did not develop as he wanted and eventually burst out crying 'It's not fair, it's not fair – you can do everything better than me.' In response to this I talked about understanding how hard it was to wait and grow up to do all the things grown-ups do.

At this time Amos had been talking a great deal at the ends of sessions about wanting to marry his mother. I attempted to reassure him that he would grow up and become a man like his dad. He agreed that today I reminded him of his dad, who seemed to be good at everything and got to stay in mum's bed. He calmed down and finished the dinosaur picture competently. A few minutes after the session he came back to my room, flung his arms around me and said 'I will have my own wife one day, won't I?' He then skipped off down the street ahead of his mother. Amos's wish to marry his mother had many meanings for him at this time, as did his severe anxiety that he would be punished for his wishes. The wish to marry his mother resonated through the various levels of his development. He could acknowledge that he wanted a permanent relationship with her. He wanted her to meet all his needs and he wanted to look after her. He wanted never to lose her and he wanted to have a grown-up relationship with her. He could accept that there was a baby part of him, a small boy part and a big boy part. He wanted to marry her just like dad and get rid of dad. The anxieties which babies experience in the earliest months include fear of annihilation and engulfment, and fear of abandonment. Later separation anxiety becomes characteristic and this anxiety of infants is replaced by a fear of loss of love of the beloved parent, fear of punishment as development proceeds and later guilt and shame. The Oedipal boy wants an exclusive grown-up relationship with his mother, and it was this part of Amos (which had been in reality painfully beaten by his father) which was terrified that his father would be angry at his wishes and retaliate by once again harshly punishing and destroying the small boy. He also heard his mother criticising his father.

Amos compared his father's body to his own, the same father who had hit him with a belt.

After some frightening intra-psychic competition with his father, the small boy resolves his Oedipus complex by giving up his wish to be his mother's partner and instead identifying with his father. He will grow up to find his own partner. For Amos all these early and later issues were present and unresolved. His primitive punitive conscience made him feel bad about some of his fears and wishes and dread the consequences of his thoughts. As a result of his problems in separating reality and fantasy, the inner and the outer world, and as a result of the abuse, Amos imagined that he had committed terrible crimes and that he was due for cataclysmic punishment in the form of further aggressive abuse and perhaps annihilation.

The process of writing about the inner world of this confused little boy is much quicker than the process by which he gradually became able to put his fears and questions into words. After some sessions in which he shared with me how much he hated being small and incompetent, Amos developed a pattern in his play. He would come into my room and show me how agile he could be. He jumped on the couch, up and down, and then tried to reach certain points across the room. He could do fantastic 'break-dancing' (black American dance form needing extreme agility for performance). We talked about the fact that in reality he felt that the grown-ups in his life only valued his school work and not the physical skills he had and which gave him great pleasure. After about ten minutes he would stop and say 'and now I want to be a baby and you be the mummy. You tuck me up in bed. I can't walk or talk, you have to know how to feed me, when to dress me. You have to cuddle me.' During the course of treatment the 'baby' game was elaborated to demonstrate how 'unloved' and vulnerable and confused he felt. He felt frail and that he never got enough food, enough presents or enough attention.

Repeatedly we worked through Amos's questions about the various parental figures in his internal world who transformed from one to the other. My task was to integrate them for him, to help him to accept the reality of the mum who sometimes neglected him and sometimes hit him. She also sometimes loved him and cared well for him, as did his father. She was sometimes busy and did not seem to value him for himself only putting pressure on him to do school work. The task of integration was long and hard for him. He would say 'the bad mummy died, she had an accident, I've got a good mummy now.' He agreed that it was confusing to be in mum's bed when dad was out and feel displaced when dad came home. It was particularly hard for Amos to accept his own conflicting wishes. He could only hold one side of his conflict in his head at a time.

During my work with Amos I kept in mind my feeling about the destructive effects of physical aggression and violence on him and developed a hypothesis that three factors in his parents' style of parenting had affected Amos:

1 the use of physical punishment and controls,
2 the fantasies his parents had about him,
3 their inconsistent, sometimes overstimulating availability.

Dennis Flynn, in his article about abused children, wrote that children who experience physical violence often try to stop themselves from feeling or thinking anything at all (Flynn 1988). When they do think and feel about their experience of parenting, this has often been elaborated and distorted by fantasies which reflect the more profound struggle of the child to come to terms with what has happened. Children will ask themselves various questions and give different answers at different times as to why they feel so confused. Why were they hit? Was it abuse, was it the devil? Was it wrong for parents to hit children? What had they done wrong? Why did it happen to them? This reflects a more healthy situation than the child who cannot allow itself to think or feel anything about the abuse. During the dynamic process of therapy and of development, the accounts a child may give about the abuse will reflect the internal rather than the external reality of the child and the need to continuously work to come to terms with the experience of abuse by developing different theories, hypotheses and explanations. During therapy both conscious and unconscious preoccupations about the abuse emerge and fantasy and reality can be disentangled so that the painful and frightening aspects of the abuse can be worked on. This process is similar to that in Kuhn's description of scientists who develop hypotheses or paradigms and then design experiments to test them out (Kuhn 1970). If further facts emerge that cannot be included in the hypotheses or paradigms, new ones must be developed to include all the new facts in the search for truth. The child is like a small scientist and the therapist has to be aware that some paradigms are conscious and some are unconscious.

After a year of treatment Amos began to play a hide and seek game frequently. This game neatly encapsulated the complexity of Amos's personality which I could begin to talk through and help him integrate. He would play hide and seek, but I was always the seeker. Sometimes I 'found' (in the limited number of real hiding places) a frightening monster, sometimes a super hero, sometimes a vulnerable bird, a baby without speech, sometimes a toddler. These were all aspects of his different experiences of himself, the self-representations in the inner world.

Sometimes it was appropriate to make interpretations, at other times it was important to help the development of Amos's ego by clarification, reassurance and boundary setting. Quite early in his treatment his fears of his own negative feelings were very clear to me, but very difficult for him to acknowledge and accept. He was unable to play or draw in this situation.

He felt hopeless and helpless. For a long time I made comments such as 'Thinking about doing something is not the same as doing it. Feeling like hitting someone is not the same as hitting them.' I was sure that he understood what I said at some level and felt that his own terrifying experiences of his sexualised wishes, the reality of his physical punishment and the religious ideas and exorcism, were too difficult and painful for him to face. It was my job to keep in mind these different experiences and put them into words for him in the sessions when he was able to allow himself to listen to me. He liked it when I said that he was not a monster, that having monster feelings sometimes was not the same as being a monster, that he had never been a monster. In normal development, magical thinking makes no differentiation between wishes, fantasies, thoughts and reality. Amos did not outgrow this mode of thinking as it was reinforced at home. In between the sessions in which he was inaccessible to interpretations and clarification, Amos would use his super hero or monster character to enact his feelings. Sometimes the 'super hero' was not available for dialogue or discussion. Amos would rush around the room scared, anxious, desperate, leaping from bed to table, and I could only empathise out loud at the urgency of his task and the fact that he might become out of control and that my job was to keep him safe. For a long time he could not consider how he enjoyed the over-excited state and it took him even longer to accept the fact that he used this state to avoid feeling sad, hurt, lonely, helpless or frightened.

I worked on the principle that only by acknowledging these feelings could he become really strong, but it is very difficult for a boy of this age, brought up in this society where boys are still expected to be physically and emotionally strong and flawless, to accept these facts. There were many opportunities to talk about Amos's negative experience of his parents, both their frightening aspects and their insensitivity to his needs. When resistant, Amos would dismiss my connections of his present play and his painful experiences with 'They don't hit me now.' Gradually he became able to bear the idea that he had different feelings and different aspects of himself, and in the same way, his parents were also complicated. Mummy and daddy sometimes found it hard to be parents and did some painful, frightening, confusing things, but they were not bad, they were not monsters or superhumans.

Work with the Parents

There is no space here to go into any detail about the subtleties of and thematic changes in Amos's parents. All through his treatment our team has worked with both parents on issues to do with differences between adults and children, on setting realistic expectations, on parenting, on their relationship with each other as parents. This has involved some individual exploration and consideration of both parents' childhood experiences. We have had several whole family meetings working both psychoanalytically and behaviourally on the events leading to physical violence. We have also spent time considering the family's experience of racism in general and their feelings about the schools Amos attended. These discussions sometimes included school staff.

Slowly the family became more consistently able to identify Amos's difficulties and their own and to see these as separate. The parents were thus better able to clearly manage and understand Amos. They also became more confident in asking for support in dealing with authority when they felt that Amos was being treated unfairly. An important part of this work was encouraging the parents to talk about their culture and childhood experiences with their children, in particular to talk about the particularly valued aspects of their culture and to compare these with the culture of school, etc.

Amos's parents certainly felt that they needed reminders about Amos's inner world, and some discussion about what he could and could not cope with. They agreed they really needed help in assessing what pressure it is realistic to place on him and this was a large part of our work together. The combination of psychotherapy for Amos and work with his parents were both important in bringing about change and moving Amos's development towards achievements more in line with his age in emotional, intellectual and social terms.

It was only after seven months of treatment that Amos began to acknowledge his real feelings. After a year of treatment, he continued to need individual support to help him learn in the context of school, although the school felt he had improved enormously and they themselves had had many staff changes during the year. They felt Amos would do better in a small class, but his parents were keen that he should not be separated from his peers and enter the special education system. Ironically, in a small supplementary school organised by the community, he learned and played well and received glowing reports. Eventually a mainstream school with small classes was found.

Conclusion

From this portion of therapeutic work with one small boy, I hope that some of the particular effects of physical aggression on a developing child can be seen. The effects of the physical aggression interact with the depriving, inconsistent and emotionally abusing aspects of the parenting style in such a way that it is almost impossible to separate out those effects that are specific to the physical aggression. The story of Amos also illustrates the way in which a child's confusion and misunderstandings about their internal and external experiences can be unravelled by techniques of child psychotherapy. This can result in change not only in the child's behaviour but also in his feelings about himself and others and his capacity to think and see the world clearly, in touch with reality. In spite of particular vulnerability to his punitive conscience (including difficulty in taking responsibility for his actions) and changes in his self-esteem resulting from external and internal changes, Amos became more able to make sense of the world and to manage his life experiences with their normal internal and external rooted anxieties, in an age-appropriate way.

At the beginning of his treatment Amos presented as a much less mature child than would be expected from his chronological age, and this immaturity emerged in every facet of his development. Amos could not allow himself to think clearly. He was afraid of the omnipotent power of his feelings and used this defensively through his endless super hero games, and also to avoid acknowledging the infantile, helpless aspects of himself. He experienced adults as terrifying and monstrous, or as inconsistent, withdrawn and weak. This extract from the work with Amos has underlined how his potential to work through normal internal conflicts by using fantasy was seriously compromised by his parenting experiences. The physical aggression had a disorganising effect on his development and served to make him less in touch with reality and less trusting of adults and peers.

Some way in to the treatment it became clear that issues and concerns from the past and the present existed alongside one another, muddled up in Amos's mind. The mode of communication that had been described as psychotic at the time of his assessment was, I felt, much more a communication of his very chaotic inner world and the persistence of a style of magical thinking.

The interpretation of Amos's conflicts was only part of my task. I had to contain his anxieties by being firm, clear, reassuring and supportive, and slowly he began to internalise this ego-supportive therapeutic style. Different aspects and qualities of Amos's past and present relationships with parental figures in his life were brought to the therapy sessions through the transference. Slowly we were able to find words for the positive and negative aspects of the transference in relation to me.

During his early development the context prevented Amos from experiencing his own feelings and making sense of them. He developed verbal language late according to his mother, and I noticed that he tended to enact his feelings rather than verbalise them. This had painful and frightening consequence for him and paradoxically inhibited his development of the verbal language that would have helped to express and contain these feelings. This also increased his isolation from other children. Because his parents' increased use of physical aggression coincided with his Oedipal phase, it resulted in a boy remaining locked in a world of fantasy until such time as he could feel less helpless in relation to his parents. He was not helped to manage and contain his aggressive and sexual feelings and fantasies, and thus felt little and different and no good. In this environment he could not develop the capacities for self-control and reflection.

In addition to the social stresses of racism, economic hardship and cultural difference, Amos had to contend with the fact that during the first two years of his life there were many specific pressures on his mother, as described earlier. These led her to be alternatively seductive, withdrawn and punitive with her second son, a cocktail of parental style that did not contain his developmental anxieties, but functioned to exacerbate and fixate them, preventing him from working them through. From Amos's story, as it emerged during his treatment, the 'real', self-doubting Amos took a long time to emerge from his defensive pretence that everything was well and that he was all-powerful, like Superman. The first defence illustrates how hard it was for him to look at the painful realities. The second defence was overdetermined by both his identification with what he saw as the aggressive, all-powerful adults in his life, who obliterated danger by force and 'magical' power (the priest performing exorcism, for example), and his own feeling that his actions must be devilish to deserve the violent and bewildering punishments.

We can formulate many questions about how a small anxious boy who has experienced cumulative trauma, some in the form of physical aggression, can learn to express and manage his aggressive feelings verbally rather than physically. How does a boy who clearly uses fantasy as a way to avoid unpleasant reality (rather than just to master reality) learn to use fantasy creatively to come to terms with reality? How does he learn not to enact his anxieties but rather to communicate them so that he can be reassured? How does the same boy learn to deal with his anxieties, to express and acknowledge them and to connect the overwhelming experiences of anxiety to their causes?

As a psychotherapist I often wonder how a child develops the state of peace of mind necessary in order to learn. There must be some repression from consciousness and the build-up of other productive defences to ward off the experience of continuous anxiety, guilt and shame. Amos failed to develop sufficient peace of mind to manage in school. His fantasies disorganised his thought. His efforts to repress failed because he was not only attempting to repress age-appropriate anxieties, but also the continuing traumatic realities including his parents' aggression, and the fantasies that resulted from that. He experienced intermittent containment and non-containment from the adult world.

Amos was preoccupied with villains and monsters. It is a good question to enquire whether or not he believed that these were real or a figment of his imagination. (A. Freud 1982). This belief or disbelief has meaning for assessing on the one hand the seriousness of his disturbance, and on the other the potential success of therapeutic intervention. Freud talks of the way in which neurotic people both believe and disbelieve their creations (S. Freud 1907). In Amos's case there were many links between the monsters of his internal fantasy and his traumatic experiences in reality. While Anna Freud writes about the positive effects of anxiety in development, it is interesting that she links the panic of children with phobia to the panics of the traumatised child. The phobic child avoids panic while the traumatised child has no mechanism to avoid it.

Anna Freud draws attention to the way in which the child's diffuse anxieties and fears are often compressed into one encompassing symbol which represents danger left over from all developmental levels. This would be a phobia. These are dealt with by avoidance. Amos could not do this. When a child has in reality experienced trauma, abuse or physical aggression it is the work of the therapy to unravel the child's fears and separate out fears that are realistic from externalisation of internal anxieties similar to phobias from the remainder of past traumas. The difficulty of this task serves to underline the confusion in the inner world of a physically abused child who may behave as if they are borderline of psychotic. This was the case for Amos.

In situations such as that of Amos, where there is a delay in the developmental structure, no sophisticated mental mechanisms are available and their place is taken by muscular action (as in infantile tantrums) resulting in aggressive outbursts, self-injury, atypical or borderline manifestations (A. Freud 1942). Through the consistent, regular meetings over a long time, and through the other aspects of the child psychotherapy technique, Amos's particular difficulties could be acknowledged, faced and worked through.

It is a curious and complicated task for a child to make sense of physical pain, parental and social boundaries and beliefs when he has not yet completely mastered words or his own emotions. It is especially difficult when cognitively he is still at the stage of concrete operations (Piaget) and not yet capable of abstract thought. I hope I have raised some questions here about the effects of physical aggression on the internal world of children. Physical aggression obviously will have different specific effects on older children and different effects on different individuals, depending on the context of the abuse. I hope I have made clear that physical aggression by parents to children is always damaging. Hitting children is not productive or desirable if we want a society peopled with emotionally healthy adults who are capable of being healthy parents.

Valerie Sinason (1989) emphasises that the more parents can bear powerful feelings, the sooner the child will learn about his or her own destructiveness. Where parents are taken over by feelings, the child can experience him/herself as the innocent victim with all the hostile feelings neatly placed in the parent, or vice-versa, with serious consequences. This is the situation with the child I have described. Children are overwhelmed by powerful, destructive feelings that they can act out, especially if they have been periodically neglected and misunderstood, as was the case with Amos. The feelings of little children feel all-powerful and magical, able to cause life and death as the super heroes and monsters in the comics.

I have tried to show here that the effect of powerful adult feelings and actions on children do not necessarily cause a healthy conscience to develop nor a substantial morality. Parents often feel helpless in the face of their children's difficult, violent behaviour (Minuchin and Fishman 1981). Parents may need help and support for themselves in order for them to facilitate the development in their children of the skills required to manage their strongest feelings. It took a great deal of time to disentangle the many roots of Amos's difficulties. I can only hope that Amos's story adds to the increasing volume of literature and opinion that argues against the use of physical aggression on the next generation.

NOTES

1. Particular thanks to Jill Hodges for discussion on the theoretical psycho-analytic issues relevant here and to Liz Aitchison for her practical help and her orderly mind.
2. For brevity, I shall use 'she' and 'her' throughout this chapter when making general points. All these points are, of course, equally applicable to male and female children.

REFERENCES AND FURTHER READING

Asen, K., Evan, G., Piper, R. and Stevens, A. (1989) 'A systems approach to child abuse: management and treatment issues', *Child Abuse and Neglect* 13: 45–57.

Blos, P. (1985) *Son and Father: Before and Beyond the Oedipus Complex*, New York: Free Press.

Boston, M. and Szur, R. (eds) (1983) *Psychotherapy with Severely Deprived Children*, London: Routledge & Kegan Paul.

Child Abuse Inquiry Report (1985) *A Child In Trust*, Report of the Panel of Inquiry into the Circumstances Surrounding the Death of Jasmine Beckford, London Borough of Brent.

——(1987a) *Whose Child*, Report on the Death of Tyra Henry, London Borough of Lambeth.

——(1987b) *A Child in Mind*, Report on the Death of Kimberly Carlisle, London Borough of Greenwich.

——(1988) *Report of the Inquiry into Child Abuse in Cleveland*, London: HMSO.

Department of Health (1988) *Protecting Children – A Guide for Social Workers Undertaking Comprehensive Assessments*, London: HMSO.

DHSS and the Welsh Office (1988) *Working Together*, HMSO, 1988.

Epstein, C. (1987) *Spirals of Violence, Mothers and Children, Therapeutic Implications of the Spiral Model*, PhD thesis Brunel University.

Evert, K. and Irne, B. (1987) *When You're Ready – A Woman's Healing from Childhood Physical and Sexual Abuse by her Mother*, Walnut Creek, CA: Launch Press.

Ferenczi, S. (1933) 'Confusion of tongues between adults and children: the language of tenderness and of passion', *International Journal of Psychoanalysis* 30: 225–30.

Flavell, J. H. (1963) *The Development Psychology of Jean Piaget*, New York: Van Nostrand Reinhold International Student Editions.

Flynn, D. (1988) 'The assessment and psychotherapy of a physically abused girl during inpatient family treatment', *Journal of Child Psychotherapy* 14 (2).

Freud, A. (1923) 'The relation of beating fantasies to a daydream', *International Journal of Psychoanalysis* 4: 89–102.

——(1963) 'The concept of developmental line', *The Psychoanalytic Study of the Child* 18: 245–65.

——(1965) *Normality and Pathology in Childhood Assessments of Development*, vol. 6, New York: International Universities Press.

——(1974) *Beating Fantasies and Daydreams: Introduction to the Psychoanalytic Writings of Anna Freud I*, New York: International Universities Press Inc.

——(1982) *The Psychoanalytic Psychology of Normal Development*, London: International Psychoanalytical Library, Hogarth Press.

Freud, S. (1907) 'Obsessive actions and religious practices', Standard Edition Vol. IX, Strachey (ed.), London: Hogarth Press.

——(1910) 'Psychoanalytic notes on an autobiographical account of a case of paranoia (*Dementia Paranoides*)', Harmondsworth: *Penguin Case Histories II*.

——(1919) 'A child is being beaten', Standard Edition Vol. XVII, Strachey (ed.), London: Hogarth Press.

Furman, E. (1986) 'Aggressively abused children', *Journal of Child Psychotherapy*, 12 (1).

Garbarino, J. and Burgess, R. (1982) 'Doing what comes naturally? An evolutionary perspective on child abuse', in D. Finklehor *et al.*, *Issues and Controversies in the Study of Family Violence*, Beverly Hills, CA: Sage Publications.

Garbarino, J. and Ebata, A. (1983) 'The significance of ethnic and cultural differences in child maltreatment', *Journal of Marriage and the Family*.

Garbarino, J. and Gilliam, G. (1980) *Understanding Abusive Families*, Lexington, MA: Lexington Books.

Giovannoni, J. M. and Becarra, R. M. (1979) *Defining Child Abuse*, New York: Free Press.

Gordon, L. (1988) *Heroes of their own Lives: The Politics and History of Family Violence*, London: Virago.

Hall, J. G. and Martin, D. F. (1987) *Child Abuse: Procedure and Evidence in Juvenile Courts*, London: Barry Rose Books.

Herzberger, S. D. (1983) 'Social cognition and the transmission of abuse', in D. Finklehor *et al.*, *The Dark Side of Families*, Beverly Hills, CA: Sage.

Korbin, J. E. (ed) (1981) *Child Abuse and Neglect: Cross-cultural Perspectives*, Berkeley, CA: University of California Press.

Kuhn, T. S. (1970) *The Structure of Scientific Revolutions* (2nd edn), Chicago, IL: University of Chicago Press.

Miller, A. (1987) *For Your Own Good: The Roots of Violence in Child Rearing*, London: Virago.

Minuchin, S. (1967) *Families of the Slums*, New York: Basic Books.

——(1984) *Family Kaleidoscope*, Cambridge, MA and London: Harvard University Press.

——(1989) Unpublished paper presented at the Day Conference on Child Abuse and Family Systems Theory, The Instituted of Family Therapy, London.

Minuchin, S. and Fishman, H. C. (1981) *Family Therapy Techniques*, Cambridge, MA: Harvard University Press.

NSPCC (1989) *Child Abuse Trends in England and Wales 1983–1987*, London: NSPCC.

Parton, N. (1985) *The Politics of Child Abuse*, London: Macmillan.

Sandler, A-M. (1975) 'Comments on the significance of Piaget's work for psychoanalysis', *International Review of Psychoanalysis*,.

Sarnoff, C. (1971) 'The ego structure in latency', *Psychoanalytic Quarterly* 40 (3) 387–413.

Schreber, D. P. (1903) *Memoirs of My Nervous Illness*, London: Dawson.

Shengold, L. C. (1979) 'Soul Murder: Child Abuse and Deprivation', *Journal of the American Psychoanalytic Association* 27 (3) 533–59.

Sherrick, I., Keraney, C., Buxton, M. and Stevens, B. (1978) 'Ego strengthening psychotherapy with children having primary ego deficiences', *Journal of Child Psychotherapy* 4 (4).

Sinason, V. (1989) 'Spare the rod and a thought', *Guardian*, 12 August.

Yorke, C. and Wiseberg, S. (1976) 'A developmental view of anxiety: some clinical and theoretical considerations', *Psychoanalytic Study of the Child* 31.

7

THE UNBEARABLE TRAUMATOGENIC PAST: CHILD SEXUAL ABUSE[1]

Gerrilyn Smith

This chapter will attempt to examine the consequences for the child of sexually abusive experiences. Frequently the experience remains a secret one, shared between the abuser and child. Often, despite obvious and gross indicators of sexual abuse, it goes undetected not only by those people in the child's family but also by other adults within the child's network. The secret nature of the abuse itself and society's equivocal response to it, makes the recovery process extremely difficult. It is a grave state of affairs that Roland Summit's observation, 'survival is better served by dissociation than by disclosure' (Summit 1988: 55) is still the case for the vast majority of children.

Child sexual abuse is not a new phenomenon. Its historical legacy has been well documented elsewhere (Rush 1980). Yet only in the last ten years has it been included in Department of Health circulars and guidelines (Mrazek *et al.* 1981).

INCIDENCE AND PREVALENCE

Variations exist in estimates of incidence and prevalence. This is due to a host of methodological considerations in gathering data (Wyatt 1985; Wyatt and Peters 1986a and b; Kelly 1988; Kelly 1989). These include definition, sample selection, method of data collection to name but a few. Most researchers agree that they are more likely to elicit false negatives rather than false positives when questioning individuals about sexually abusive experiences. (That is people saying they have not been abused when they have rather than people saying they have been abused when they have not.)

As a psychologist and feminist, self-definition of personal experience takes precedence over legal and other more restrictive definitions of

130

sexual abuse. This approach helps to reflect the complexity of experience that comprises sexual abuse (Kelly 1989) as well as providing a vital starting point in the therapeutic process.

The data on incidence and prevalence clearly identify the scope of the problem and the necessity for mental health workers to have a good knowledge base and training in dealing with the psychological consequences.

A postal survey to professionals who would be most likely to come into contact with child sexual abuse through their routine work produced a very low incidence figure of 0.3 per cent of the population (Mrazek, Lynch and Bentovim 1981). The data was collected for the period between June 1977 and May 1978. It would be interesting to see if the same postal survey conducted ten years later (in effect) generated the same figure. Professional awareness has undoubtedly increased over the last decade.

The often quoted MORI Poll (Duncan and Baker 1985) reported a prevalence figure of 12 per cent of women and 8 per cent of men who had experienced sexually abusive touching (clearly defined in their study) before they were 16 years of age. This is frequently averaged out to 10 per cent of the population.

Incidence and prevalence figures climb when the definition of what constitutes sexual abuse is broadened, questionnaires are replaced or followed up with interviews, interviewers are trained and matched for gender and race to their interviewees. In studies that employ these techniques much higher rates are reported such as 48 per cent of women in a GP practice (Nash and West 1985), 54 per cent of women in a random sample in San Francisco (Russell 1983), and 62 per cent of black and white women in a random urban sample (Wyatt 1985). With figures as high as this, it makes sexually abusive experiences in childhood almost the norm for women.

Reporting in Britain is still not mandatory and professional workers, especially those in the mental health field, may give priority to client confidentiality over child protection issues (La Fontaine 1987). When researchers have concentrated on mental health clients the results are quite staggering. Jehu (1988) summarises some of these results.

Without listing all of the studies he reported, the percentage of sexual abuse among women in clinical samples ranged from 13 per cent in a general psychiatric out-patient population (Herman 1986) to a staggering 90 per cent in both a sexual dysfunction clinic (Baisden and Baisden 1979) and a clinical sample of women suffering from multiple personalities (Bliss 1984). The implications for clinicians are clear. Child sexual abuse has far reaching psychological consequences for a significant proportion of those who experience it. Unfortunately, we do not have a way of knowing what that proportion is, so it would be wrong to assume that sexually abusive experiences in childhood necessarily generate long-term psychological disturbances. Despite this uncertainty we can be sure that there will be a significant proportion of clients, both children and adults, for whom sexual abuse plays a major role in their current disturbance. This may not necessarily be known at the time of referral.

GENERAL PATTERNS OF ABUSE

Knowledge of general patterns of sexual abuse and its effects is essential for mental health practitioners. It is clear from research that the child is targeted, groomed and systematically abused over a period of time usually by someone they know and trust(ed) (Smith 1986; Wyre 1987). The majority of abusers of both boys and girls are men. Despite outstanding questions regarding under-reporting it is clear that girls are still abused more frequently than boys.

There is increasing evidence of more widespread sexual abuse of boys. Under-reporting of sexual abuse by boys may be explained by a number of factors including the male ethic of self-reliance, notions of youthful male sexuality, different familial patterns of supervision of boys and gender-mediated responses to the abuse (Peake 1989).

Female perpetrators clearly exist. Recently researchers have begun to question the long held belief that the overwhelming majority of perpetrators were men. Despite increasing reports of female perpetrators it seems the pattern of abuse is still strongly mediated by gender factors (Russell 1986). Unlike men women rarely abuse alone, but often in conjunction with male partners or groups of paedophiles. A lone woman abuser is often suffering from a frank psychiatric/psychotic disturbance. Home Office Criminal Statistics between 1975 and 1984 indicated that 99.05 per cent of convicted perpetrators were male. A significant proportion (50 per cent) of women convicted of sexual offences were involved in 'aiding and abetting' (Wyre 1987).

Actual violence is rarely necessary because the perpetrator is known to the child. Clearly psychological force is used but it is often subtle and well disguised. A skilled abuser will clearly manipulate the onus of responsibility on to the child and encourage the child's feelings of complicity. There is clearly a softening up process employed by abusers (Wyre 1987). Often it follows a pattern of befriending, involvement in nurturing and non-abusive touching moving to ambiguous touching through to exploitative abusive touching often with some form of penetration as the ultimate goal (Conte *et al.* 1987). The illusion that the child controls the process is fostered by the abuser.

It is important to stress and constantly emphasise that children rarely lie or fabricate accounts of sexual abuse. There are many good reasons why they do not tell. It is often a wonder that they do (Peake 1989). When they disclose their experience they are more likely to minimise it, often disclosing in stages and leaving the worst bits until they know how the person they have told is going to respond.

What happens following a disclosure of sexual abuse varies tremendously. There is no doubt that the experience is mediated by a range of factors. Often these are unrelated to the child and their experience. More frequently they are factors relating to the alleged perpetrator. Finkelhor (1984) did not find class and race distinctions in the detection, reporting and conviction rates of sexual abuse crimes committed in the United States. He did not analyse the data in relation to the gender of perpetrator. However Clarke and Lewis (1977), in researching reported rapes in Toronto, Canada, found clear evidence that the disposition of the case was mediated by a range of factors. They described this filtering process in detail. There is no doubt that a similar filtering process happens in child sexual abuse cases. The race, gender and class of the offender seem to strongly influence the course of action taken by professional agencies.

CONSEQUENCES

For the child the consequences of sexual abuse are often traumatic and distort the developmental process. Clearly various factors influence the consequences. If the abuse is short-lived, terminated by effective action either by the child and/or the non-abusing parent, the child is believed and supported by their family and community, the negative consequences are minimised. For most children this is not the case. The abuse remains secret causing inner turmoil and confusion that often wreaks havoc long after the abuse has stopped.

Roland Summit (1983) described the process of the child learning to live with the sexually abusive experience. He labelled this process the Child Sexual Abuse Accommodation Syndrome. He identified five separate but consecutive stages of the accommodation process. They are the establishment of secrecy, engendering a sense of helplessness, entrapment by the abuser and accommodation by the child, delayed and often unconvincing disclosure often followed by retraction.

The establishment of secrecy is of primary importance. Often this is achieved by introducing an element of danger, especially danger of disclosing. For example a child may be told no one will believe them or something awful will happen to them if they tell.

Case A
A young white girl's father fed her pet rabbit to his snake in front of her. The message to the 4-year-old was quite clear despite the fact it was not articulated by her abuser but demonstrated – if you tell this will happen to you.

This display of power or superior strength smoothes the way forward to the next stage of engendering a sense of helplessness. The feelings of powerlessness experienced by the child are thought to contribute to the traumatisation. Finkelhor and Browne (1985) list powerlessness as one of the four traumatogenic dynamics of child sexual abuse. They identify two main components of this powerlessness. The child's sense of control and mastery over their experience is repeatedly shown to be false and overruled. Additionally the child may fear that they will be seriously hurt or destroyed. The 4-year-old girl witnessing her pet's demise must have seriously feared for herself. Indeed, this very effective threat was periodically reinforced by intermittent references to the rabbit; thus maintaining the potency of both the implicit message and messenger alike.

Having established a secrecy around the sexual abuse and engendered a sense of powerlessness in the child, the abuser effectively shifts the burden of coping with the sexual abuse onto the child. The child must learn to live with it! This is labelled the third stage of entrapment and accommodation.

Entrapment is the successive limiting of options as perceived by the child. Children are dependent on adults, especially their parents, for their needs, both physical and emotional, to be met. However, unlike adults in families, who may also be dependent on children to meet their needs, children have fewer options outside of the family. Parents play a major role in shaping a child's perception of the world and relationships. They can define abusive experiences as loving and/or caring. Children are often told the sexual abuse is a special experience yet at the same time they sense the tension and anxiety of discovery that often accompanies the secret exploitation. Confronted with a limited range of responses or alternatives to abuse, it is no wonder that children learn to accommodate the sexually abusive experience.

Ferenczi described this process clearly in 1932 (quoted in Summit 1988): 'the misused child changes into a mechanical obedient automaton or becomes defiant but unable to account for the reasons of his [sic] defiance'. Attempting to cope with sexual abuse can serve the dual function of trying to both resolve the problem and regulate emotional distress. Not all coping mechanisms are adaptive. Haley (1976) clearly conceptualised symptoms as responses to problems, that in time often became identified as the problem. This is frequently the case in sexual abuse.

Symptoms serve a function for the individual who manifests them. Over time these solutions can become dysfunctional and it is often these 'solutions' that bring a child to professional attention rather than the sexual abuse itself (Smith 1987b).

Case B

A 13-year-old black girl was referred for difficulties in school. She was an excellent attender and came to school even when she was on the run and had not spent the night at home. She always produced work of a high standard. She had a history of running away. This started at age 5 and was labelled 'wandering off'. She frequently had large sums of money, the source of which was not known. She wrote sexually explicit poetry and stories which she handed in to school teachers. When much younger she had brought pornography into school in her 'kissy sexy book'. She was extremely difficult with male teachers and boys. She clearly had better relationships with female members of staff and girl friends. Her mother reported long-standing difficulties between the two of them. She felt unable to reach her daughter. She reported that her daughter always slept with a knife under her pillow. She attacked a boy on the bus with a knife for 'looking at her'. She refused to wear her school uniform, preferring instead heavy make-up, jewellery and expensive grown-up clothing. She was consequently easily identifiable and totally dissimilar to any of her classmates. Her taste in clothing was completely at odds with her peers and not age-appropriate. The clothing was not bought by her mother. She made no disclosure of sexual abuse. At 14 she was picked up by the police for soliciting.

This young girl was demonstrating many of the signs one would expect a child to exhibit if they had been sexually assaulted. The index of suspicion is extremely high. The evidence of her involvement in prostitution was there prior to the police arresting her. Despite this no professional alerted the child protection services. Referral to a specialist agency was because she was difficult in school, not because someone suspected she was being sexually abused.

Children who are sexually abused come under enormous pressure from their abusers not to tell. They are exposed to habitual double-bind patterns of communication (Bateson *et al.* 1956), that is, receiving contradictory messages at different levels of communication. This causes enormous internal confusion. In double-bind patterns of communication, the individual, in this case a child, is unable to comment on the discrepant messages they are receiving.

To communicate the problem they are experiencing, without breaching the injunction to remain quiet, requires ingenuity and immense effort on the part of the child. Many describe clearly the hints they were giving to adults in the hope someone would ask why they were behaving as they were. If someone guesses what is happening, the child literally remains innocent of the forbidden telling.

Cases E, F, I, J

When asked to list the signs they gave prior to disclosure, four girls between the ages of 14 and 16, all white, generated the following list:

1 Avoiding the abuser.
2 Marked changes in the way they behaved – from being very cheerful to sad, sociable to a loner.
3 Being scared of boys.
4 Spending lots of times with boys.
5 Running away.
6 Messing around with drugs and glue.
7 Stop eating.
8 Overdosing (usually paracetamol).
9 Losing friends.
10 Not going to school.
11 Staying out.
12 Staying in.
13 Staying closer to your sister.
14 Sleeping around.
15 Not talking about abuser.
16 Cutting up.
17 Complaining of being ill all the time.
18 Jumping in front of cars or buses.

(Peake and Smith 1987)

As can be seen from this list these girls were trying very hard to let someone know they were in trouble. In only one case did professionals suspect sexual abuse prior to the young woman disclosing (see Table 7.1). Even in that one case, the girl's disclosure was not prompted by a child protection investigation but by the girl herself.

Many of the young women exhibited several of the signs listed. Clearly those who stayed out, for instance, did not list staying in as a sign. The same is true for items three and four. Usually the girls did one or the other, not both.

What is disturbing is that the girls disclosed not as a result of professional concern but because they felt they had to. They all expressed exasperation at caring adults not recognising or picking up their hints that something was wrong. Despite wanting to share their secret, they found no one who was really interested enough to ask what was going on. Their experience is not unique.

All of the above signs are clear examples of symptoms as solutions to the problem of being sexually abused. For many of these girls, they coped with their abuse by employing the tactics above. So the signs served the dual function of attempting to alert people to the problem and thereby resolve it and regulating their emotional distress.

Messing around with drugs and glue was seen as a way of blocking out the experience. In effect it is the adolescent equivalent of self-medication. Unfortunately, over time, these patterns of adaptation or accommodation can become maladaptive. This is because they become a more generalised way of coping rather than a response to a particular stressor. They often increase the child's vulnerability to additional sexual assaults. As they are not under the child's conscious control they are consequently activated in inappropriate circumstances. Paradoxically, rather than protecting the child, they can cut them off from potential sources of protection and support. Case N is a clear example of this.

Case N
This 10-year-old white boy was received into care following an episode of fire-setting in his adoptive home. A year previously the family's home had been gutted by fire. The cause was said to be faulty wiring. However, N was playing with matches by the settee. He left the house and watched TV at a next door neighbour's house whilst the rest of the family was evacuated by the fire brigade.

Historically, concerns had been raised about this young boy. His mother failed to bond with him. He was often neglected and any level of parental protection was absent. He was referred, at 4, to a mental health facility as an arsonist. His mother's brother, a schedule one offender, was living with N and the family. Mother was the victim of domestic violence from her boyfriend who also physically abused N. The case notes record several disclosures by N regarding mother's boyfriend. He alleged that he was beaten and sexually assaulted by this man. No child protection measures were taken, nor was an investigation mounted. Mother wished to marry her violent abusive boyfriend. Pressure was put on N by mother to say to social services that he had previously lied about boyfriend's behaviour and things were alright now between him and his prospective step-parent. The 6-year-old child refused. A week later, whilst playing with matches, he set the sofa alight. Mother's flat was gutted and he was received into care. He never returned home to his mother's 'care', nor did he have any future contact with his abuser.

At 10, during assessment, he made clear re-statements of his earlier physical and sexual abuse. These disclosures were detailed. His index of suspicion based on current behaviours was also high. He had received intensive psychotherapy prior to and following his reception into care when 6 years old; despite this he was not recognised as a child who had been sexually and physically

Table 7.1 These girls were all referred to a Girls' Group following disclosure of sexual abuse. Case E and Case I disclosed longstanding abuse by stepfather after being in care for six months. They were all aged between 14 and 16; two were black (one Caribbean, one Asian) and six were white.

	Abusers – including legal disposition	Girls' place of residence		Previous professional involvement (i.e. Social Services Child Guidance)
		Following disclosure	Six months later	
Case C J.N.	Father – parents divorced No prosecution	Living at home with mother	At home	Longstanding psychiatric involvement CSA[1] not suspected
Case D L.P.	Father – parents divorced No prosecution	Received into Residential Care	Res. Care	No previous involvement
Case E J.R.	Raped by group of boys (4) Unknown prosecution pursued following commencement	Already in Residential Care	Res. Care	Previous SSD[2] involvement. Received into care as beyond parental control. CSA not suspected Disclosed stepfather whilst in care
Case F T.L.	Stepfather No prosecution	Received into Residential Care	Foster placement	Long-term SSD involvement CSA suspected

Case	Abuser	Action	Placement	Previous involvement
Case G T.R.	Father No prosecution	Received into Residential Care	Foster placement	No previous involvement
Case H A.R.	Raped by adolescent male acquaintance Convicted	Living at home with both parents	At home	Professional involvement regarding educational needs
Case I K.B.	Stepfather No prosecution	Already in Residential Care	Res. Care	Previous SSD involvement as beyond parental control. Vol. r.i.c.[3] CSA not suspected. Disclosed in care.
Case J L.H.	Stepbrothers (3) No prosecution	Received into Foster Care	Home (Brothers rehoused)	No previous involvement CSA not suspected

Source: Peake and Smith (1987)
Notes: 1 CSA = Child Sexual Abuse.
2 SSD = Social Services Department.
3 Vol. r.i.c. = Voluntary reception into care.

abused. He was seen as neglected, deprived and a difficult child to manage.

His playing with matches, reflecting poor parental vigilance given his age, becomes labelled prematurely as fire-setting. However, it becomes an effective way for him to control and master difficult situations. By 10 years old his fire-setting has become out of control and uncontainable. His initial verbal disclosures offered no protection. His behaviour did.

In the short term the effect of sexual abuse for the individual child is an increase in feelings of fear, depression, anger and hostility, aggression and sexualised behaviour (Finkelhor and Browne 1985). Case B (see p. 134) presents many of these features.

In the long term these feelings are exacerbated if untreated and/or the child does not find adaptive ways of coping. Long-term sequelae can be self destructive behaviour, anxiety, isolation and stigmatisation, poor self-esteem, difficulties in trusting relationships, revictimisation, substance and alcohol abuse and sexual maladjustment (Finkelhor and Browne 1985). One individual may exhibit some or all of these patterns of behaviour.

Consequences of sexual abuse can be categorised under the following areas of development.

Sense of self

A child who has been sexually assaulted for as long as they can remember may fail to even establish a sense of themselves. Typically this is manifested as an over-intrusiveness on their part with little or no understanding regarding privacy or personal space. For children who are sexually abused after establishing personal boundaries, the feelings of violation and intrusion are often much greater. They often feel as if they are 'damaged goods'. Indeed Sgroi (1982) goes so far as to label it the 'damaged goods syndrome'.

Self-esteem

Self-esteem is generally very low. Some children who have been sexually abused perceive their self-worth only in terms of their sexuality. They feel valued only as a sexual object and relate to the world through sexual activity sometimes exclusively. In the absence of caring adults picking up the clues children are giving, feelings of self-worth are low. It is not uncommon for children who have been sexually abused to feel insignificant, worthless, and almost invisible.

Affective range and expression

The secrecy and confusion that surrounds the sexual abuse makes it difficult for the child to express the whole range of feelings they experience. Their affective range often becomes very restricted. Much of their anger and hostility whilst being abused must be repressed as it does not facilitate the accommodation process that is necessary for survival. Anxiety, fear and depression are often overwhelming yet the child's outward expression can be flat, and they can show a numbed responsiveness. Explosive outbursts of feelings are often the only blips on an otherwise flat range of affective expression. These can be dramatic suicide attempts or violent outbursts as in Case B, attacking the boy on the bus with a knife. Some children only operate within a limited range of angry, aggressive behaviour. Frequently deemed out of control, they experience many moves of placement and keep people at a distance through their violent outbursts.

Capacity to judge people and situations

The sense of betrayal felt by children who have been sexually abused by adults in caring roles, such as parents, should not be underestimated. The consequence of this betrayal is often an impaired ability to judge the safety of other people and situations. If a child is sexually assaulted at home, running away and sleeping in a stranger's house may seem a safe alternative. In this way one can see the increased vulnerability of children who have been sexually abused. What should be safe is not. How, then, can one begin to make judgements about other people and other situations? Their own abusers may appear to be pillars of the community, responsible adults or loving parents, to people outside the abuse. For some children this teaches them to rely exclusively on their judgements based on personal experience. These children usually possess a degree of self-confidence that allows them to both make and believe in their own assessments.

Sense of responsibility

The child's sense of responsibility is frequently distorted. Sometimes an overdeveloped sense of responsibility is exhibited. They feel responsible for everything and are frequently overwhelmed by guilt. Other children, who internalise the victim role completely, can become totally irresponsible and refuse to recognise that their own actions do have consequences that they must be accountable for. Everything becomes someone else's fault. The feelings of loss of control and powerlessness they experienced whilst being abused annihilate any element of choice or individual free will.

Morality

Often coupled with the issue of responsibility, moral development is clearly affected by sexually abusive experiences. Clinical experience indicates this is not always in a negative way. Many of the children who have been sexually abused show a very highly developed sense of what is right, wrong, just or fair. This seems to be because they have had to make their own evaluations based on their experiences of sexual abuse. They know that you cannot tell what someone is like merely by looking at them. This is based on personal experience, i.e. if you could see/meet my dad, you wouldn't believe me because he doesn't look like a sex offender. Consequently they become reluctant to judge people by appearances or reputation alone. Some white children who have been sexually abused have demonstrated a better understanding of racial and gender discrimination as a consequence of their experience.

For other children, sexually abusive experiences make moral judgements difficult because they are confused by what is right and what is wrong. Because our society has institutionalised discrimination, it allows and encourages people to project bad feelings onto whole categories of people. For the child who has been sexually abused, it might be all men. It may also be related to a particular feature of the abuser as in Case E, a white girl who was raped by a group of black and white boys. She chose to vent most of her fury at the black boys and was provided with ample racist material from friends, family and society to support her arguments. She will need help to separate out her justifiable anger at being raped and her unjustifiable anger at issues of race.

Case H
A 14-year-old black girl is raped by an older black boy. He is cautioned. She is then sexually abused by her half-brother. He is not prosecuted. A few months later she is picked up by the police whilst defending a friend on the tube. This incident results in her hitting a plain clothes officer. When it comes to Court, two friends also involved in the episode are not charged because they are under 14. She pleads guilty, is fined and receives a two-year Supervision Order. Both her abusers have received no penalty for the crimes they committed.

What is this young black woman learning about morality? What did the eight girls listed in Table 7.1 learn about morality when only one of the thirteen known perpetrators was brought to justice?

Making and sustaining relationships

For many children, the sexually abusive experience demonstrates blurred role boundaries between adults and children, parents and children, and often men and women. All children see role confusions as they are almost unavoidable, but sexual abuse is one of the most extreme forms of boundary violation. Children may be frightened to trust, fear intimacy, show extremes in dependency needs, vacillating from being totally dependent to totally independent.

Sgroi (1982) identified pseudo-maturity coupled with failure to accomplish developmental tasks as one of her treatment impact issues. The pseudo-maturity often leads to relationships developing prematurely and moving quickly into sexual intimacy. This is often because children who have been sexually assaulted do not know how to relate other than in a sexualised way. Consequently many of their relationships become sexualised. Same-age partners contribute to the notion that their sexual activity is developmentally appropriate. It is often through observing consistently inappropriate partners and/or sexualised approaches to foster parents and/or residential care workers, that adults recognise the child's limited range of social skills and total ineptness at negotiating relationships other than in the way they have been taught by their abusers. Societal messages about making and maintaining relationships are also quite confusing as sexuality is frequently emphasised.

Communication skills

Relationships are very closely bound up with an individual's capacity to communicate.

The disclosure and/or discovery of sexual abuse should be the first step in the process of recovery and healing. Yet all too frequently it leads to further trauma to the child. This is often because they are not believed. As Summit points out in his paper on the Accommodation Syndrome (1983), disclosure is often delayed in that it rarely follows the first abusive episode. In the Clarke and Lewis study on rape in adult women (1977), delay in reporting increased the likelihood that women would not be believed. Children's disclosures are often quite tentative and are often construed as being therefore unconvincing.

A women's affect when reporting rape significantly affected the likelihood of belief. If she was calm and collected at the time of reporting she was less likely to be believed (Clarke and Lewis 1977). It appears, although there is little empirical evidence to support this, that misconceptions and assumptions like this also affect the likelihood of children being believed: 'The menace of the perpetrator is typically effaced by focusing morbid attention on the silence and implied complicity of young participants' (Summit in Wyatt and Powell 1988: 43).

Of the fourteen cases presented in this paper only one resulted in a conviction. Many of the young people and children described in this chapter felt it was they who had been punished.

Early in this chapter, reference was made to Bateson's (1973) double-bind patterns of communication. Child sexual abuse frequently fulfils the necessary and sufficient conditions of double binds (Smith 1987b). These are:

i A dependent relationship which is subjected to repeated experiences that come to be perceived as habitual
ii Contradictory messages are given at different levels of communication, such as a verbal message that is contradicted by non-verbal behaviour. Disobeying one or the other of these injunctions will result in punishment.
iii An inability to comment on the contradictory messages and an inability to leave the relationship.

(Bateson *et al.* 1956)

Once subjected to the characteristic sequential pattern of interaction, the recipient acquires mental habits which accommodate and attempt to make sense of them (Bateson 1973: 179–97). It is further postulated that the complete set of ingredients for the double bind is no longer necessary, once the recipient has 'learned to perceive their universe in double-bind patterns. Almost any part of a double-bind sequence may then be sufficient to precipitate panic or rage. The pattern of conflicting injunctions may even be taken over by hallucinatory voices' Bateson (1973: 179).

The hallucinating voices referred to, frequently take the form of persecutor and often express thoughts and feelings the child could not overtly express.

Case K

A 14-year-old white girl, with a high index of suspicion of sexualisation, but no disclosure, left an exam at school and was unable to continue. The reason she gave was that she could not concentrate as the voices in her head were too loud. They were saying she was being sexually abused.

Case L

A 20-year-old black woman disclosed to the police at 14, her sexual abuse by her half brother. Following disclosure she was rejected by her family and received into care. She regularly heard persecutory voices. They would taunt her, tell her she was dirty, evil and wicked. Their content was exclusively centred on her experience of sexual abuse and many of the statements were made in reality by members of her family.

It is therefore, extremely important for workers to recognise that children who have been sexually abused over a long period frequently have distorted communication and that they are prone to catastrophic disconnections from reality (Smith 1989b).

These disconnections are frequently labelled psychotic or a result of a schizophrenic illness without proper recognition being given to the original trauma of sexual abuse.

For these children, the real meaning of any communication always seems obscured and/or contradictory. Additionally double-bind communications produce a confusion between literal and metaphoric communication. Within the context of therapy, this confusion can be explored. Metaphorical communications, such as drawings, can be used as means of addressing the traumatic material without the child being overwhelmed by its potency. If a young person cannot learn to discuss and assess the communication of others realistically, they become victim to a never ending systematic distortion of human communication (Bateson 1973:183). Without a secure base, from which to explore the various contradictions they have become trapped in, there often seems no alternative but suicidal despair.

Double-bind communications push an individual to find solutions to the perpetual no-win situation.

Case M

This 16-year-old white girl was sexually assaulted by her brother. She was received into care and referred for therapy after numerous placement failures, overdoses and episodes of severe self-mutilating. In addition to showing many of the consequences already listed, she had difficulty in verbalising her psychic pain. In therapy, when considering her options she *wrote* them as follows:

Option 1 Be the dutiful daughter and accepted by my family.
Option 2 Suicide.

Caught between these two extremes, she vacillated between intense and idealised attachment to her family followed by bouts of self-mutilating and suicide attempts. As therapy progressed a third option emerged as she began to examine her previous perceptions. She wrote her new understanding as follows:-

Option 1 ~~Be the dutiful daughter and accepted by my family.~~ Not for me.

Option 2 ~~Suicide.~~ That's not an option I want.

Option 3 Find myself and fight like hell to get it. That's the one I've chosen.

From the above example the emergence of a third alternative is apparent. She also demonstrates the literal/metaphorical confusion, often experienced by young people who have been sexually abused, by the crossing out of Options 1 and 2. Her written comments beside each option show she is beginning to learn to comment on her own communications.

Bateson was not totally pessimistic about the outcome for those who experienced double bind-communication. If pathology could be warded off or resisted, the experience could enhance creativity as it pushed the child to find solutions to what appear to be insoluble dilemmas.

Sexual development

Many people assume that sexual abuse will affect sexual development. The common lay assumptions are that boys who are sexually abused by men (sexual abuse by women is often not considered possible) will become homosexual and girls who are sexually abused by men will become frigid. These concerns are frequently expressed by parents of children who have been sexually abused. These assumptions carry some nonsensical gender differentations. The traumatic sexual experience is seen as creating a compulsion in boys and a revulsion in girls. Additionally it suggests that homosexuality is not a matter of individual choice but rather something one is forced into by circumstances beyond individual control.

The logic seems to follow this pattern. Sexual abuse will affect sexuality. It will pervert normal sexuality. What is seen as perverted sexuality in our society but homosexuality. This is overtly stated for boys and implied for girls. It reflects society's underlying homophobia. It also over-simplifies both the consequence of sexual abuse on a child's sexual development as well as homosexuality itself.

Finkelhor and Browne (1985) discuss traumatic sexualisation in their traumatogenic dynamics model of sexual abuse. It is important to recognise that many children are sexualised by their experience of sexual abuse. This is because they have been exposed to sexual behaviour and contact that is developmentally inappropriate. Unfortunately, once they have this sexual 'knowledge', it cannot be taken away. This exposure frequently heightens their interest in all sexual matters (Adams-Tucker 1981, Friedrich *et al.* 1986).

Many children are rewarded by the abuser following episodes of sexual abuse. In part this is to ensure their silence. However, it also conveys to the child a sense of how they are valued by this adult in particular. Often the child generalises and believes all adults will only value them for their sexual behaviour. They can also become very confused about the difference between love and sex.

Sex can become a means of getting needs fulfilled. Many children experience their abuser's love as contingent upon the sexual abuse. Multiply victimised children have experiences which reinforce this view only too clearly. Their 'needs' may have been met in exchange for sexual activity. Unfortunately our society is keenly attuned to and values sexual commodities. For children who have been exploited sexually, selling themselves can seem a way to regain control.

The focus of attention on genitals and genital contact frequently leads the child to develop a distorted body image. This is frequently demonstrated by children who, at a very young age, will expose themselves to their peers in a developmentally inappropriate way (i.e. it is contextually abnormal and not part of mutual exploration). At worst this can lead to fetishised and fixated attitudes to their own and other people's genitals. This is frequently displayed in children's drawings where sexual parts are drawn, often in a large exaggerated manner.

Clinical experience indicates that sexually abusive experiences do not provide children with functional sexual knowledge despite the fact that sex instruction is one of the most common ruses adopted by perpetrators. Abusers control the information and often purposely mislead children. 'All daddies do this with their children' is a very common example of this. Children who have been sexually abused find it difficult to ask questions or seek clarification regarding sexual matters.

Another by-product of sexual abuse for some children is that any sexual intimacy in later life becomes a trigger for intrusive memories of the sexual abuse (Smith 1989b). A high prevalence figure for sexual abuse in childhood of 90 per cent of the women attending a sexual dysfunction clinic (Baisden and Baisden 1979) bears this out. Some young people and adults who have experienced sexual abuse may choose to avoid sexual intimacy as a way of minimising unwanted flashbacks.

It is also important to recognise that some children's sexualisation leads them into perpetrating sexual offences themselves (Becker 1988). There seems to be a gender difference in that this is more likely to occur in boys. However, with the younger age group (under 12) the ratio of girls to boys who sexually victimise other children is higher. Perhaps this is because the girls' gender socialisation has not progressed far enough to extinguish the notion of females as overt sexual predators. If a child violates their gender stereotype, reactions are often more punitive. It is almost expected that boys will go on to victimise and girls to be victims. Empirical evidence is needed that demonstrates exceptions to these patterns, most importantly boys and girls sexually victimised in their childhoods who become neither victim nor perpetrator.

It is not surprising that a child exposed habitually and repeatedly to sexually deviant behaviour runs a high risk of being perverted by it.

Authority issues

Much has been written and researched about the sexual aspects of sexual abuse. There is, however, a paucity of literature on power and authority in relation to child sexual abuse. This is despite the fact that many researchers see the need to dominate as an important motivating factor in perpetrators. The misuse of power and authority is often central to many people's understanding of the phenomena of sexual abuse. Yet translating this theoretical knowledge to actual clinical practice has proved difficult.

Family therapists are currently grappling with this issue in relation to their clinical work with violent and abusive families (Dell 1989). All therapeutic models, whether systemic, behavioural or intrapsychic, usually employ the authority of the helper as a means of bringing about change. Because authority has been irresponsibly and exploitatively manipulated in sexual abuse, mental health practitioners may want to consider and reflect on their own use of professional authority (Smith 1987a).

What do children learn about authority and power as a result of their experience of sexual abuse? Many children who have been sexually abused come to view the world as comprised only of abusers and victims. The dilemma for them is which role will they occupy as they grow up. Is it inevitable that they remain victims? Is the only way out of perpetual victimisation, to become a perpetrator? The responsible exercise of authority is unknown and consequently also unrecognisable. For some, to exercise any power is to be an abuser. If an abuser is a hated person the only choice, as they perceive it, is to remain a victim. A victim is defined as someone who has no power rather than someone who has had their options limited or been unable to exercise choices. For others, who want to reject their victim position, the only other role as they perceive it, is to become a perpetrator. Some children clearly articulate this dilemma: 'I want to hurt other people like I was hurt'; 'No one will victimise me anymore because, if anyone is going to be abused, I will be the one doing it' are two examples of this.

Unfortunately, society often glorifies sex offenders such as Peter Sutcliffe or Jack the Ripper. Media coverage of sexual offences against children, whilst limited with regard to what can be said about the child, tends to focus on the abusers' alleged innocence or moral depravity. Headlines are more likely to contain lurid details of the actual abuse as well as the rationalisations, minimisations and other cognitive distortions of the alleged abuser. This conveys to many children a clear message that they will not be heard, inaccurate and misleading things will be said about them and they will have no right of reply. Despite the fact that they are not actually named, within a small community it is often obvious who the articles refer to. To many children this is further evidence of the abuse of authority of adults. This increases their feelings of powerlessness and often makes them wish to 'become adults' quickly so they too can have access to this authority.

Additionally children who have been sexually abused are often very perceptive regarding power hierarchies in foster families, residential units, classrooms, in fact any social gathering. They can be quite adept at manipulating and 'working the system'. This need not be dysfunctional. They are often quick to point out inconsistencies regarding rules, to challenge authority or show disrespect for it. This may take the form of 'What gives you the right to tell me to do anything?' Many children who have not been sexually abused also do this. For those who have, there is a much deeper understanding perhaps of how, why and where adults derive their authority over children. For adults, working or living with these children can be profoundly disturbing. Other adults often find it difficult to categorically state that the adult who sexually abuses children is wrong. Children who remain living at home with non-abusing parents, often demonstrate a lack of respect for those parents' authority. One parent sexually abusing a child undermines both parents' authority. Unfortunately all too often professional interventions also undermine the non-abusing parent's (usually mother's) authority as well, at a time when it needs to be reinforced and strengthened. The message for the child rather than being 'your mum made some mistakes or may have missed important things and we're going to help her sort it out' is often received as 'your parents are both failures – your father for sexually abusing you, your mother for failing to protect you'. Generalised, this misinterpretation can engender feelings that authority is really illusory so there is no need to take it seriously or that it is rigid, inflexible and to be blindly obeyed.

One-up, one-down relationships, or those based on power imbalance are endemic in our society (Smith 1989a). We all experience them and we may occupy both positions, up or down, at different times. Often therapy, especially individual work, inadvertently or unconsciously replicates the abusive relationship in the unequal and unchanging power balance between client and helper (Miller 1985; Smith 1987a). The consequences for those who have been sexually abused who are seeking help, is that they begin to feel the secrecy, helplessness and entrapment of their abuse being replicated. They learn to accommodate in therapy, finish treatment and often break down as their essential pain remains untouched. Therapy has, without meaning to, retraumatised them.

Clearly more work and research is needed in this area. More attention needs to be paid to authority issues in both investigative and clinical work. Sgroi (1982) usefully raises some of these issues.

Most children whether they love or hate their abusers perceive them as powerful. This traumatic definition of power will undoubtedly shape the child's future perception of it.

INTERVENTIONS

Interventions must aim to help a child make sense of the experience of sexual abuse. Additionally they should concentrate on reducing the secrecy that surrounds the experience and the consequent vulnerability of the child. It is important to recognise that once a child has been sexually victimised their vulnerability to subsequent victimisation is increased.

Some workers maintain that perpetrators often target vulnerable children, suggesting that the vulnerability is already there. Whilst in some cases this may be true, such as targeting children with special needs or learning disabilities it is important for professionals to remember that the targeting of potential victims is based on the individual predilections of the perpetrator. A vulnerability then might be blonde hair and blue eyes.

There is also some confusion frequently expressed between aetiological factors and consequences. It is not uncommon for professionals who assess a very sexualised child, to see the sexualisation as a mitigating circumstance in the genesis of the sexual abuse. Children will also internalise these beliefs. It is important to help the child differentiate between the consequences of the sexual abuse on them and their own individual characteristics that may have become distorted by the abuse.

Belief

In order for any treatment work with children who have been sexually abused to be effective, belief in the child's disclosure is essential. It must be recognised that the vast majority of sexual abuse is traumatising for the child and produces far-reaching psychological consequences. It undoubtedly shapes the developmental processes of the child and in some cases will prevent the unfolding of those processes considerably.

Affirmation of feelings

Treatment work must help the child articulate their feelings about the abusive experience. This may include some disturbing positive as well as negative feelings towards the abuser and/or the abuse itself. Challenging the child's perceptions too early in therapeutic work, may block the healing process. Another aim of this intervention would be to broaden the child's affective range of expression; for angry children to facilitate the expression of sadness or loss; for depressed children the expression of anger. Children should not be given prescriptions about how they should feel.

Increase self-esteem

It is important that the child learns to value themselves, and not just in terms of being a sexual object. The stigmatisation of sexual abuse, especially incestuous abuse, often leaves children feeling dirty, shameful, guilty and worthless. They may need help in establishing appropriate boundaries and private personal space. Regular, predictable sessions with no intrusions conveys to the child that they are important and deserve individual (or group if that is the treatment modality) attention and space.

Recognition of abuser's responsibility for abuse

This is crucial. It may be necessary to explore with a child why they *feel* responsible, but it is very important to convey that all adults, and parents in particular, have a duty and responsibility towards protecting children. Adults have the power and authority to make choices and to prevent situations with children from becoming exploitative. This will help the child be clearer in terms of judging people and situations, as it clarifies issues of responsibility. Additionally, it aids their moral development and helps clarify confusions regarding authority.

They need clear statements from other adults about adult wrong doings.

Removal of blame

Many children who have been sexually abused blame themselves for what happened. This may make them feel more in control but it is important that these misperceptions are corrected. Messages that the adult perpetrator must bear full responsibility for individual actions they have committed, must be reinforced. This also helps prevent the cycle of moving from the position of victim to that of perpetrator.

These five interventions should form the essential elements of any therapeutic work. In addition they need to be coupled with an effective child protection plan. The child, to begin recovering and making sense of the sexual abuse, above all needs to be safe. These issues can be effectively raised in individual and/or group work settings. It is also useful to restate them openly at family sessions. Primary carers including, where appropriate, non-abusing parents, need to reinforce the messages given above. Where the primary care-giver is a non-abusing parent, this helps to realign and maintain their authority as custodial and protective parent.

Some children will need substantially more intensive therapeutic help. These children may be suffering from post-traumatic stress disorder (American Psychiatric Association 1987). Their symptomatology is often more extreme and sometimes bizarre. In addition to the five interventions listed above, more detailed and focused work will need to be undertaken. Sgroi (1982) proposes a similar two-stage model of treatment intervention.

Identification and recognition of survival tactics

The coping strategies the child employed whilst accommodating the abuse need to be identified. Some of these strategies may well have been functional. Children referred to mental health workers are more likely to have employed dysfunctional ones.

The child may need help with their guilty feelings for accepting bribes or participating in the sexual abuse. It may be necessary to look at what options are actually available to a young child. Often the child will describe numerous avoidance tactics they employed with varying degrees of success. It is not uncommon for children to have made previous disclosures that were not believed or followed up. A picture will emerge of a young child struggling, often alone, with a very big problem. The passivity they may initially present is the predictable outcome of many failed efforts to resolve the problem. To demonstrate their active and not so active resistance to them helps them to begin to view themselves as survivors. The solutions that may be most effective in avoiding abuse either literally by running away or metaphorically by getting 'glued up', are also most frequently deemed the most maladaptive. Workers must ask what tactics the child employed before moving on to more drastic and dangerous measures. Undoubtedly the child has moved to more desperate solutions as others have failed to provide relief.

Externalisation of coping patterns

Children may not recognise that their current symptomatology may have served a protective function for them. More frequently they view the current disturbances as more evidence of their essential badness. Often they are inflicting damage on themselves because they have completely internalised the notion that they are deserving of punishment. The original trauma that drove them to such drastic solutions may no longer be accessible to them. They do 'x' because they have done for so long. It often becomes their identity as in cutters or sniffers or runners. Workers need to help the child identify the pattern, or repetitiveness of their actions. It needs to be seen as triggered by the sexual abuse. Having established this pattern, predictability is the logical next step. 'X' will happen again when you are reminded of your abuse by feelings, family or other circumstances.

Identification of triggering factors

Workers need to help identify what preceded the episode of maladaptive coping or symptomatic behaviour. Often it is something that powerfully reminds the child of the original trauma. It could be a letter or card from the perpetrator, a phrase or expression used during the abuse. Each person will have their own unique triggers to the experience. The longer an individual with dysfunctional coping mechanisms has struggled unaided with overcoming their experience of abuse, the more likely that the triggers, often environmental, will be generalised and almost pervasive – any contact with any man rather than specific contact with the abuser.

Identification of communication patterns

The distorted communication patterns that so often accompany the experience of sexual abuse have been detailed in this chapter. Case K gives clear examples of work specifically aimed at her communication skills. Because children who have been sexually assaulted have been coerced into secret and furtive interactions, their communication skills often become equally obscure, secret and furtive. Clearly this has implications for making and sustaining relationships including the therapeutic one. It is not uncommon for children to present the opposite of what they are actually feeling. It is important that workers recognise this and comment on it.

Development of alternatives

All this work must be geared towards developing alternative strategies to replace the old dysfunctional or maladaptive ones. Workers must be aware that until new ways of responding to stressors are developed, children will continue to employ the strategies they have always used in the past. This should be anticipated, perhaps even predicted by the worker, as often an episode of symptomatic behaviour in the course of treatment can be taken to indicate treatment is not working or is too stressful to continue.

CONCLUSION

Throughout the whole of this process, the child needs reassurance. Belief in their experience, so crucial to first stage work, must be maintained and restated at various intervals throughout the therapeutic work. For the child does not assume that belief will be forthcoming. Indeed they are more likely to think that belief, like so many things in their lives, is conditional or dependent on their behaviour.

Undetected sexual abuse increases not only the vulnerability of the individual child who is being sexually abused, but also that of the whole community of children in proximity to that perpetrator. Children's misbehaviour, which is the consequence of the sexual abuse, is frequently labelled the problem, leaving the real problem to continue, causing more confusion, pain and suffering.

Unrecognised, child sexual abuse forces the child into the secret, furtive world of the perpetrator. Often it is a life disconnected from reality. It is frequently distorted by the misinformation of the perpetrator. A child may purposely cut off from all experience as a means of eliminating or reducing the impact of the sexual abuse. The developmental process that combines maturation with a physiological and psychological readiness is wilfully violated and perverted.

The traumatogenic potential of childhood sexual abuse is unbearable. For so many children, despite giving caring adults clues to the existence of an unspeakable problem, are left with little choice but a psychic retreat into the self. This depressed numbness or manic madness is often infinitely preferable to the reality they are forced to live with, and then keep secret.

NOTES

1. The title of the paper comes from a lecture by Ferenczi in 1932 published in English in 1949. International Journal of Psychoanalysis. Vol. 30. pp 225–230.

REFERENCES

Adams-Tucker, C. (1981) 'A sociological overview of 28 abused children', *Child Abuse and Neglect* 5: 361–7.

American Psychiatric Association (1987) *Diagnostic and Statistical Manual of Mental Disorders* (Revised 3rd Edn), Washington DC.

Baisden, M. and Baisden J. (1979) 'A profile of women who seek counselling for sexual dysfunction', *American Journal of Family Therapy* 7: 68–76.

Bateson, G. (1973) *Steps to an Ecology of Mind*, London: Paladin.

Bateson, G., Jackson, D., Haley, J., and Weakland J. (1956) 'Towards a theory of schizophrenia', *Behavioural Science* 1: 251–64.

Becker, J. (1988) 'The effects of child sexual abuse on adolescent sexual offenders', in G. Wyatt and G. Powell (Eds) *Lasting Effects of Child Sexual Abuse*, London: Sage.

Bliss, E. (1984) 'A symptom profile of patients with multiple personalities including MMPI results', *Journal of Nervous and Mental Disease* 172: 197–202.

Clarke, L. and Lewis, D. (1977) *Rape: the price of coercive sexuality*, Toronto: Women's Press.

Conte, J., Wolff, S. and Smith, T. (1987) 'What sexual offenders tell us about prevention: preliminary findings', paper presented at the Third National Family Violence Conference, Durham, New Hampshire, July.

Dell, P. (1989) 'Violence and the systemic view: the problem of power', *Family Process* 28: 1–14.

Duncan, S. and Baker, T. (1985) 'Child sexual abuse: a study of prevalence in Great Britain', *Child Abuse and Neglect* 9: 457–67.

Ferenczi, S. (1949) 'Confusion of tongues between adults and the child: the language of tenderness and of passion', *International Journal of Psychoanalysis* 30: 225–30.

Finkelhor, D. (1984) *Child Sexual Abuse: New Theory and Research*, New York: The Free Press, a division of Macmillan Inc.

Finkelhor, D. and Browne, A. (1985) 'The traumatic impact of child sexual abuse: a conceptualisation', *American Journal of Orthopsychiatry* 55 (4): 530–41.

Friedrich, W. Urquiza, A., and Beilke, R. (1986) 'Behavioural problems in sexually abused young children', *Journal of Pediatric Psychology* 11: 47–57.

Haley, J. (1976) *Problem Solving Theory*, London: Jossey Bass.

Herman, J. (1986) 'Histories of violence in an out-patient population: an exploratory study', *American Journal of Orthopsychiatry* 56: 137–41.

Jehu, D. (1988) *Beyond Sexual Abuse: Therapy with Women who were Childhood Victims*, New York: Wiley.

Kelly, L. (1988) 'What's in a name?: Defining child sexual abuse', *Feminist Review* 28: 65–74.

——(1989) Surviving Sexual Violence. Cambridge: Polity Press.

La Fontaine, J. (1987) *A sociological study of cases of child sexual abuse in Britain*, ESRC Report.

Miller, A. (1985) *Thou Shalt not be Aware: Society's Betrayal of the Child*, Trans. by Hildegarde and Hunter, Hannaum, London: Pluto Press.

Mrazek, P., Lynch, M. and Bentovim, A. (1981) 'Recognition of child sexual abuse in the UK, in P. Mrazek and H. Kempe (eds) *Sexually Abused Children and Their Families*, New York: Pergamon.

Nash, C. and West, D. (1985) 'Sexual molestation of young girls: a retrospective study', in D. West (ed.) *Sexual Victimisation*, London: Gower Press.

Peake, A. (1988) 'Issues of under-reporting: the sexual abuse of boys', paper presented at British Psychological Society Annual Conference.

——(1989) *Why Many Children Cannot Tell About Sexual Abuse and How Some do Tell*, London: The Children's Society.

Peake, A. and Smith G. (1987) Unpublished raw data from a group work programme.

Rush, F. (1980) *The Best Kept Secret: Sexual Abuse of Children*, Englewood Cliffs, NJ: Prentice-Hall.

Russell, D. (1983) 'The incidence and prevalence of intrafamilial and extrafamilial sexual abuse of female children', *Child Abuse and Neglect* 4: 133–46.

——(1986) *The Secret Trauma: Incest in the Lives of Girls and Women*, New York: Basic Books.

Sgroi, S. (1982) *Handbook of Clinical Intervention in Child Sexual Abuse*, Lexington MA: Lexington Books.

Smith, G. (1986) 'The power of intrusion: child sexual abuse', *Adoption and Fostering* 10: 13–18.

——(1987a) 'Is there a feminist therapy? Power and the therapeutic process in sexual abuse', paper presented at a conference on Child Sexual Abuse: Towards a Feminist Professional Practice, Polytechnic of North London, April.

——(1987b) 'Right solution, incorrectly applied. Maladaptive coping in sexual abuse', paper presented to the British Psychological Society Annual Conference.

——(1988) 'The traumatic response cycle', paper presented to the North West Thames Division of Clinical Psychology.

——(1989a) Collusive women: power and sexual abuse in the family' paper presented at Institute of Family Therapy, London, June.

——(1989b) 'The traumatic response cycle: working with adult survivors of childhood sexual abuse,' *Clinical Psychology Forum* 22: 38–43.

Summit, R. (1983) 'Child sexual abuse – "The Accommodation Syndrome"', *Child Abuse and Neglect* 6: 177–93.

—— (1988) 'Hidden victims, hidden pain: societal avoidance of Child sexual abuse', in G. Wyatt and G. Powell (eds) *Lasting Effects of Child Sexual Abuse*. London: Sage Publications, pp. 39–59.

Wyatt, G. (1985) 'The sexual abuse of Afro-American and white American women in childhood', *Child Abuse and Neglect* 9: 507–19.

Wyatt, G. and Peters, S.D. (1986a) 'Issues in the definition of child sexual abuse in prevalence research', *Child Abuse and Neglect* 10: 231–40.

——(1986b) 'Methodological considerations in research on the prevalence of child sexual abuse', *Child Abuse and Neglect* 10: 241–51.

Wyatt, G. and Powell, L. (eds) (1988) *Lasting Effects of Child Sexual Abuse*, London: Sage Publications.

Wyre, R. (1987) *Working with Sex Abuse: Conference and Workshop Papers*, Oxford Publications.

8

THE SECRET LIFE OF HYPERACTIVE CHILDREN

Alan Franklin

Hyperactive children are frequently misunderstood. Because the way they react or behave in any given situation differs significantly from their peers, other people observing them attribute the causes of their behaviour to factors which they have preconceived, which in fact may be very different from the actual causes. I believe that they mostly react automatically or instinctively without pre-thought for the consequences of their actions and this frequently disturbs those closely associated with them. Yet much of this behaviour is part of their nature and can be considered to be congenital. The chief reason for believing this is that the problem of hyperactivity begins in very early infancy, or even earlier still, in the womb in some cases, and a secondary reason is that these children behave in an almost predictable way so that the features which go to make up hyperactivity form a syndrome. This is not totally consistent, in the Procrustean sense, or that would exclude environmental influences which I think are also very important.

The word hyperactive has become in Britain a very common word to try to explain badly behaved small children but in its original sense the word has social, emotional and educational implications as well. One of the earliest accounts of what we now call hyperactivity is to be found in G.F. Still's (1902) Goulstonian Lectures on 'Some abnormal psychical conditions in children'. But I would like to use Barkley's (1982: 6) definition.

Hyperactivity is a developmental disorder of age-appropriate attention span, impulse control, restlessness and rule-governed behaviour that develops in late infancy or early childhood (before age 6), is pervasive in nature, and is not accounted for on the basis of gross neurologic, sensory, or motor impairment, or severe emotional disturbance.

DIAGNOSIS AND CAUSATION

This definition implies a number of factors which can be used for the diagnosis. First, that the onset is very early in life, usually within the first year and may even pre-date that because the motor aspects of this are often complained about by the parents of these children, that they kick vigorously within the womb and they are very uncomfortable children to carry. In my own series of thirty cases (Franklin 1988: 54) one-third of the mothers were aware of overactivity in the child from birth and just less than two-thirds thought their children were hyperactive by the age of eighteen months. Second, there need to be persistent complaints from either parent or teacher of inattentiveness, restlessness or impulsiveness extending for at least a period of twelve months or more; the behaviour of the child must differ significantly from the range of normal behaviour for a child of the same age. Third, the Conners Rating Score (Barkley 1982: 108) should be in excess of 16. This is a method of assessment devised by C.K. Conners in the USA based on a parents' questionnaire of forty-eight items, ten of which he thought were significant and could each be scored from 0 (minimum) to 3 (maximum). A score above sixteen would therefore suggest that problems in behaviour will appear in 50 per cent of a number of given situations. A similar rating applied to the school has also been devised for teachers. Before attempting such a diagnostic exercise however, it would be important to exclude problems of mental retardation, epilepsy, deafness or severe emotional disturbances. It has been suggested that, on the basis of these criteria, between 2 and 3 per cent of children are likely to be hyperactive so there is likely to be one in every classroom in the land. One common mistake is to associate sleeplessness with hyperactivity. These I believe are two quite separate conditions although both may exist in the same child and hyperactive children tend to be restless in their sleep. There are one or two other factors which are commonly seen in these children, for example excessive thirst; this was something discovered by Colquhoun (Barnes and Colquhoun 1984: 15), who is the chairman of the Hyperactive Children's Support Group, through her questionnaire sent out to over 200 members of the Group whose children were hyperactive. Aggressive behaviour, specific learning disabilities and depressive symptoms occur in some of these children, particularly as they get older. The majority of them are boys; the ratio is approximately 5:1 boys to girls. Many of them seem to be, in Britain, fair-haired and blue-eyed irrespective of the hair colouring of their parents, and many appear to come from atopic family backgrounds and have physical symptoms in association with the behavioural problem. This was brought out by the Great Ormond Street Children's Hospital survey (by Egger *et al.* 1985: 540) and in my own series (Franklin 1988: 52) both of which showed a greater than expected number of allergic symptoms both in the children and in their parents. This could be taken to imply an environmental triggering factor, based on a genetic predeterminant. Whilst a number of triggering factors have been identified, such as food chemicals, synthetic plastics, environmental aeroallergens, etc., the genetic factor has not been determined so far.

THE PARENTS

Hyperactivity and attention deficit disorder is therefore, by definition, a problem behaviour associated with compliance whether it be to parents or to teachers. It can only be measured or observed while the child is awake and person-to-person relationships become of the utmost importance. It is therefore worth spending a brief while looking at the parents, who are the ones that most of all complain about their children. Here I find myself agreeing with Barkley (1982: 291) that the effect of parents on children is bi-directional and other workers have reported that, in classroom-type situations where behavioural tasks are set, the parents tend to be less active when the child is hyperactive and it is as though the child is trying to stimulate the parent to be more involved in their activities. However, in their review (Whalen and Henker 1980: 109) refer to other studies which suggest that there is an increased psychopathology in the parents of hyperactive children and that, in particular, fathers have an important role and in hyperactive families there is a greater use of physical means for discipline and of non-involvement of the father in the children's upbringing. At the same time a hysterical personality in the mother was also more commonly found. Also up to 20 per cent of the hyperactive children's parents would probably have been diagnosed themselves as hyperactive in their own childhood. The inference that parents have a bad influence on these children has become fairly widespread and most unfortunately, it tends to be particularly prevalent in social service, educational and other child management services. But in fact not all parents are stupid and, in addition to being in the best position to provide information about their children and implement intervention programmes, parents of hyperactive children have had unique experiences and have evolved intriguing coping strategies worthy of further study (Whalen and Henker 1980: 349).

THE CHILDREN

I have already indicated that parents of hyperactive infants have found that the child was overactive in the womb, in fact 50 per cent of the parents in my own study did so. Their mothers described them as being uncomfortable infants, trying to kick their way out. In very early infancy these babies behaved differently from others in relation to their restlessness, degree of wakefulness, excessive crying and poor feeding. This was despite having average or better than average antenatal and perinatal care, having births which were relatively uncomplicated (26 out of 30) and being the children of stable marriages (28 out of 30). The general misery which they displayed was also reflected in the fact that the parents found them difficult to cuddle or to comfort and the poor feeding also was associated with increased vomiting, diarrhoea and colicky abdominal pain. The parents often described cuddling their babies as like getting involved in a fight with them: the baby would fight to get away and to be loosened, disliked being wrapped up and held tightly.

As infancy progressed these problems developed further. The colicky abdominal pains continued. They became very finicky feeders and often chose an inadequate diet: this inadequacy being either in total quantity i.e., calories, or in quality, usually an excess of refined carbohydrate or milk in preference to anything else. An excessive thirst began around this time and they became increasingly fidgety, moody, demonstrating temper tantrums and head banging behaviour. They also appeared fearful and clinging at one moment, antisocial and demanding the next. They normally demanded immediate gratification and would not tolerate being told to wait a moment, this commonly being the signal to start a temper tantrum. Some of them carried their wakeful restlessness into the night and some woke with colicky pains during the night. Many developed catarrhal symptoms which may have impaired hearing and developed glue-ear requiring the insertion of grommets. Some, however, developed habits of loud shouting so that they never listened to what was said to them and could therefore not respond as they apparently did not hear. Selective treatments were clearly able to assist some of these children. For example, those with abdominal symptoms frequently responded to the removal of cows' milk from their diet as did some of those with catarrhal problems and the relief of partial deafness caused by glue-ear clearly improved their hearing ability, so they were able to respond to their parents' voices more accurately. Those with aggressive and volatile behaviour often became much calmer when food colourings were reduced in their diet and their lifestyle became more regularised and predictable.

EARLY CHILDHOOD

In early childhood, by which I mean a period extending from after the child has learned to walk up to about the age of 7, the child's hyperactive characteristics increase yet further. This is most marked by the fact that the child runs everywhere and often runs away from his parents or carers. He becomes very rapidly and easily excitable which leads to uncontrollable and unpredictable behaviour. He tends to be very impulsive, changing interest and activity so fast that the parents have great difficulty in keeping up with him. If he gets into difficulties he panics easily and cries often. He appears fearful and timid, especially in new, untried situations. When frustrated or challenged he will become very angry, very negativistic and will scream and be destructive, throwing any movable object to hand, either at the person he is angry with or just indiscriminately, causing further damage. He appears to have little understanding of the consequences of his behaviour and will climb out of first-floor windows, or run across roads without stopping to look at all. I admit that many of the foregoing are perhaps just exaggerations of normal post-toddler behaviour, but I think it is to be noted that in degree they are excessive and, furthermore, they tend to persist much longer than in a non-hyperactive control group. In addition some of the children develop compulsive touching habits which tend to frighten children of their own age. Some develop this into compulsive aggression which makes them even more unpopular both with the children and with their families, so that the hyperactive child tends to lose his friends and feel cut off and isolated. His demand for immediate gratification continues. He shows extreme jealousy and resents competition especially from those of his peer group who are close to him in age. He tends to become obsessional, resenting sleep and having no time to sit and eat; quenching his excessive thirst appears to take the place of eating.

In a school situation he shows a very noticeable lack of attention and degree of impatience which causes much distress amongst school-teachers. He has a short attention span, is very easily distracted, but can be very difficult to divert if he has his mind set on doing any particular activity. It would seem as if the child's mind could cope with only one train of thought at a time – like a train on a single track line. Almost any diversion would switch the train on to a deviation from the main track, and he would have to be brought back again by some external force. If left alone the mind wanders aimlessly being frequently switched by each new stimulus. As a consequence work is hardly ever completed, or else is hurried and careless resulting in a lower achievement than the IQ would suggest should be possible. In an organised schoolroom situation he can be very disruptive. Punishment appears not to be effective unless it is to isolate the child, which would tend to decrease his self-confidence and further limit his already poor attainments within a schoolroom setting. Undoubtedly, one-to-one teaching relieves much of this attention-seeking behaviour and will enable the child to learn at his own pace but this is extremely difficult in most normal classrooms.

161

His degree of selfishness and self-interest seem quite extraordinary for a child so young especially as, in many cases, these are not the characteristics of his parents.

It is difficult to interpret how the child feels about this phase. He is very sensitive about injustices and can be extremely resentful of any accusations which turn out, to him, to be false and in fact may indeed be so. On the other hand he is quick to take advantage of any lapses of discipline that may present themselves. The world appears to be full of opportunities and so many things are there for him to explore and understand and find out about. He explores everywhere and has a great drive to touch and handle everything within reach. Things placed out of reach are a challenge to his ingenuity and he will often climb on chairs and tables to reach 'inaccessible' objects. He hates secrets and wants to know what every box or drawer contains. In fact he seems to want to know about everything, but all at a rather superficial and rapidly passing level. He appears to have very little sense of the value of property, even his own sometimes, and appears to take the view that if something breaks or is destroyed, well, then it was not worth having anyway and we just leave it alone and move on to the next thing. Yet, although he has this great spirit of adventure, he does not wish to tread the path alone but prefers the company of one other person, preferably adult, or at least an older child. He seems to demonstrate very clearly the old proverb, 'two's company and three's a crowd', because in the presence of two older persons he will adopt any means within his power to draw one away from the other and to have their exclusive attention focused upon himself. With his chosen companion and without any sibling competition he can be charming, loving, helpful, in fact a thoroughly nice companion but rivalry appears very quickly whenever a third person comes on the scene, whether that third person is another member of the family such as a sibling, or a friend. Frequently it is the mother who receives the worst of his aggressive and antisocial behaviour. It is as if he blames his mother for allowing, or even causing, all the distressing things which he has to face, be they competition, or loneliness, or frustration, lack of friends or lack of opportunity to do as he wants to do; and, as more hyperactive children are boys, there appears to be some degree of male chauvinism in this behavioural characteristic. The late Dr Winnicott (1984: 125) in discussing the deprived child and the antisocial tendency, suggested that the antagonism towards mother which can be manifest as either aggression, or greed, or stealing, may be an attempt to recapture a form of love which he felt it was his right to own and which he experienced as a baby in early infancy. Winnicott describes how the baby first of all has to create the mother and then go on to 'create' the world and that he should only experience the reality of the objective world slowly and one step at a time, or confusion results; the fact that his imaginary mother and his real mother do not necessarily tally also provides him with some confusion. He went on to suggest that some of the aggression, therefore, was an attempt to bring the real mother into line with his imaginary mother and so complete a sense of reality in his own mind. Failure to achieve this produces anxiety which is expressed as anger or non-compliance.

LATER CHILDHOOD

The hyperactive child at school is still physically on the go all the time 'as if driven by a motor', as described by a child psychiatrist colleague, Ian Menzies (Franklin 1988: 80) who also goes on to describe these children as being clumsy, jerky, even stuttering, often showing a tremor, whereas sensory oversensitivity is characterised by increased sensitivity to noise, light, chemicals, scolding, correction and indeed almost all external stimuli. Paradoxically, these tension-ridden children also collapse into fatigue states, fatigue which is not alleviated by rest (Speer 1958: 207), in which they present as irritable, sullen and easily annoyed by trivial incidents. They may respond very negatively to parents and exhibit sleep disturbances with restlessness and nightmares. They have variable mood states, sometimes associated with compulsive behaviour and at other times with paranoid ideation and may show considerable destructiveness and excitement, surprising cruelty to playmates and attention-demanding behaviour. Some chatter constantly using a high-pitched, strangely different voice, and parents often report bizarre, silly behaviour, emotional lability and mental sluggishness. Such children often appear as emotionally retarded children. In this age of the 'pack-animal' such children seem to stand out. They reject rules, they behave in an immature, impulsive, intolerant and impatient manner. They become easily frustrated which manifests in anger, loss of temper and slamming of doors. In any activity which they undertake they demand instant success and if this is not forthcoming to their satisfaction, often with quite high standards, the activity is rejected outright or destroyed. They seem to experience this as further loss of confidence and it leads to further loss of self-esteem. The same often applies to school work where, because of poor concentration which leads to poor achievement, loss of self-esteem again manifests as disruptive and sullen behaviour.

In order to deal with this behaviour in a classroom situation it may be necessary to single out the child for special help. The provision of a welfare assistant may help to make the child feel 'special', and take the pressure off the rest of the class. Such discrimination may not be welcome either to the parents or the education authorities unless the syndrome is recognised and classified as a genuine handicap. But in child-guidance circles such a child will be assessed according to his perceived mental age rather than his biological (chronological) age and a therapist would then seek to meet him at this age level and treat him individually and not as a member of a group. This approach contrasts with the teacher's normal group approach to children, even though in theory education should be given to each individual child according to need. Personnel and finance dictate that this will rarely be possible.

What is the alternative? One strategy which has been worked out is that of a small school where the teacher–pupil ratio is much lower than in most state schools and where regular assessments are made using electrical devices to first assess, then, improve concentration, relaxation and stability of hand and eye movement. And where poor learning achievement, aggression and hyperactivity are all present most of the time, the cautious use of stimulant drugs, especially methyl phenidate (Ritalin) is made paradoxically, to reduce the distraction rate in school and improve learning time and achievement. The drug is given in the minimum effective doses, up to 10 mg per day for children under 7 years of age to 30 mg per day for children up to 12 years of age, once or twice daily and subsequently slowly withdrawn, according to the child's response. By improving the child's learning achievement, his self-esteem will also be improved, and although the time after school may be explosive, parents will need to be counselled to cope with this for a few years – and their compliance with this strategy will be crucial.

Paradoxically, again despite their own lack of self-appreciation, hyperactive children, seem to have acute insight into relationships involving other people which makes them overly critical or fearful and quite neurotic about their own personal disabilities or minor passing illnesses. Because they are often rejected by their peer group they may seek friendship with younger children or seek an association with an older friend, usually of the same sex, with whom they can share confidences.

ADOLESCENCE

The adolescent shows all the normal characteristics of adolescence but to a greater degree in many respects. They may have rather violent mood swings from being very depressed to sudden manic outbursts. Such moods may spill over into physical aggression and/or abusive language. Within the home they frequently display non-compliant negative behaviour. They may often display intensely selfish and amoral or delinquent behaviour which to outsiders appears to be totally antisocial though here Winnicott (1984: 123) regards the antisocial tendency as implying hope and he sees these moments of hope as important in the way that such children are managed.

He goes further to say that the treatment of the antisocial tendency is not psychoanalysis but management, a going to meet and match the moment of hope.

Trying to meet these almost outlandish demands can of course be very costly to parents. The cost is mainly in terms of time and devotion and a not giving-up on them but, on occasions, the cost may be financial also. One mother in tears once confessed that her junior-aged child had wreaked over £700 of damage to her living room and to be the successful mother of a hyperactive child demands an unusual degree of self-sacrifice and devotion, for often in our society the time when the child is being most hyperactive is the time when the mother, if she is working at all, would be looking for advancement and therefore having to give more time and effort to her employers.

Another sign of the immature insecurity of these children is seen in their hatred of secrets especially family secrets. They have an overwhelming desire to know every detail about other members of the household, what they do, who they speak with, who they know, what they keep in their rooms, in their drawers, in their cupboards, in their secret places. Nothing must be kept secret from them but they must have access to and knowledge of all that is within their house. Compulsive touching may again be manifest at this age, possibly another sign of their own insecurity. Their natural fearfulness and timidity has to be covered up at this stage, often by impetuous, very foolhardy behaviour. Not only do they reject rules but they are prepared to challenge authority at every level though not within their peer group with whom they must identify even though they are often rejected by them. This seems to cause an acute tension within them and a great fear of being socially isolated. One young person once said that they resisted authority and resented discipline because it was like being put in a cage and you were trapped and you couldn't get out and so you fought like mad against this imprisonment. At such moments, to be free, seemed to be the value above all others that they most wanted. This freedom however has to be defined by them and not by others. Despite many of these apparently socially negative characteristics, such people often have very high personal standards for themselves and experience considerable remorse and attempt, sometimes quite desperately, to make amends by exacting forms of self-discipline and self-punishment that other people would not consider at all reasonable.

HELPING THE HYPERACTIVE CHILD

I believe that there are strategies for helping such children to get round their considerable internal difficulties and social handicap but I think we need first to recognise both the genetic and the environmental effects which impinge upon them and both aspects must be tackled simultaneously. Despite the dislike of labelling which some people have, it is important to acknowledge the Hyperactive Syndrome as a discrete entity so that appropriate therapeutic measures can be applied. Of course the edges will be blurred, because hyperactivity also occurs as part of other recognisable states such as mental retardation from many causes, autism, deafness, child abuse and deprivation, cerebral anoxia, etc. but, having excluded these, we are left with a child who is disturbed without a cause. If cows' milk and other basic foods cause problems to young babies we have substitutes for them. If food chemicals, such as colours and sugars found in many children's foods, cause them to lose control of themselves we can manage without them. Changing family patterns by parents spending more time with the family in the home rather than at work amassing a large bank balance or saving for holidays abroad may make the difference between coping or not coping with their child, and may prove eventually to have the greater value.

I would especially appeal to fathers to take a greater interest in their young sons and to support their wives throughout in terms of behaviour and disciplinary measures. Utter consistency, strong management and absolute fairness are key words in the management of a hyperactive child. Mothers particularly need to analyse the way they attempt to deal with the child. It helps to write down the sequence of events especially when things go wrong, so that through the analysis, with a counsellor if necessary, they can try to plan a different approach next time the situation arises. For example, try to avoid nagging – the child quickly learns to switch off a nagging voice – the instruction or sanction should be given clearly once, and then when ignored positive action should be taken. Be careful with threats – they should be carried out if issued. But here is a situation where actions speak louder than words – control should be by a 'hands on' technique – the child should be touched, guided or led by the hand rather than simply told or shouted at from a distance. This will give much more authority to the parent and reassurance to the child that the parent means what she says and cares also. But the management must be firm and strong or the child will subconsciously escalate his demands until he experiences it. The recognition of this child's deep needs, usually much greater than non-hyperactive children, will mean that more time and effort needs to be spent for this child in order to maintain fairness within the family. Various techniques of behaviour modification as well as drug treatment are available, but the details are beyond the scope of this chapter. Barkley for example (1982 ch. 6–11) devotes nearly half of his book to explaining some of these methods, and many other books and articles have been written on the subject (e.g. Taylor 1985; Flack 1987; Rapp 1979).

CHILD INTO ADULT

Many believe, or would like to believe, that hyperactivity disappears with the passing of childhood. Unfortunately it is not always so. Whalen and Henker (1980: 322) point out that it is a myth to believe that hyperactivity vanishes with adolescence as this conclusion is not supported by recent outcome data, such as that by Borland and Heckman (1976: 669) in their paper on a twenty-five-year follow-up study, or Weiss, Heckman and Perlman (1978: 438) describing hyperactivity in young adults over a ten-year follow-up period. But they do admit that problems tend to change in form and decrease in intensity, even if social and attentional problems often persist.

For the adolescent or adult who may be troubled by food intolerance or addiction leading to brainstorms and other disruptive behaviours, there is the option of allergy desensitisation, especially a method known as enzyme potentiated desensitisation as pioneered by Dr L.M. McEwen in London (Brostoff and Challacombe 1987: 990) or by hypoallergenic dieting (Egger 1985: 674) and followed by enzyme potentiated desensitisation (Egger unpublished recent clinical trial).

The following was written by an intelligent lawyer when she was in a bad (food allergic) phase:

Hypoactivity produces more less the opersit feeling to brain fag. Everything becomes sharper , the feeling of pain, cold heat as if the nerves are tort. But like brain fage thereis an absance of fear. It starts oftern slowly, but not nesesarlly so, and yhe feeling is like running round and roun an anormouse spring sometimes seeing to sliral upwards, or feeling as is one is an aturntable with someone starting to turn it egain faster & faster. Alough one pftern feelstired the brain starts to speed at the same time demandingaction and however tired you fail to obay at your peral, the longe you mage to stop the action the more intence it will be.

The driving forse within the brain feels very like a strong wind, you may desperatly wasnt to stop but can't. Rather like a kite on a string your main object, disire is to sail into the clear blue shk dipping and swerling with the sthere joy of speed. Only conventions, (ruls) or the frustrating handicap of a grownup(children) stops you doing just that. Excitement, move-ment are a must, to stop causes the brain to (sceam) The slower the pace the more frustratedgthe feeling. Like a person sitting on the bumper of a train, travinling at speed the fe eling of exsilation canselsout any fear. WhilleI do not condone rapeI feel the feeling of compustion ust be very similar. Whille you feel out of control the brain pushes to move faster and faster.

YOu can build a mountain, but if anyone asks you why you would like to hit them, dig the garden from end to end, but anything that takes the slightest thought like wher to put a pland is quit impossible. Normally I weed with great care but when HA find I tare at the weeds. I can do the housework at increadable speed, butfind I tend to knok thins over and if the slightes difficulty arises I stop & do somethig else. People become like salt on a woud as they moveso slowly and want to talk.

I have fund the best way is to try to use the speed doing thins that requir no thought, I have not trid dancing(Moden) when I now know I am H A but I have done so in the past & find it helped. As an adult I felt that I must be able to try and think my way through it but have only tried once, never again, I thought I was going mead. An Adult should have more. control that a child for them it must be hell, an adult can keep away from people a child can't. Whille I realise that some restrant must be tried, the hell this must cause is indiscrible.

Any form of ristrant will only add fule to t he fire, as they pit htere wits against yours getting wilder and wilder. Rather like a boat on a river, out of control being pushed with the currant, sometimes resting for a moment against a rock, and then driven free. No effert in running jumping climimg is spared, but as the brain is filled with the drivning forse there isno romm for any thought. If the child must be contained may I sujest a padded cell. One of the main problems isthe desire for excitment,speed. When thebody says stop, the brain scea s GO I found t e wind exciting, it se med to stir me to run faster and faster. The person apears to have increadable enery, bright alert, smilling with ease, the life and sole of the party, untill that is you dare to go against them in however small a way. Then ither they slam out, cut the conversation dead or begin to tornt you, when repeated it sounds like a joke, but its the way that its done, neddling you untill you snape, then say you have no sence of humor. One thing is very clear to a HP pesron they are never at fault it's alwas the other person. They oftern look as is thy are high, as with drugs. I never go to a lector in t is state as I will not learn anything, and will only antagisze the speacher by stiring having to speak to get ride of the pentup felling Whille the activity sounds great to many people it is the feeling of being driven with the lack of control that creats the feeling of desparation, the knowalde that however tired however the paperwork piles up the feeling of being driven faster and faster, so that when you finaly crah the brian fag, somby-like state, is oftern a reliefe., particulary I'm sure to the parents.

Finally we can recognise that many adults who were hyperactive as children have become very successful in their own sphere and successful parents at the heads of families as well.

REFERENCES

Barkley, R.A. (1982) *Hyperactive Children: A Handbook for Diagnosis and Treatment*, Chichester, New York: Wiley & Sons.

Barnes, B. and Colquhoun, I. D. (1984) *The Hyperactive Child*, Wellingborough: Thorsons.

Borland, B.L. and Heckman, H. K. (1976) 'Hyperactive boys and their brothers – a 25-year follow-up study', *Archives of General Psychiatry* 33: 669–75.

Brostoff, J. and Challacombe, S. J. (1987) *Food Allergy and Intolerance*, London: Ballière Tindall.

Egger, J. *et al.* (1985) 'Controlled trial of oligo-antigenic treatment in the hyperkinetic syndrome', *The Lancet* (9 March) 540–5.

Flack, S. (1987) *Hyperactive Children – A Parents' Guide*, London: Bishopsgate Press.

Franklin, A.J. (1988) *The Recognition and Management of Food Allergy in Children*, Carnforth: Parthenon.

Menzies, I. (1988) 'The role of food intolerance in child psychiatry', in A. J. Franklin (ed.) (1988) *The Recognition and Management of Food Allergy in Children*, Carnforth: Parthenon.

Rapp, D.J. (1979) *Allergies and the Hyperactive Child*, New York: Sovereign Books.

Speer, F. (1958) 'The allergic-tension fatigue syndrome in children', *International Archives of Allergy* 12: 207–14.

Still, G.F. (1902) 'The Goulstonian Lectures I–III', *The Lancet* 1: 1008–12, 1077–82, 1163–68.

Taylor, E. (1985) *The Hyperactive Child – A Parents' Guide*, London: Dunitz.

Weiss, G., Hechtman, L. and Perlman, T. (1978) 'Hyperactives as young adults: school, employer and self-rating scales obtained during ten-year follow-up valuation', *American Journal of Ortho-psychiatry* 48: 438–45.

Whalen, C.K. and Henker, B. (eds) (1980) *Hyperactive Children*, New York, London: Academic Press.

Winnicott, D.W. (1984) 'The antisocial tendency', paper read before the British Psychoanalytical Society in 1956, reprinted in *Deprivation and Delinquency*, London, New York: Tavistock Publications.

9

ON RELATING TO VULNERABLE ADOLESCENTS

Anton Obholzer

ON ADOLESCENCE

There are many different ways of defining adolescence. For example:

by age
by social criteria
by physiological (pubertal) development
by state of mind
or by a permutation/combination of the above

Definition of adolescence by age is at best a very rough marker. Such definitions generally cover periods in the age-range of 12 to 20 years. They fail because they take no account of the state of mind of the person involved. Thus, is a pubertal 15-year-old with the state of mind of a latency child and with no evidence of negotiating any psychosocial transitions an adolescent, or an adolescent with no adolescent phenomena? To enrich our understanding of adolescence, we have to incorporate the approaches inherent in other definitions.

Eric Erikson in *Childhood and Society* (1965) describes adolescence as 'a psycho-social moratorium'. This definition, in my view, best captures the essence of the social type of definition, for it emphasises on the one hand the spheres of personal development (psychic and social), while on the other hand paints in the backcloth of society's response by his use of the word 'moratorium'. Borrowed from the world of banking, it means a specifically designated period during which a debtor is given the chance to put his house in order while being free of the normal processes of foreclosure, and being subject to having to pay for the consequences of his actions. Translated into adolescent terms, it therefore means a period during which ordinary social sanctions do not generally apply.

This definition of adolescence, as a transitional state between childhood and adulthood is peculiar to modern western societies. Up until the

Second World War 'adolescence' as defined above was the prerogative of the well-off few. There was, generally speaking, no 'transitional space' between childhood and adulthood, and in many communities children started doing 'adult' work the moment they were capable of it. It was only after the social changes in the period following the Second World War (during which, incidentally, many teenagers were catapulted into adulthood) that the idea of a developmental space for adolescents gained general acceptance.

Physical and sexual changes associated with growing up of course happen whether there is a socially sanctioned period of adolescence or not. In the former approach, coming to terms with one's sexual identity and with sexuality is of course an integral part of development. In the latter approach, the transition is often marked with one or other puberty or initiation ceremony.

Definitions of adolescence by body change alone, usually based on the signs of puberty, again are not very helpful. There are rare cases of individuals who have delayed or absent pubertal development on account of hormonal dysfunction, but who fully experience adolescent mental and social phenomena. Much more commonly, there are adolescents who experience full pubertal development but without any accompanying change in state of mind, nor any change in their social functioning. In fact, they continue with a latency state of mind which often becomes transformed into 'as if' adult functioning. That leaves us with attempting to define adolescence as a state of mind – in itself no easy task. It is of course made more difficult in that an adolescent state of mind often does occur in someone who by no other definition falls into the category of adolescence. For example, a 50-year-old might function in a fundamentally adolescent way, both in mind and in social relationships. An adolescent state of mind refers to an approach to self and others that is characterised by some or all of the following phenomena: mood swings, uncertainty about self both mentally and physically, inconsistency or at times rigidity about one's 'weltanschaung', fickleness in social relationships, self-preoccupation to the detraction of relating to others, etc. The list of attributes is endless. The state of mind, however, is one of a preoccupation with self in mind and body, and an ongoing attempt to find a self, partly by identifying with the peer group and partly by rejecting previous role models, usually the parents.

It is important for us to have some agreed personal (and professional, if we function in that role) definition of adolescence in our mind, so that we can use that as a benchmark against which adolescent phenomena can be roughly measured and thus judged as to whether they are essentially 'on line' developmentally speaking, or not.

I would suggest that any effective working definition of adolescence would need to include elements of all of the above-mentioned definitions, and would therefore include mental and social phenomena in the context of physical development within a relatively circumscribed time period. The absence of any one of the factors would therefore lead to concern and possible intervention, as would the presence of some of the elements either in a different time context or over an unduly spread out period of time.

ADOLESCENCE – THE TRANSITIONAL YEARS

A key to understanding adolescence as a developmental phase is the reality that adolescence is the successor to childhood and the predecessor to adult life.

Individual behaviour in adolescence therefore has to be seen in the context of the earlier development of children. The parent who brings a hulking 14-year-old with violent outbursts for consultation complaining that 'he was such an angelic 3-year-old, I only had to tell him "no" once and when I smacked him he stopped and was good as gold', has obviously missed the developmental link between childhood 'training' and adolescent behaviour, for the essence of the example given is that 'might is right' and 'you get your way by force' – a lesson learned only too well by the nearly grown-up child who now has the physical strength to try out and apply that particular philosophy of life.

The importance of the first three years of life is by now well researched and understood, and child researchers, whatever their orientation and training, are agreed about the crucial importance of the first years of life.

It is in this period that the child builds up his basic picture of what sort of place his world is, how he relates to others, what response and understanding he can get from them. It is also the period in which a whole range of vital attributes are first tapped and in part put to the test, so that by the time the child reaches the social arena proper, be it nursery school, playgroup, school, etc., he comes with a whole personal inner world that is then either confirmed or not by his experiences in the new setting and re-enacted with the people in this world. The inner world he brings with him of course also influences the way he perceives the world, and so there is at the same time an opportunity for confirmation of his picture of the world and the possibility of change or growth.

The child therefore reaches adolescence with a long history of struggle, growth and, one hopes, development. In adolescence all the previous psychic and social processes are given an additional boost by the adolescent process – part hormonal, part family, part social.

The learning, or mislearning for that matter, of the pre-adolescent years is therefore now reworked in the service of creating the foundations for adult life.

The inner world of the child with accompanying skills and problems is now put to the test. Like the earlier example a child that has a 'good enough' (to borrow Donald Winnicott's term) experience of the world, and a capacity to communicate with and to love others, will now embark on the opportunities and stresses of adolescence to enrich his inner world and to lay the foundations for adult functioning. The deprived child, too, will have an opportunity to re-enact his deprived state of mind and way of relating. And, in turn, he will be met with either the same response he has had before, either from the same people, his parents, or others who stand in their place, or, with luck, he will have an opportunity of a different response and thus the chance to review his picture of the world.

This emotional 'work' then forms the basis of the individual's capacity to cope with and develop the opportunities and stresses arising from adult life. And, in adult life, as mentioned at the beginning of this chapter, this adolescent part of the personality is often powerful in influencing the adult's response to the adolescent process in others, whether they be family, friends or clients.

NEGOTIATING ADOLESCENCE AND ITS 'TASKS'

In negotiating adolescence, there are a series of what might loosely be called 'tasks' that have to be addressed *en route* to adulthood. Some of these tasks arise from the unfolding of the growth process, both physical and emotional – others are determined by the expectations arising from family, community and societal pressures. As mentioned before, all of them are based on previously developed childhood skills, and will be needed in the service of adult development.

Most important is the development of a sense of self, of personal identity. Associated with this is the matter of sexual identity and, later, of work identity.

The work of establishing one's personal identity has as its raw material the inner world 'dowry' from childhood, and this is used in the new climate of adolescence – a climate created by a combination of family and social space, 'spiced' with the hormones of puberty.

Much of the early process of establishing identity has more to do with what the adolescent is not, than what he is. 'If I turn out like you dad, I'll shoot myself!', 'What utterly bourgeois values, yuk!', and many more rude comments are ways of distancing oneself from parents and adults alike. This 'pushing away' from and rejecting parental values is essential if a natural 'line of cleavage', emotionally speaking, is to be found between adolescent and adult, and if the adolescent is to escape the fate of being 'trapped' in his family or living in a symbiotic lifestyle with the parents. For adolescents who don't manage this break with their parents, the crunch often comes with the death of the parents when the creation of an adult lifestyle and state of mind is of course so much harder to achieve, as none of the social devices of that age are geared to that particular transition. Alternatively, compliance with parental and family values can lead to a pseudo-adult lifestyle, sometimes affected by emergent or re-emergent adolescent issues during a 'mid-life crisis'.

The formation of a separate identity in adolescence is of course often not accompanied by overt rebellion as described above. In assessing whether or not an adolescent in his development is 'on line' for the expected growth and development, or not, the ability to stand up for himself and for separate ideas and values from the parents is an important indicator of healthy development.

I would regard an adolescent who shows no signs of differentiation as outlined above as being as worrying as one who cannot do anything but constantly rebel.

It is the experience of many working in the field of adolescence that little is as frustrating and interfering of adolescent growth and development as a parent who does not provide the opportunity for the adolescent to have views and rules that can be kicked against and broken. An example of this would be a parent who would regularly modify his views in order to fit in with the views of youth, and in this way to attempt to curry favour or acceptance. Nothing could be further from the truth, and such a parent is only likely to be perceived as weak and pathetic. This does of course not mean that the other extreme of gross inflexibility on the part of the parent is to be advised. What is hoped for is the opportunity for a clearly stated point of view on both sides of the divide, with the possibility of debate of the issues.

In another instance, parents wished to show their open-mindedness by setting no time-limit for a teenage girl going out for a much sought-after date – 'we trust you darling, come home whenever you feel like it' – thus in one fell blow undermining their daughter's capacity to say no to advances about which she felt in two minds, and removing her face-saving, 'I have to be in by X o'clock.'

At the same time such parental 'generosity of spirit and understanding' is more often than not interpreted as uncaringness on the part of the parents, thus adding to the confusion.

The adolescent's need to find his own identity requires not only the presence of parents or of parent-surrogate adults who are prepared to perform that role, it also requires the presence of a peer group as a basis of support for the adolescent/rebelling-against-the-parents part of self. In the eyes of the adolescent, nothing can be a higher endorsement of peer group value and support than a parent's comment about the unsuitability of someone as a companion. Such an epithet is almost guaranteed to ensure the thus named person a special relationship with the adolescent and in the peer group, for after all a prime purpose of the peer group is to service the function of being 'unsuitable' to the parental aspirations.

Adolescent peer groups give the opportunity for experimenting with individuality in an emotionally safe environment, whilst at the same time providing a chance of anonymity. Most obvious is the preoccupation with dress. A Nazi cap is worn nonchalantly with a Che Guevara T-shirt and Buddhist sandals, allowing experimentation in both dress and state of mind of all philosophies connected with the outfit.

ADOLESCENCE – THE SPRINGBOARD TO ADULTHOOD

Work on the 'tasks' of adolescence as outlined previously is of course never 'completed' in the sense that no further emotional work need be done on them. Not only are there the issues thrown up by the vicissitudes of life that affect various aspects of how we see ourselves, there is also the ongoing issue of ageing, so that the sexual identity of a 50-year-old would appropriately be based on his previous adolescent sexual identity, while at the same time taking into account the ageing process.

The adult's capacity to cope with the tasks of adulthood is, however, dependent to a large degree on the foundations he has laid down in earlier life. If these are good enough and in touch with the various aspects of the particular area of development, then the adult has a good chance of coping with relevant issues in adult life and later. If not, the defective foundation of adolescence often creates the conditions for a subsequent collapse in response to the additional pressures of adult life or of the adolescence of any offspring.

A young woman, the oldest child in a rural Catholic family, lost her mother when aged 14, and from then on took on the role of substitute mother for the father and her seven siblings. This led to a life of misery and deprivation, with no opportunity for adolescent pastimes and heterosexual pairing. At 28, the youngest surrogate child/sibling having left school, she became pregnant by an older man and, though in conflict about the match, married him. Thoughts of sexuality, doubt about the marriage, the social system, religion, etc., were banished from her mind. She lived her life as if she had had a personal adolescence and had grown to become an adult – in fact, she had emotionally done neither.

The adolescence of her daughter, and the latter's questioning of all the issues that she herself had suppressed, led to a depressive breakdown in the mother, requiring her hospitalisation – the daughter's adolescence had 'detonated', as it were, the previously dormant and

THE SECRET LIFE OF VULNERABLE CHILDREN

unresolved aspects of mother's adolescence, as well as the loss of her own mother.

A man of 45, a stockbroker in a small firm taken over by a large consortium, was made redundant. He had gone straight from school to the City and this had been his first and only job.

In helping this man overcome his self-doubt and subsequent despair, it became clear that he had hardly any foundations of work identity to fall back on. He had never 'messed about' as adolescents do, and thus had not learned from the experience of changing jobs. He had never had to apply for and been rejected for jobs – a whole area of 'skills' had in fact been missed by him, and these adolescent/early adult skills now had to be painfully learned at a much later age.

THE ADOLESCENT AND HIS FAMILY

That the family has expectations of the new baby, even prior to birth, is evidenced by the phantasies expressed by them about the sex and nature of the child, even while intra-uterine. After birth, family comments about the new baby and its characteristics might well be described as a family projective test – each person seeing in the child quite different aspects, often of self or of those previously assigned to a sibling. The choice of name itself often comes with some or other, often unconscious, family expectation of what the child will be like. The child grows up, hopefully held, but also restricted within this framework of family expectations and assumptions.

In adolescence, the time when it is appropriate for the individual to confirm his own identity, the time often comes when the child effectively says – by word and action, sometimes even by a choice of a different name – I am myself, I have a different identity, I no longer am going to go along with your ideas of who I am and how I am to behave. It is not uncommon at this point for parents to complain about this change or to bring, or attempt to bring, the adolescent to Child Guidance or related services. In dispute at this point often is the matter of who is going to determine the sort of person the adolescent is going to be – the adults or the adolescent himself. Either party, whether adult or adolescent, gaining complete control of the process, is likely to create major problems. Adult hegemony is likely to cause a blighting of the adolescent's development of self, and delay the development of adult maturity – sometimes forever. On the other hand, an unmitigated adolescent takeover puts the whole process in the hands of the adolescent, who by definition does not have an adequate psychic apparatus to deal with it – the end result can be the development of a personality that is 'adolescent' forever, particularly in regard to what are perceived to be authority figures or establishment structures.

The family is best seen as an interconnected system of conscious and unconscious assumptions about each other. In this interlinked state, members perform emotional functions for each other and on behalf of the system. This unconscious mechanism happens by a process of projective identification – thus a process in which aspects of one person are 'kept' and perceived in the other.

This process, described by family therapists of all persuasions, might be illustrated as follows. A father, having grown up in an orphanage, had his delinquency knocked out of him by fierce disciplining. A fierce disciplinarian himself now, he nevertheless has a remaining encapsulated defiant aspect of his adolescent personality – an aspect that is rebellious, defiant, contemptuous of authority. To be in touch with this intra-psychic conflict between these incompatible aspects of self is both tiring and disturbing to the father. The problem can, however, be 'easily' and unconsciously 'resolved' by the mechanism of projective identification. By this mechanism, father projects his defiant self into his adolescent son who thus, in a sense, has a double load to carry – his own developmental one and his father's unresolved one. At the same time, the son can use father as a repository for his own 'managing authority' aspects of himself. Both father and son thus carry disowned and unacknowledged aspects of the other's personality, and in the disowning can gain a self-righteous satisfaction. Father can thus at an unconscious level encourage son's defiance and delinquency, while also vicariously gratifying his own repressed and disowned adolescent remnants; at the same time he also has the satisfaction of self-righteous indignation at 'what youngsters get up to nowadays'. The son in turn acts out the delinquent aspects of father while having the satisfaction of witnessing the functioning of authoritarian behaviour in father.

In work with adolescents and in thinking about the adolescent process, it is important to distinguish between what is authority and what authoritarian. The former refers to a sense of values of responsibility, of dialogue in the service of decision making, the latter to a sense of abusing power to impose one's will to achieve a personal non-negotiated goal. The process is of course not only confined to the male coupling described above – it also applies to other members of the family who, in turn, might use, or be used by, other members of the family as repositories of psychic qualities. The above family, in fact all families, could thus be described as a system of mutually interlocked projective identifications.

In thinking about an adolescent within his family, it is therefore essential that we take into account the person, not only as an individual with a personal history, but also as a member of a family system in which he has 'served' a variety of psychic needs, probably from before birth. The manifestations or qualities that are observed in the individual's personality therefore need to be seen as a combination of

177

personal qualities and projective identification 'attached to', as it were, the outcrops of these qualities in his or her personality.

It needs to be remembered, though, that not only supposedly 'negative' attributes are treated in this way – any qualities can be. Thus, in the above family it is quite possible, for example, for the mother to have to carry the tenderness on everyone's behalf, the daughter/sister academic excellence or sexuality or some other quality. We are thus talking about a family that is so intimately interlinked that they can really only be 'whole' when they are together, and then by definition they will of course be caught in interpersonal differences.

This type of functioning makes it very difficult for the adolescent to grow up, to 'gather up' his different aspects of self from amongst the family members, and to leave.

In looking at the adolescent process in the family context, it is important to realise that any change in the projective system – for example, the adolescent working at disengaging himself from the system – also means that those who use this self-same adolescent as a repository for aspects of self need to, as a consequence, again assume responsibility for their own projections.

Thus, when the defiant delinquent boy described above changes, father is likely to get more in touch with the previously split-off aspects of self and to have to deal with them in their new manifestations, say, within the marriage or at work.

THE ADOLESCENT AND INSTITUTIONAL PROCESSES

Families, of course, are ongoing institutions, and so it is not surprising that the family projective process described above also occurs in institutions. This is most likely to occur in institutions specifically set up to deal with adolescents – Children's Homes, Boarding and Day Schools, Adolescent Treatment Centres and Units, etc. In these, too, an institutional process manifests itself, in which the adolescent acts out, or is at risk of acting out, one specific or a series of, institutional roles, 'allocated' unconsciously to the most 'talented' or 'receptive' individual. It is in the nature of the institutional process that all the various qualities and characteristics that make up life, particularly life in adolescent institutions, are allocated on the basis of an ongoing unconscious process of auditioning and allocation of parts. This process includes not only the adolescents, but all members of staff as well so that, for example, a confrontation between a 'delinquent' teenager and a 'rigid' member of staff, whilst no doubt involving aspects of the personalities of both, also very much contains elements of institutional function, e.g. delinquency versus authority, or at times authoritarianism, within the context of adolescent growth. One of the key 'tasks' of adolescence, as mentioned previously, is the task of achieving a personal identity, including a sense of personal authority and the capacity to manage oneself and one's own boundaries. The above 'dispute' is therefore very much on line for the tasks one might expect to be tackled in adolescent institutions.

As mentioned above, all members of the institution staff are likely to be caught up in the process. In order to counteract the negative elements of the institutional process, it is essential for the staff to have adequate training, a support system for them in role, and preferably outside consultancy – the outside consultant being less likely to be caught up in the institutional process and therefore more likely to be able to intervene and 'free' members of the institution from some of the processes endemic in institutions.

PARENTS AND ADOLESCENTS

Perhaps the most important point to bear in mind in relating to adolescents (whether delinquent or not) is that the key part of oneself in this process is the adolescent part of one's own personality. Keep this in mind, and you are likely to survive, even manage, a relationship with an adolescent – lose touch with this fact, and no amount of theory, advice or training will help to salvage the contact.

It is a platitude to remind parents that they too were adolescents once. Somehow parents seem to only too often lose touch with this fact – because they had a 'different' adolescence, because they 'didn't have' an adolescence, or lived in a 'different' culture, or because teenagers 'didn't behave like this in my day'. Whatever the supposed or proferred reason, parents 'forget' about their own adolescence and do so at their peril. For their own adolescent self, if available, helps them to understand the adolescent's point of view and therefore puts them into the advantageous position of being in touch with both an adolescent and an adult (both aspects of self) point of view, and from this base to reach an understanding and the capacity to act on it in such a way that the growth processes in both parties can continue. For it is of course not only a matter that the parents need to help the adolescent children to 'grow up' into adults, the adolescents too need to help the adults to grow up into more age-appropriate behaviour. Perhaps the best late adolescent/early adulthood example of this sort of family developmental log-jam is one in which the parents bemoan the fact of becoming grandparents, 'we're not ready yet'. Translated, this can at times mean, 'we're not ready yet to hand over adult sexual procreativity and to move on to having children symbolically rather than in the flesh'.

There are thus often quite heavy parental pressures in adolescence for the children not to grow up, and therefore to maintain a 'frozen in time' state of adulthood for the parents.

At this point in the family, it is also not uncommon for the children to be negotiating their personal sexual and work identities at approximately the same time as the parents are required by social and physiological pressures of mid-life and the menopause to review these aspects of self. It is at times like this that the quality of the adults' work in these areas during their own adolescence counts. Ongoing or encapsulated problems are inclined to re-surface and make it doubly difficult for the adults to cope with their own resurgent difficulties, while also being available to help their adolescent children with similar problems.

At times adult identity is lost, and it feels as if there are only adolescents in the house – at other times there is even a reversal of roles.

The X family were offered an appointment at an Adolescent Out-Patient service in response to a request from a teacher who had noticed a marked increase in irritability in Betty, aged 16.

At first interview Betty arrived in a two-piece grey flannel coat and skirt, Nigel, her brother (18), in a pin-striped suit and carrying a briefcase. Father wore a T-shirt, stone-washed jeans, rope-soled shoes and a gold ear-ring, mother a tight sweater and mini-skirt. The story soon unfolded into the children being concerned about the parents' whereabouts, never knowing whether and when they were coming home at night, etc. In fact, a complete case of role reversal with the parents 'hogging' the adolescent behaviour and the children being pushed into a pseudo-adult role.

Both parents had come from restrictive families, had never had an adolescence and had married young. They were now in the grip of a mid-life crisis and desperate to make hay while the sun still shone. In doing so, they usurped the adolescent 'space' of the children who were thus deprived of an opportunity to work out their adolescent transitional issues and instead forced into a premature and pseudo-adult behaviour.

Being in touch with one's own adolescent self is therefore of great importance if one is to communicate well with adolescents – be it one's own children, or in a professional role. The adolescent part of the self gives one an opportunity to identify with the adolescent to a degree, and therefore to further understanding. At the same time, one's own and one's adolescent peer group experiences give one a norm of sorts, as well as access to a personal study of outcome, as it were. This 'study', limited and personal, of course also needs adjustment for cultural change. It is nevertheless the best hallmark we have and has the advantage of being immediately to hand (or, more appropriately, to mind), whenever we are in a position of having to deal with an unrehearsed or unprepared contact with an adolescent.

Adolescents have an uncanny capacity to home in on one's Achilles heel. It is just as well to have some indication of what the nature of one's particular weakness is, before rather than after such adolescent contact.

It is a common mistake for parents and workers alike to attempt to 'guide' adolescents into a style of life that is supposedly best for them. On closer examination it often turns out that this 'guidance' is often based much more on the adult's unconscious wish to have another chance at adult life – and to do it differently this time – than it has to do with being in touch with the adolescent's state of mind and what would seem right for him or her.

In the same way, it is very common for parents to try and have adolescents learn from their (the parent's) experiences. This approach is guaranteed to be a failure and a sure way of alienating parent and adolescent alike.

The best one can hope for is a situation in which the adolescent is of a sufficiently mature state of mind for him to be able to learn from his own experience. Parental presence in the background, when needed, is a support, parental breathing down the adolescent's neck to facilitate the 'learning from their own experience' can only blight the potential growth available from the young person's experience.

SOME PROBLEMS OF ADOLESCENCE

Very few adolescent problems appear *de novo* without some indication in earlier life – in the case of this being supposedly so, it is much more likely that the problem has been denied. Parents understandably take their children to be reflections on themselves – whilst often quick to take credit for so-called achievements, we are less keen on taking on board difficulties. The most common way of dealing with difficulties is therefore one of 'turning a blind eye' – not seeing the difficulty and hoping that it will disappear. I believe that it is this mechanism which explains the fact that we as parents so often see difficulties in others' children and are aware of their difficulties, sexual acting out and drug taking, while blissfully unaware of exactly the same, often very destructive processes happening under our very own roof.

So, how does one detect the problem under one's own roof? I believe that the most helpful indication is a change of the adolescent's previously established pattern of personal behaviour and interaction with the family.

By the time one's child reaches adolescence, one has a pretty good idea of his lifestyle, ways of coping with stress, etc. Any change of this pattern should be viewed as a warning sign; whilst inexplicable moodiness, rudeness, 'boredom', etc., might be a manifestation of the 'bite' of the adolescent process, it would in my view be a mistake to necessarily see it as such. It might also be an indication of a more deep-seated problem and/or a developmental block.

When it comes to 'assumptions' about the behaviour of one's adolescent and what they are up to, the approach 'my Emily (or William, or whoever) would never do such a thing' is in all likelihood part of the above-mentioned 'turning a blind eye' process. The problem with this approach is not only that it takes so much longer for the parents to grasp what is going on – often leaving it very late, if not too late. It also makes it much more difficult, if not impossible, for the adolescent to turn to the parent(s) for either help or consolation, because the latter have by now made it clear that they neither expect such behaviour, nor are prepared to acknowledge problems arising from it or to discuss it with their child.

From an emotional point of view it is therefore much more manageable to assume that your child is likely to a degree to participate in matters of adolescent experimentation, and that these would include areas of sexuality, delinquency and experimentation with alcohol and other drugs.

The assumption that these processes are at play obviously causes the adult a degree of ongoing anxiety throughout the period of adolescence, but this is only realistic as regards the risks of the processes, and in any case is likely to be substantially less than the 'anxiety' experienced by the adolescent in negotiating these same processes. Adolescence is a process not only for the adolescent to cope with – but also for the siblings, parents and the extended family circle.

Boredom is often a manifestation of a depressive process. Adults often view adolescent depression with alarm and wish to 'shake' the adolescent out of it. To assume that depression is necessarily a bad thing seems to me to be a mistake – it may be so, but not necessarily so. It would seem to depend on how long it lasts, whether the state of mind is one of thoughtfulness and learning, or one of angry blame of others.

At some times depression would appear to be the most appropriate response, say to the loss of one's childhood, of one's looks, one's self-idealisation, etc. It may also be to the loss of a boyfriend or girlfriend, or other family matters.

Depression as such is therefore not a bad thing. Obviously one would need to distinguish between the adolescent who is constantly in the grip of suicidal thought and at risk of attempting suicide, and the adolescent who at times dreams in a self-indulgent and melodramatic way of suicide. The latter state is by no means uncommon and not necessarily worrying.

It is clear though that a parent who is himself by nature depressive, and who had difficulties of this nature in adolescence, would naturally be much more concerned about such manifestations than a parent of a different make-up and with a different history.

Delinquency essentially means a state of mind in which society's norms, whether internalised in the mind or in society as such, are defied and broken. Whilst this state of mind is not uncommon in children from a very young age, the process itself is often not recognised until adolescence. This is to a large degree because it is only in adolescence that the child has the physical and social skills to be able to act upon and carry out delinquent acts. It is also often only in adolescence that there is enough of a gang 'support system' to encourage the perpetration of delinquent acts.

In viewing such acts, they need to be seen as an acting out of inner world phenomena in the perpetrator. They also need to be seen in a family and group context as described earlier.

Finally, we need to own up to the fact that delinquent acts and their perpetrators are also an aspect of our society – for example, that football hooligans might be perceived as present-day mercenaries contracted unconsciously by the rest of the population to perform jingoistic acts such as were previously contracted to merchant-adventurer-pirates, Falkland heroes, etc.

So-called 'psychotic' symptoms in adolescence, whilst recognised as potentially devastating of the personality, also need to be understood as not necessarily having the same consequences when manifest at this age, as opposed to mature adulthood. Drug experimentation and group pressures are at times factors that tip adolescents into transiently psychotic states. A period of observation, lasting from a few hours to a maximum of a week, for the pattern to become clearer and the adolescent to 'settle down', should this happen, is essential. During this time a careful history should be taken. My preference is for understanding to come from parents, siblings, if appropriate peers, and certainly the patient himself, in order to get the full picture.

Diagnosis and treatment is thus a matter of discussion and consensus involving participation by the patient whenever possible, rather than a process whereby symptoms and history are elicited by the doctor who makes 'the decision' and decides on the treatment.

It is my unshakeable view that electroconvulsive therapy is never justified in adolescence.

Other conditions in adolescence, such as drug addiction, acting out, difficulties in performing school or work tasks, need to be seen as ways of expressing personal inner world issues that need addressing through therapy and social intervention.

As mentioned previously, many of these have their origins in earlier life and only reveal themselves openly in adolescence.

Psychotherapy of one sort or another is the treatment of choice. It is relatively rare for adolescents to whole-heartedly embark on psychotherapy of their own will, but it is not uncommon for them to accede to it as part of an initial phase of help, and once this is weathered, progress is often good. Psychoanalysis over a period of years is the most intensive form of treatment and indicated in certain cases. Brief counselling, family therapy and group therapy are other options that at times help to restart growth and the developmental process. Apart from as described previously, drug treatment is not a solution, except in the rare cases of psychoses manifesting themselves in adolescence.

It is understandable that a diagnosis of biochemical, genetic, hormonal, or even dietary imbalance is more 'palatable' to many a parent. It leaves them free of the 'blame' that they themselves so often (and, unfortunately, professionals too at times) place on themselves, and leaves the cause as nothing to do with them.

In spite of what is supposedly said by many experts in the field, there is no evidence so far of processes due solely to the above factors. In all instances there is at least an interplay of the above factors with family and social circumstances, and in the majority of cases no evidence of such specific factors existing at all.

SUGGESTED READING

Aichhorn, A. (1951) *Wayward Youth*, London: Imago Publishing Co.
Erikson, E.H. (1965) *Childhood and Society*, Harmondsworth: Penguin.
Shields, R. (1971) *A Cure of Delinquents*, London: Heinemann Educational.

10

THE ART OF COMMUNICATING WITH VULNERABLE CHILDREN

Francis Dale

INTRODUCTION

For many of us, the act of communicating with someone else is synonymous with the notion of 'imparting information from one person to another'. However, whilst the imparting of information – either consciously or unconsciously – is always an aspect of communicating with others, in the field of human relationships, communication is about more than merely using words to convey meaning. It is essentially, about 'being in contact' with another human being; about having an idea about what they are feeling, experiencing or thinking. That is, it is about *making contact* or having rapport with, someone's 'internal state' – with the way they are experiencing themselves. Communication of this kind, in which another person feels understood, 'held' in someone else's thoughts, where experiences of an intimate nature are shared and acknowledged, is a transforming experience. It moves one from relating 'on the outside' to relating 'on the inside'.

Furthermore, a communication which 'reaches us', which makes an impact, is essentially one which has an emotional significance for us. We are never in a neutral position to it. With this kind of communication we say things like: 'I felt *understood*', or 'I was touched', or 'It got through to me' – all of which are ways of indicating a 'reaching across', a 'getting through to' or a 'making contact' with a certain depth of feeling or shared experience where one feels understood and *recognised*.

However, before developing any of these themes further, it may be useful to look at some of the key words in the title and at some of the assumptions underlying their popular usage.

Beginning with the last first, what do we mean when we say that a particular child is 'vulnerable'? Looking back on my experience of working with children whom I would describe as vulnerable, they all seem to share some or all of the following traits: of being easily hurt or wounded, and lacking in self-confidence, emotional robustness and resilience. There is also often a peculiar quality of fragility and brittleness about them, that makes one more than usually careful in how one relates to them. In other words, we are made more alert to the importance of the nature of what is being communicated between ourselves and the child in question.

This brings us to the question of what we mean when we talk about 'communication', and more importantly, *what* gets communicated, by whom and *how*? A major difficulty for those of us who live in technological societies lies in the over-emphasis which we typically place on the verbal component of communication. This is often to the detriment or exclusion of more subtle – but no less important – ways of communing with others. I use the phrase 'communing with others' because I want to stress the 'emotional' component of communication as opposed to the notion that it is only about imparting 'facts' and 'information'. After all, children do not become disturbed or vulnerable because they lack facts or information, but because they lack closeness and understanding.

It is important to remember that *words stand between us and 'reality'*. There is 'experience', then there is 'the recollection of the experience in imagination', then the conceptualisation and translating of this experience into words, and then the transfer of this *verbal* conceptualisation to someone else. Therefore the more we interpret experience in words, the more removed we become from the 'experience of the experience'.

It should not come as a surprise then, to realise that what we say with words can sometimes be the least important part of a communication: 'The rest will be in terms of attitude, posture, tone, gesture, look or touch – or the non-verbal signs and sounds we all make when what we feel will not go into words' (C. Winnicott 1964).

But it is probably unwise to ignore the fact that language, in its written or spoken form, is by far the most ubiquitous and effective means for the transmission of culture, knowledge and human experience that we possess. This places us in a dilemma – and a paradoxical one – for the possession of the one quality which most clearly differentiates and marks out *Homo Sapiens* (thinking man) from all other species – language – is at the same time, one of the greatest obstacles to forms of communication which lie beyond words.

It is an obstacle partly *because* of its success in greatly enhancing our ability to communicate to others in areas where experience can be objectified, classified and conceptualised. However, much of our experience cannot be expressed adequately through language alone.

For the expression of these experiences, we need to turn to the artist: the painter, sculptor, musician, dancer and poet (who uses the form and shape of language – including its rhythm – to convey feelings and sensations rather than facts and information).

If therefore, communication is about more than imparting facts and information, we need to look at those aspects of it which are more to do with communication as an 'art' than a 'science'. In doing so, I am not attempting to put art in opposition to science, or intuition in preference to a clear methodology, but more, to draw our attention to, and to redress the imbalance which exists between communication which is essentially about imparting information and communication which is about *understanding* and making contact with someone else.

BARRIERS TO COMMUNICATION

Before looking at what actually 'happens' when we communicate and at the various strategies we can adopt, we need, I think, to understand from the *child's* point of view, or even better, from our own first hand recollections of childhood, what it is like to be in a world where the people we are so utterly dependent on are so omniscient and omnipotent.

In a situation where a child's relationship to significant others – usually the parents – is benevolent and helpful, the child can develop a trusting and confident attitude towards adults which fosters the necessary openness and receptivity without which satisfactory communication with children would be difficult if not impossible.

Paradoxically, children who have not had benevolent relationships with adults and who would most benefit from being able to be 'got in touch with', are often highly resistant to any attempts at getting close to them. This is because they have learnt to distrust communication, and even to fear it as something which is dangerous, or even destructive to their fragile sense of self-integrity. Communication then, can become for the vulnerable child, not something which brings them into closer more rewarding contact with others and therefore to be welcomed, but something disturbing and even frightening. Thus it comes about that what the child most wants is most feared, and what is most needed is actively avoided.

In order to overcome the child's fear of 'being in communion' with someone else, and the attendant risk of becoming vulnerable and defenceless, it is important that, in whatever context the child is being seen (school, hospital, child guidance, residential home or nursery), the person relating to the child respects his or her need to be able to protect themselves from a relationship which they may find at times too intrusive or threatening. This does not mean that the child doesn't – at some level – *want* to be made contact with, but rather, that they cannot *own* this need until you have proved your trustworthiness to them.

From the foregoing, it is evident that 'making contact' or 'getting in touch' with the vulnerable child requires a certain degree of skill (knowledge of various techniques and how to apply them), a lot of patience and forbearance (you may not be thanked for your efforts and undergo much rejection from the child) and the ability to empathise (literally, to put yourself in someone else's skin). It is certainly much more than just 'talking to children'. It is about *how we make relationships*, how we learn to 'make contact' with the non-verbal child, the child received into care, the sick child in hospital, or the rejecting, contemptuous adolescent. All of this implies having *different levels of understanding* which one can use in order to understand what children of different ages, developmental stages, different needs and different life experiences are needing to communicate.

LEVELS OF COMMUNICATION

How deeply one delves into a particular child's inner experience depends on several factors. For example, is it likely to be a short or long-term relationship? Is it primarily managerial or caring? Is your task to teach the child or to form a close emotional bond? Is it therapeutic or giving advice? Or is it a combination of all of these?

Whatever the level at which we may need to communicate with the vulnerable child, whether it will be over a short or extended period of time, there are certain 'rules of engagement' which can facilitate the formation of a trusting relationship within which meaningful communication can take place.

One way of reassuring a child is to create a 'safe field' within which he feels he can have some say or control over what is happening. For example, when children are in hospital facing surgical procedures, sensitive doctors may create this safe field by talking to the child 'through the parent', by asking the parent's permission to talk to the child, or by talking to the child *indirectly* using a doll or teddy bear as an intermediary. This puts the child at a safe distance from what may be a frightening, even terrifying situation and allowing something else – the teddy bear – to own their anxiety. In fact, experience often shows that direct communication is only made possible *after* contact has first been established with the child by way of indirect communication.

Another important factor is the attitude or stance that you adopt towards the child. This would include many of the things mentioned above: *posture* – Do you tower over a small child in a physically dominating manner or crouch down to be at his level? *tone* – Is your voice harsh or soft? Is your use of language appropriate to the level of the child's understanding or too adult and sophisticated? Do you distance yourself emotionally from the child or do you empathise with him? Do you impose your personality on the child or do you allow the child to let you know when increased intimacy is appropriate? Perhaps most importantly, are you really *hearing* what the child has to tell you? One child in care who had had numerous fleeting and unsatisfactory contacts with adults spoke for many children when he said: 'Adults listen to us but don't *hear* us.'

Hearing the child

If one accepts the premise that communication operates on different levels: conscious or unconscious, literal or metaphoric, intentional or unintentional; then 'hearing' what the child has to say means having some familiarity with unconscious processes – especially as they are used by children. Unconscious communications are mediated via the language of the unconscious which is that of the symbol or metaphor.

A symbol is something which stands in place of, or which represents, an experience in such a way *that it can be communicated about* – either to oneself, or to someone else. Before symbol formation occurs, one *is* one's experience. After symbol formation has occurred, one is able, through the symbolic representation of the experience, to relate to the experience from a distance and is therefore able to communicate to others about its meaning. Children most naturally and spontaneously do this through their play, and it is by engaging with children in play, and understanding its significance, that the most effective therapeutic contact can be made.

The therapeutic alliance

In order to communicate therapeutically with the vulnerable child, some form of bonding or 'joining' has to occur between the adult and child. This is called the 'therapeutic alliance' and as the name implies, is a positive bond or connection that develops between the child and therapist or careworker and which is a powerfully motivating factor in facilitating and maintaining the therapeutic relationship. This 'connection' may exist at either a conscious or unconscious level, with the result that while a child's *conscious* attitude may be one of indifference or even contempt, their *unconscious* attitude may be one of affection and even dependency.

The initial contact

The way in which you initially relate to a child can often play a crucial role in shaping your future relationship with him as well as influencing the therapeutic outcome in a positive or negative way. It is important therefore, to try and get a 'feel' for how a particular child is relating to you before deciding how to interact with him. This means, at least initially, *letting the child make the running* in deciding how the relationship between you is going to develop. This does not mean becoming wooden and inert, but does imply that you do not become too active or intrusive and that you *follow* rather than lead.

Explaining and providing a context

Many children received into care, admitted to hospital or recommended for therapy, have a very partial understanding about, and almost no control over, what will be major, and possibly traumatic events in their lives. They will therefore frequently be suffering from acute anxiety, confusion and uncertainty and have little or no idea of who you are or why they have come to see you. Acknowledging these fears by saying: 'I expect you wonder what's happening and why you've come to see me' will reassure the child that you understand their situation and are sympathetic.

It is useful then, to understand, *from the child's point of view*, why he thinks he is coming to see you. If the parents are present, which ideally they should be – at least for the initial part of the interview – then it is important that the child sees that you seek their permission before speaking to him directly. This is important because it respects the family hierarchy (*they* hold the authority and trust – not you) and reassures the child that you are not doing anything without the parent's permission. This also provides you with the opportunity to explain to the child, in his terms and in simple language, *your* understanding of why they are coming to see you.

The therapeutic setting

As important as explaining to the child why they are coming to see you, is the provision of an appropriate setting or context in which to see them. This isn't always possible but at least if you know what the optimum conditions are, then steps can be taken to make the best of whatever situation the child is being seen in.

For a trusting relationship to develop, consistency in the setting and in the boundaries surrounding it, is essential. For children who are disturbed or vulnerable, familiarity and continuity are a prerequisite for open communication. This means that, where possible, you should meet in the same room and at the same time and on a regular basis. You should also ensure that the room is not too public so that neither you nor the child are distracted by noise or physical intrusions. Privacy and seclusion are the ideal although not always possible to achieve.

The items of furniture and equipment in the room should also be appropriate to the age and sex of the child. A low table, some small chairs, a sink, and sand tray are fairly basic items. In addition, play materials such as: farm set and animals, doll's house and furniture, a set of family figures, some cars, building bricks, plasticine and drawing materials are fairly standard. If possible, the room should not be cluttered with non-play material such as typewriters, briefcases or personal items. Some children need to make a mess, and it is easier for you to contain the mess – internally as well as externally – if the mess isn't being made with your personal or valued possessions.

DIFFERENT FORMS OF COMMUNICATION

Most adults who have regular and intimate contact with children, naturally change and adapt their behaviour to accommodate to the child's preferred mode of communicating. In the main, we do this without becoming fully aware of the strategies we adopt. For this reason, although much of what follows will be very familiar, it is worth restating if only to remind ourselves of the subtle, complex nature of the subliminal cues (below the threshold of conscious awareness) which shape and mould our responses to other people.

A major – although often unconscious – way in which we communicate, is through body posture and facial expression. Filmed interaction between mothers and babies reveals very clearly both the sensitivity of most mothers to their baby's bodily communications as well as the *mutually reciprocal* nature of the interactions which take place. Both mother and child are 'shaped' and 'shape' their behaviour in response to the meaning conveyed by each others 'body language'. So, by observing the way a child moves, the distance it places between itself and others, facial expression, directness or aversion of gaze, *and one's own bodily responses*, it is possible to make a connection and to begin a dialogue without having to rely on language as the sole means of communication.

Another, perhaps even more subtle way of communicating is through 'emotional contagion'. For example, when a baby screams the parent doesn't conceptualise the upset, the pain or terror, he or she *feels* it. Even more, parents respond to the distress *as if it were their own*. This is important because babies can't talk about their inner state. They can't 'put words to feelings', they need their parents to do this for them. Similarly, many vulnerable children are not able to adequately express in words what they are thinking or feeling. Like the parent with the distressed baby, they need the therapist to do this for them.

This means that in any interaction with a disturbed or vulnerable child who has difficulty in communicating with words, the therapist needs to be able to tolerate and think about the feelings which are generated in him or her and to see them as a potential communication from the child. This means that sometimes one has to go 'inside' and to examine one's *own* emotional response before one can understand what is being communicated.

COMMUNICATING THROUGH PLAY

Although it would be an overgeneralisation to say that children play in order to communicate (there are many other motives for playing: imitative learning, role modelling, working through anxieties, releasing energy, increasing one's competence in motor skills) there is no question that children *do* convey through their play their ongoing concerns and preoccupations. You could even say that the 'natural language' of childhood is play and that play is the 'Royal road' to the child's unconscious processes as Freud believed dreams were in the case of adults. This knowledge provides those who work with children an ideal vehicle through which non-verbal communication can occur.

Play takes many forms and so it is important, as outlined above, to provide sufficient materials and opportunities to enable the child to choose the form of play which suits him or her best. This brings us to the important question as to how much we should 'direct' the child in its activities.

As mentioned above, how one relates to a particular child depends on a variety of factors: is it short or long term? supportive or therapeutic and so on. However one relates to a child – whether directly or indirectly, there will be opportunities to use whatever situation one is in to discover what the child is *really* feeling. This is usually most safely brought about through *shared* experiences. As Claire Winnicott points out:

> Shared experiences are perhaps the only non-threatening form of communication which exists. They can concern almost anything in which we both participate – walks, car rides, playing, drawing, listening to something, looking at something or talking about something.

(C. Winnicott 1964)

Directive versus non-directive play

How much we direct a child's play depends on the personality of the child (some children need to be coaxed to play while others will engage in play immediately), why you are seeing them, and how *you* perceive your role in relationship to a particular child. For example, a nurse, teacher or doctor have obvious constraints placed on them by nature of their ascribed roles. They may only see a child once or, if frequently, never in a one-to-one situation. In addition, their role will be prescriptive and their aims and interventions in relation to the child, clear-cut and well defined. At the other extreme, the child psychotherapist or child psychiatrist may be seeing a child over a period of years with the very open-ended brief of helping a child to cope better with life.

It is clear, then, that we cannot apply a rigid 'rule' which could cover all the situations in which children are seen where play may be the principal mode of communication. What we can say, is that, taking into consideration the constraints of time, place and purpose for seeing the child, that one should try to be as non-directive as the situation allows. This will at least tend to limit any tendency to get the child to tell us what we want to hear rather than hearing what *the child* wants us to hear.

Although there are many ways of communicating with children in which play is not the 'shared experience' (for example, life story work with children in care) it is the most ubiquitous and readily available activity through which an adult and child can communicate and relate to each other. It can also be extraordinarily rich in the content of both unconscious material and the psychic processes which it reveals. It is for these reasons that I would like to use some play material from a boy in therapy to illustrate some of the points already made.

Case material

The boy in question was referred to a child guidance clinic when he was 7 because of temper tantrums, extremely difficult behaviour and because his adoptive parents felt he was deeply unhappy. He had been emotionally deprived as a baby – often being left by his mother to scream for hours on end in his cot or pram – until he was taken into care at 6 months. When he was 18 months old, he was adopted by his current parents who were, at the time of the referral, experiencing severe strains in their marital relationship (they in fact subsequently divorced).

As you will see, his name is important in understanding the material and I have changed it so as both to conceal his identity and retain its symbolic significance.

First session

I met Peter and his mother in the waiting room and after a brief introduction he came with me to the play room – without showing any obvious signs of anxiety at leaving her. He was wearing a thick overcoat and a woollen ski hat pulled down to just over his eyes. Once in the room, he went straight to the box of toys which were to be his as long as he was seeing me, and I then sat down next to him and watched to see what he would do.

Without taking off his coat, Peter immediately began to draw (see Figure 10.1). I waited until he had finished and then asked him what he had drawn. He said it was 'a cowboy . . . with guns'. At this point, I made my first interpretation.

Figure 10.1

Interpretation I said that I thought that Peter was showing me that he was a little anxious about being in the room with me when he didn't know who I was, what I was like and whether he could trust me. I also pointed out that the cowboy had a kerchief around his chin as if he was needing to cover himself up – perhaps to hide his identity. I wondered if Peter was needing to hide a bit of himself from me?

Now, one of the functions of an interpretation is not just to communicate to someone how *you* understand them, but also to help *them* to understand the significance and symbolic meaning that you attribute to their behaviour.

The effect of *Peter's* communication – and hence probably its function – was first, to let me know that he was anxious, and second, to let me know he could protect himself (if you like, he was saying something to the effect: 'You'd better watch out! If you try to hurt me, I've got guns!').

The effect of *my* communication, was to show Peter that I understood what he was trying to tell me, which in turn reduced the anxiety and made me a less frightening figure. He immediately began another drawing (see Figure 10.2). He said this was 'Bugs Bunny' and that he was 'angry and fighting'. I wondered why he was angry and Peter said 'Mummy and daddy. I don't like it when they fight. I fight daddy – kick and hit him.'

Figure 10.2

Internal Commentary Here, it is clear that Peter was using the Bugs Bunny character both to express *his* anger and deny it at the same time (that is, it is Bugs Bunny who is angry not him).

He then drew another picture (see Figure 10.3) and commented on it saying it was: 'Bugs Bunny in disguise', adding under his breath: 'To look tough'. At this point, I made a second, more complete interpretation of the material.

Interpretation I told Peter that I thought *he* was Bugs Bunny and pointed out that Bugs Bunny had a kerchief around his mouth like the cowboy. I added that the second Bugs Bunny also had a woollen hat pulled down over his eyes like Peter and that rabbits lived in Burrows (Peter's family name was Burrows). I said that Peter was showing me how angry he was but also how frightened he was about what might happen if the people he was angry with found out. That was why he had to disguise his anger and to make himself 'look tough'. Perhaps Peter was anxious about what I might do if he got angry here and whether I might tell his parents. At this, Peter gave a slight nod of his head.

I then told Peter that what happened in the room was private and just between us and that although I would obviously be meeting his

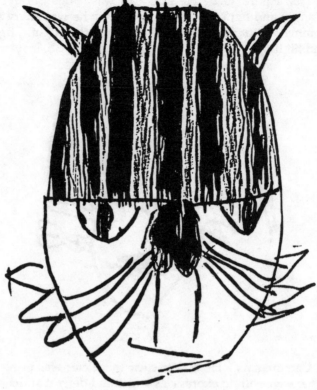

Figure 10.3

parents from time to time, that I would not tell them about anything which would harm him or make him embarrassed.

The *effect* of the interpretation plus the reassurance about confidentiality, was to lessen Peter's level of anxiety and to enable him to be more open with me: he immediately took off his hat and coat and said *sotto voce*: 'What's up Doc!' (just as Bugs Bunny does in the cartoon film). I said that he was wondering what sort of a person I was and what he was coming to see me for. I wondered what ideas he had about why he had been brought to see me. Peter's next statement revealed that he had no doubts in his mind about what *his* agenda was: 'I've come here to talk about my mummy and daddy.'

Peter then picked up a female doll and, peering up its skirt, made several comments as if he were thinking aloud: 'Boobs . . . tits . . . milk'. I wondered if there was some confusion in his mind between 'tops and bottoms' and whether there hadn't been enough milk for him as a baby. Peter replied that there had been 'too many babies' and went on to say, 'My first mummy didn't want me.'

196

We can see here, how interpreting Peter's anxiety and addressing his unconscious motivations, has enabled him to feel less defensive and to begin to communicate on a deeper level.

Peter spent the rest of the session modelling in great detail the figure of a woman in appropriately different coloured plasticine. He made breasts, eyes, hair; and then knickers, bras, skirt and top and told me how he slept in the same room as his mother and saw her 'boobs' and didn't like the 'the hanging skin'.

Commentary   In this first session, I felt that Peter revealed how, at an unconscious level, he has an ongoing preoccupation with his first mother and the reasons for his abandonment. In making such a detailed and 'real' model of his 'mother' he is showing how concretely she is represented in his phantasy life [concrete thinking is typical of much younger children where the 'thought' about the object – its mental representation – and the object itself, are seen as equivalent (Segal's symbolic equation) and precedes the capacity to separate the object – in this case the mother – from its symbolic representation, the doll which symbolises the mother].

His dislike of the 'hanging skin' (the 'empty breasts') of his adoptive mother, is about his defensive anxiety regarding unacceptable feelings of rage, emptiness and loss which he unconsciously experiences at an *infantile level* with regard to the mother who abandoned him (and possibly his phantasied attacks on the breasts which didn't 'feed' him).

Second session

The feedback that I had from Peter's mother after the first session was about how much he had enjoyed it and how keen he had been to come today. She also said that he had begun to ask if he could see his real mother again. At this point, Peter, who had been listening stated quite forcefully: 'Not to *see* her, to *talk* to her!' which suggested that he was aware of his adoptive mother's ambivalence about him renewing contact and was letting her know that he wanted something more intimate than a superficial meeting.

In the room, Peter began by drawing a rather squashed up sad looking cat (see Figure 10.4). I asked him if he had a cat. He said that he did and that it was called Moses.

Internal commentary   At this point it occurred to me that Moses too had been an abandoned child and that Peter may have projected into his cat some of his own feelings of abandonment.

I gently suggested that the cat looked a little sad, to which Peter replied: 'He's sad because he hasn't got a mummy. She's gone behind

Figure 10.4

a door – up some secret passage.' I asked Peter if he knew about Moses and the bulrushes. He said that he did, and then drew a picture (see Figure 10.5) of a cat with a boy's head growing from the back. He then added: 'Its claw is in a puddle,' and continued: 'Moses is in the stream – she's cooking.' He then drew a face with an angry expression and big teeth (see Figure 10.6).

Interpretation   I said that I thought that Peter was telling me what he thought had happened when he was a baby. The squashed, sad little cat was how the 'baby inside Peter' felt about losing his mummy. One part of him felt that his mummy had been a good mummy – like Moses's mother who had been cooking for him and who really loved him; but another part of him felt terribly angry, like the cat with the big claw in the puddle or the angry face with the big teeth. Perhaps he was telling me about an angry attacking monster part of him which he feared had bitten mummy's breast and made her reject him.

He then drew a mouse-like animal with enormous ears (see Figure 10.7) which I interpreted as showing that he was listening very carefully to what I was saying, to which he replied that he had never known his mother, before drawing a 'jelly man' (see Figure 10.8). He then drew another picture (see Figure 10.9) and asked me to guess what it was. I wondered if it was a penguin. He said: 'No, it's a blackbird eating a worm/snake.' I said he was telling me about something biting and dangerous – like a 'willy-snake'. He laughed and drew a 'willy' on the bird's neck and said that it was 'peeing on the snake'. I commented that the bird's beak looked sharp, like scissors cutting off the dangerous willy/snake.

Figure 10.5

Internal commentary Here I think, Peter is telling me something about his Oedipal anxieties in relation to his adoptive father. He has already in the first session openly expressed the wish to 'kick and hit' him which, added to the fragile state of his parents' relationship, is likely to make him feel that his phantasy of getting rid of his father – and having his mother all to himself – could actually come true. In this situation, it would hardly be surprising if he wasn't afraid that his father

Figure 10.6

(symbolised by the blackbird) would retaliate by cutting off and eating this dangerous 'willy/worm/snake' which was trying to usurp him.

Acting on an intuitive hunch, I asked Peter what his father did. He said that he was a butcher and began another drawing. I kept my thoughts about all the cutting and chopping up that butchers do to myself as I thought it might make him too anxious if I made the connection too explicit. This time, Peter drew a picture of Superman (see Figure 10.10). I asked him if he knew what had happened to Superman. Peter said he didn't want to say.

Interpretation   I pointed out that Superman was very much like Moses. He too had been abandoned by his parents, who tried to save him from their planet and home being destroyed in a terrible explosion, by sending him to Earth in a spaceship like the cradle or basket in which Moses had been placed. Like Moses, he had been found by people who had wanted to keep him and bring him up as their own child. I then pointed to the difference between the 'jelly' man and Superman and said that perhaps 'inside' he felt like the jelly man – all wobbly and falling apart – so that he made himself into Superboy on the outside so that he was tough and strong and couldn't be hurt – just like Superman, when he was ordinary, was a bit weak and jelly-like, like Clark Kent (Superman's alter ego).

Peter's response to this interpretation was very revealing. He told me how, when Superman was found as a baby by his future adoptive parents, he lifted up their truck so that the wheel could be changed. He then added: 'I really *do* come from Krypton – bits of me are still there.'

Figure 10.7

Commentary Here we can begin to see both how Peter has attempted to understand and come to terms with his early childhood experiences, as well as the nature of the defences he has erected in order to protect himself from the knowledge of what *actually* happened. His defence is one of omnipotent denial. He was *not* abandoned by his mother. His parents loved him and sent him away *in order to protect him*. He is not a vulnerable and defenceless baby, a wobbly jelly with no insides, but strong, powerful and invulnerable – like Superman.

Figure 10.8

Third session

Peter came to the third session with a wooden egg which was hollow inside. He commenced by playing in the sand tray making 'scenery' with hills, lakes and rivers. It was apparent that he was trying to find a way of communicating something with the shapes but could not find an appropriate composition or configuration of the sand to 'release' whatever it was that he was wanting to express. He eventually constructed a pointed mound with a river beside it saying that it was a pyramid with the Nile beside it. He then covered the 'pyramid' over with sand saying there were 'people buried inside'.

Interpretation   I said that I thought he was telling me about something which had happened a long time ago – perhaps when he was a baby. Something got buried, hidden, and now needed to be uncovered. I pointed out that special people were buried in pyramids and that they were called 'mummies'. Peter had lost his mummy and now, like Moses, was wanting to find her again.

Following this interpretation, Peter left off his play in the sand tray and I understood this to indicate that he had heard enough for the time being and needed time to digest it.

Fourth session

Peter began playing in the sand tray but this time, placed little wooden houses on the sand before covering them up with 'dust' (that is, sand which he sprinkled on top). He then made a dome shape by pressing an inverted saucer with a hole in the centre on top of a mound of sand. He then filled a cup with sand and started throwing a small wooden stick into the sand in an attempt to knock it out of the cup before stabbing the stick into the cup so that it was sticking out like a lance or spear. This was followed by him making a circle of sand and throwing 'a dart' (i.e. another wooden stick) repeatedly into the centre of the circle.

Internal commentary   The rather aggressive way in which Peter thrust the stick into the cup, or threw it into the circle, coupled with his earlier statement about sleeping in the same room as his mother and not liking to see her breasts, suggested to me that in his play he was communicating his anxiety about some real or imagined sexual intercourse which had stirred up his envy and rivalry of his father.

I told Peter that I thought he was 'knocking daddy out of mummy'. He said it (i.e. the stick) was 'Pinocchio's nose'. I thought it might make him too anxious if I made the obvious connection between Pinocchio's nose, which grew longer and longer until it had to be cut off, and a sticking out penis which a daddy butcher might cut off (see material above regarding the blackbird eating the 'worm'). Instead, I followed the other association and reminded Peter that Pinocchio was a boy who had been made out of wood and who had desperately wanted to be a 'real' boy. Peter then said that Pinocchio had been made real by a fairy to which I replied that Peter, like Pinocchio, did not feel 'real' because he felt he had been 'made' and not born.

Commentary We can see here how Peter's current anxiety concerning the poor relationship between his adoptive parents is activating much earlier anxieties which have been 'covered up' but not resolved. This boy has never felt 'real', and in the play between us, a 'story' is gradually unfolding in which he reveals how, in his unconscious phantasy life, he has tried to make sense of it. As an adopted child, he is a 'made' boy and cannot become real until he has parents who love him enough (as in Pinocchio where, as a result of the toymaker's love, the puppet was made real). However, first, he has to 'find' his parents. They are lost or hidden away – his mother has 'gone behind a door – up some secret passage' (see Session two).

One is reminded here of Winnicott's (1975) notion of a 'false' versus a 'true' self. Peter has developed a false self. He does not relate to people with his 'true' self because he doesn't have one – it has been stolen; like Pinocchio, he doesn't experience himself as a 'real' boy.

Peter then returned to his play in the sand and made houses, 'like Pompei' which he covered up with sand. I asked Peter if he knew about Pompei and he replied that it was an 'old Roman city which got covered up by dust by volcanoes.' I then asked him if he knew what had happened to the people and Peter replied: 'They all got buried and discovered hundreds of years later.' I wondered if he felt that a bit of him (possibly his 'real' self) had got buried and now needed to be uncovered.

Peter then put the saucer with a hole in the middle on top of an upturned cup and said it was a volcano. I made a link between feeding breasts and angry breasts and said that he was telling me about an angry volcano breast which had destroyed him as a baby and buried him.

Commentary As a small baby, Peter's primary relationship to his biological mother would have been to the breast and his feeding relationship to it. Both metaphorically and literally, small babies 'take in' the world through the breast. Thus in early life, the breast, and what it stands for in our unconscious phantasy life, assumes a significance and importance which it would be hard to overestimate. In Peter's case, the breast has become associated with destructive events of unimaginable consequence (i.e. the loss of one's mother *is* the loss of one's world) to

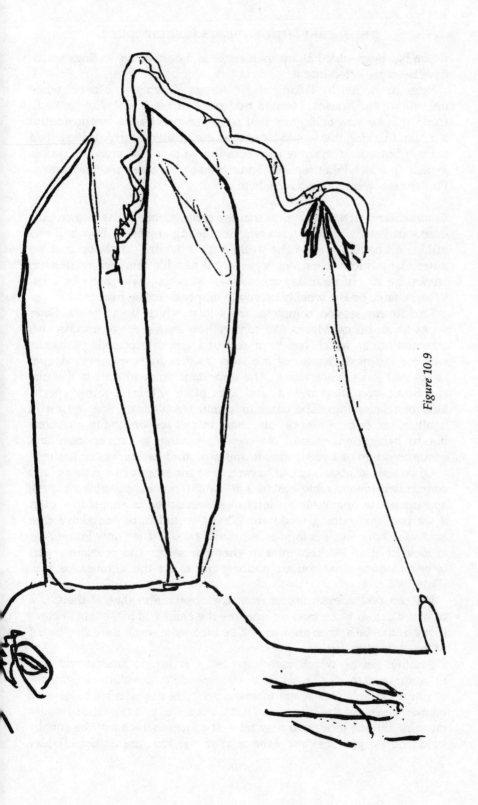

Figure 10.9

which has been added all his own anger and destructive feelings which have been projected into it.

Peter continued by talking about 'Mummy's bras – no boob' while uncovering the houses. He said that some of the houses 'had rotted'. I said that he was telling me that something had gone bad inside (in Kleinian thinking this would be seen as the result of internalising a 'bad breast') but added that the ash from the volcano did preserve people inside. To which Peter replied: 'Some tried to run away and they rotted. Plaster casts were made out of them.'

Commentary It would appear that the consequence of the catastrophic events in Peter's infancy have left him feeling empty, hollow and bad inside. All he has to meet the world with is a 'shell', a plaster cast, an outer skin which holds him together. When his omnipotent defence works, he is – in phantasy anyway – a superboy who can't be hurt. When it fails, he is a wobbly jelly with empty or rotten insides.

This fourth session completes the 'story' which began when Peter spoke about his cat Moses. We can see how each piece of unconscious communication which has been received and interpreted, paves the way for the next chapter of the story as it unfolds into ever deeper layers of Peter's inner world. The important point to note is that the communication arose out of, and took place within, a rather special kind of relationship. The communication wasn't from one person to another, but *between* two people. Peter wasn't responding to questions but to being understood. We weren't having 'a conversation' but communication of a very intimate and profound nature was occurring.

Of course, it goes without saying, that for most of us coming into contact with vulnerable children it would not be possible or even appropriate to engage in an intensive therapeutic relationship – even if we had the training to do so. What I would hope the above case shows, is how much *is there to be communicated* – if we only know how to look for it and to recognise it when we see it. The problem seems to be to 'notice what you are noticing and to see the significance in it' (Dale 1984).

We can take some comfort from the observation that, if there is a communication to be made, somehow the child will make itself heard. If one 'route' fails, then another will be tried either until the adult 'hears' or the child gives up.

Another factor which can help us in trying to understand and to communicate to the child, is the 'overdetermination of symbolic communication'. This refers to the capacity of any symbol to operate on many levels at the same time. If, for example, you miss the symbolic meaning on one level, you may hit it at another which may be equally valid from the point of view of the child's overall communication. To take

Figure 10.10

an example; a child's play with a crocodile could convey the following meanings:

1   The need to be able to defend oneself from attack (symbolised by the thick skin).
2   One's aggressive, angry feelings (symbolised by the rows of sharp teeth).
3   Insatiable greed, possessiveness or hunger for love (symbolised by the gaping mouth).
4   Ambivalence (symbolised by being half in the water and half on land).
5   Secretiveness (symbolised by the crocodile's ability to hide or disguise itself).

PRIMITIVE FORMS OF COMMUNICATION

There are however, other, less obvious ways of communicating which are exceedingly subtle and consequently harder to detect. Most primitive forms of communication occur without the mediation of either non-verbal or verbal symbols. At the *pre-symbolic stage*, babies (and some psychotic children, e.g. those suffering from autism) 'communicate' through the arousal or evoking in *another* person of intensely felt emotional states which cannot be processed or understood at an intellectual level. The recipient is then left with an experience: rage, fear, emptiness, confusion, etc., which, although originating from someone else, has now become their own.

Earlier, mention was made of 'emotional contagion' a primitive form of communication – typically seen to occur between infant and mother – in which the mother's emotional state resonates to that of the baby, so that she experiences the baby's emotional state *as if it were her own*. This brings us to a consideration of those forms of communication which occur by way of projective mechanisms.

Projective mechanisms in communication

Strictly speaking, in the psychoanalytic sense of the word, projection implies the ejection into the outside world – usually into a person or thing – of qualities, feelings, wishes or even 'objects' which the person cannot own or tolerate as belonging to himself (Laplanche and Pontalis 1973). It is an unconscious mechanism of a primitive origin and its purpose is not to 'communicate' as such, but rather to 'get rid of or to expel'. However, if the recipient – the mother of a baby for example – cannot just receive but also tolerate and even attempt to understand the projection (what Bion (1977) refers to as 'alpha function') then what is being projected: fear, anger, falling apartness, can be seen as communicating something about the other person's feelings or state of mind.

The most primitive mode of evacuating or expelling unwanted or unbearable parts of the self into another object (here an 'object' can stand for another person or an aspect of them) was initially described by Melanie Klein (1952) and given the name *Projective Identification*. It is essentially a primitive mode of defending the self from unacceptable thoughts or feelings – for example, the intense hatred a baby can have towards the breast which frustrates it; by splitting them off from the self and inserting them into the 'object' – the mother – in order to control her 'from the inside' and thus protect the self from (a) unwanted feelings and (b) phantasised persecutory attacks from the damaged object. In its pure form, it is essentially a psychotic form of defence and one which is usually associated with people who are either very unintegrated (e.g. young babies) or whose ego structures have become fragmented or disintegrated – as with very disturbed individuals such as psychotics.

Although very few of us will have to deal with psychotic children, the notion that *what we are made to feel* in relation to a particular child may be telling us something about the internal state of the child, is a very powerful concept, both for understanding the child and in our attempts to help.

In conclusion, perhaps the most precious quality any of us can have to offer the vulnerable child, is an openness to *experiencing their experience*, the ability to tolerate another's pain and distress, and the optimistic belief that helping a child to attain a better understanding of their predicament in a *shared relationship* is better than sailing alone.

REFERENCES

Bion, W.R. (1977) *Learning from Experience*, in *Seven Servants*, New York: Jason Aronson, Inc.

Dale, F.M.J. (1984) 'Baby observation: some reflections on its value and application in the clinical setting', paper presented at Esther Bick Commemoration Day.

Klein, M. (1952) 'Some theoretical conclusions regarding the emotional life of the infant', in J. Riviere (ed.) *Developments in Psychoanalysis*, New York: Jason Aronson, Inc.

Laplanche, J. and Pontalis, J.B. (1973) *The Language of Psychoanalysis*, London: Hogarth Press.

Segal, H. (1986) *The Work of Hanna Segal: A Kleinian Approach*, London: Free Association Press and Maresfield Library.

Winnicott, C. (1964) 'Communication with children', *Child Care Quarterly Review* 18 (3).

Winnicott, D.W. (1975) *Through Paediatrics to Psychoanalysis*, London: Hogarth Press.

NAME INDEX

Adams-Tucker, C. 146
Aichhorn, A. 184
American Psychiatric Association 152
Asen, K. 94

Baisden, J. 131, 147
Baisden, M. 131, 147
Baker, T. 131
Barkley, R.A. 157–9 *passim*, 166
Barnes, B. 158
Barocas, C.B. 76, 77
Barocas, H.A. 76, 77
Barton, N. 35n
Bateson, G. 135, 144, 145
Bean, P. 95
Becarra, R.M. 105
Becker, J. 147
Beckford, Jasmine 94, 105
Bentovim, A. 131
Berger, M. 76
Berne, E. 35n
Bick, Esther 55, 57
Bion, W.R. 58, 59, 208
Bliss, E. 131
Blom-Cooper, L. 94
Blos, P. 127
Borland, B.L. 167
Boston, M. 108
Bowlby, J. 17n, 18n
Brostoff, J. 167
Browne, A. 134, 140, 146
Burgess, R. 128

Cantwell, P. 18n
Carlen, P. 96
Carlisle, Kimberly 105
Carlson, G.A. 18n
Challacombe, S.J. 167

Clarke, L. 133, 143
Colquhoun, I.D. 158
Conners, C.K. 158
Conte, J. 132
Covitz, J. 76
Cytryn, L. 18n

Dell, P. 148
Department of Health 79, 97, 105
DHSS 79, 105
Dickson, J. 35n
Dodds, E.R. 35n
Duncan, S. 131

Ebata, A. 128
Egger, J. 158, 167
Epstein, C. 101, 107, 110
Erikson, Eric 170
Evert, K. 102

Faludy, G. 35n
Ferenczi, S. 101, 134, 154
Field, N. 35n
Finkelhor, D. 133, 134, 140, 146
Fishman, H.C. 127
Flack, S. 166
Flavell, J.H. 107
Flynn, D. 108, 121
Fraiberg, Selma 76, 94
Franklin, A.J. 158, 163
Freud, A. 103, 113, 126
Freud, S. 34n, 108, 126
Friedrich, W. 146
Furman, E. 115

Garbarino, J. 76, 78, 93, 106
Gilliam, G. 78, 106
Giovannoni, J.M. 105

Glasser, M. 35n
Goldstein, J. 93, 94, 96
Gordon, L. 105
Graham-Hall, J. 78, 79

Haley, J. 134
Hall, J.G. 128
Heckman, H.K. 167
Henker, B. 159, 167
Henry, Tyra 105
Herman, J. 131
Herzberger, S.D. 107
Herzov, L. 18n
Higgins, R. 35n
Hinshelwood, B. 35n
Hodges, J. 78, 95

Irne, B. 102

Jehu, D. 131
Jephcott, E.F.N. 35n
Jones, A. 17n
Joseph, Betty 60
Jung, C.G. 18n

Kelly, L. 131
Kennedy, H. 76
Kerenyi, C. 18n
Khan, Masud 76, 80
Klein, Melanie 18n, 41, 209
Knight, D. 18n
Korbin, J.E. 106
Kuhn, T.S. 121

La Fontaine, J. 131
Lambert, L. 78, 95
Laplanche, J. 206, 208
Lewis, D. 133, 143
Lynch, M. 131

McEwen, L.M. 167
McKnew, D.H. 18n
Martin, D.F. 78, 79, 128
Meltzer, D. 50, 56–8 passim
Melzak, S. 77
Menzies, I. 163
Miller, A. 76, 149
Millham, S. 95, 97, 98
Minuchin, S. 94, 106, 127
Mrazek, P. 130, 131
Murphy, M. 35n

Nash, C. 131
NSPCC 101

O'Shaughnessy, E. 59

Parton, Nigel 105, 106
Peake, A. 132, 136, 139
Perlman, T. 167
Paters, S.D. 130
Piaget, J. 107
Plutarch 104
Pontalis, J.B. 206, 208
Powell, L. 144

Rapp, D.J. 166
Reich, Wilhelm 32, 35n
Rich, Adrienne 77
Rush, F. 130
Rushton, A. 95
Russell, D. 131, 132
Rutter, M. 18n
Rycroft, C.F. 17n

Sandler, A.M. 108
Sarnoff, C. 114, 118
Schreber, D.P. 108
Segal, H. 197
Sgroi, S. 140, 143, 150, 152
Shengold, L.C. 76, 108
Sherrick, I. 117
Shields, R. 184
Sinason, Valerie 127
Smith, G. 132, 134, 136, 139,
    144–9 passim
Speer, F. 163
Still, G.F. 157
Summit, R. 130, 133, 134, 143,
    144
Szur, R. 108

Taylor, E. 166
Tizard, B. 78, 95
Tustin, Frances 54–8 passim

Waddell, M. 17n
Wallerstein, J. 77
Weiss, G. 167
Welldon, E.V. 35n
Welsh Office 79, 105
West, D. 131
Whalen, C.K. 159, 167
Winnicott, C. 186, 192

Winnicott, D.W. 17n, 35n, 54,
58, 93, 96, 162, 164, 204
Wiseberg, S. 113
Wyatt, G. 130, 131, 144

Wyre, R. 132

Yahraes, H. 18n
Yorke, C. 113

SUBJECT INDEX

abuse, *see* emotional abuse, physical abuse, sexual abuse
adolescence 170–84; defined 170–72; depression in 182; establishing personal identity 173–5; and the family 176–8; and institutional processes 178–9; parents in 179–81; problems of 181–4; and projective identification 177–8; as transitional phase 172–3
anger, depression and 12, 13
attachment 78; to abusers 77
autism 37–61; absent object and 59; Normal Primary Autism 54; and projective identification 56, 57, 60; used as conscious defence 53

bereavement 62–74; acceptance of death 67; grieving in 65; reactions to 67–8; school life after 71–3; therapy for 71
body image, sexual abuse and 147
body language: as communication 191; as displacement 27–8

case histories: adolescence 175–6, 180; autism 37–61; communication through play 192–208; depression 2–16 *passim*; emotional abuse 80–94; neuroticism 22–33 *passim*; physical abuse 108–27; sexual abuse 133–45 *passim*
Child Abuse Enquiry Report 105
children's drawings 28, 41, 42–4, 46, 194–207 *passim*; sexual abuse and 147
clinical material, *see* case histories

communication with vulnerable children 185–209; barriers to 187–8; different forms of 191–2; initial contact 189–90; levels of 188–91; limitations of verbal 186–7, 191–2; through play 189, 192–208; primitive communication 208–9; projective mechanisms of 208–9; therapeutic setting for 190–91; unconscious 189
compulsive repetition 31–4
counter-transference, autism and 57–61

death: acceptance of 67; child's picture of 18n; parental 7–8; *see also* bereavement
denial, secrecy and 17n
depression 1–19; in adolescence 182; and anger 12, 13; and denial 17n; and diagnostic classification 18n; and hopelessness 11; hyperactivity in 15–16; loss as trigger for 9–11; parental 'protection' from 2–3; vs. sadness 3–5; and sexual abuse 11; substitution behaviour in 15
displacement: through body language 27–8; secrecy and 25–7
double bind communication 135, 144, 146
drawings, *see* children's drawings

emotional abuse 75–99; attachment to abuser 77; children in care 95–7; clinical case study 80–94; defined 79; and physical abuse 103; privacy and the family 94–5; societal

approaches to 78–9; statutory
    context 79–80; types of 76–7

grieving 65

hyperactivity 157–69; in adolescence
    164–5; into adulthood 167–9;
    defined 157; in depression 15–16;
    diagnosis and causation 158–9; in
    early childhood 160–2; help for
    child 165–7; in infancy 159–60;
    in later childhood 163–4; and the
    parents 159; in school 161–4 passim

internalisation of objects 12–13
introjection 29

latency developmental phase 113–14,
    117
loss, and depression 9–11

moral development, sexual abuse
    and 142

neuroticism 20–36; defined 34n;
    as displacement 25–8; as paranoid
    style 29–31; as repetition 31–4; as
    splitting 21–4

Oedipal material 119, 120, 199

paranoid style, secrecy and 29–31
parental death 7–8
phobias 26–7; A. Freud on 126
physical abuse 101–29; case history
    of 108–27; and emotional abuse 103;
    legislative aspects of 105; locus
    of responsibility for 105–6;
    therapeutic help for 106–7; working
    with parents 122–3
play, communication through 189,
    192–208; see also children's
    drawings
projection 29; autism and 56;
    in communication 208–9
projective identification 29, 209;
    adolescence and 177–8; autism and
    56, 57, 60
Psychoanalytic approach: child

communication through play
    192–208; development latency
    113–14, 117; Oedipal material 119,
    120, 199; theory of normal
    development 116–17; treatment of
    autism 37–61; treatment of physical
    abuse 108–27
psychotherapy, child 102–3; in
    adolescence 183–4; for physical
    abuse 106–7; for sexual abuse
    149–54; therapeutic alliance in 189;
    see also psychoanalytic approach

repetition, secret forces in 31–4

secrecy (child) 6–7, 11, 20–1; and
    body language 27–8; conscious vs.
    unconscious 5–6; and denial 17n;
    and displacement 25–7; and the
    paranoid style 29–31; and repetition
    31–4; and splitting 21–4
separation 41; effects of on child 7–9
sexual abuse 11, 130–56; abuser's
    responsibility 151; and affective
    expression 141; authority issues in
    148–50; and body image 147; case
    material 133–45 passim; and
    communication skills 143–6, 153;
    consequences for the child 133–54;
    entrapment in 134; establishment of
    secrecy 133; gender characteristics
    of 132; general patterns of 132–3;
    incidence and prevalence 130–2;
    interventions in 150–4; and
    judgement 141; and moral
    development 142; powerlessness in
    134, 148–50; passim; and relationship
    success 143; and sense of
    responsibility (abused) 141–2; and
    self-blame 151; and self-esteem 140,
    151; and sexual development 146–8;
    survival tactics in 152; triggering
    factors in 153
splitting 35n; secrecy and 21–4
suicidal attempts 13–14

therapeutic alliance with children 189
transitional objects 26